Sincerely,

Harnett T. Kane

QUEEN NEW ORLEANS

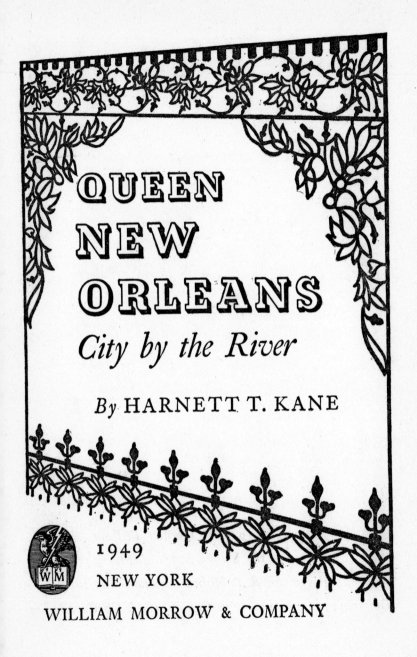

QUEEN NEW ORLEANS

City by the River

By HARNETT T. KANE

1949

NEW YORK

WILLIAM MORROW & COMPANY

 CONTENTS

Part III *LUSTROUS TOWN*

 ILLUSTRATIONS

PAGES 86-87

Jackson tips his hat as he rides past the cathedral

Ursuline Convent: Centuries have mellowed the walls

Marigny "Casino": The gay Bernard was good to all the ladies

Pontalba Buildings: The red-headed baroness had temper and taste

Claiborne Courtyard: The fanlight is studied grace

Cabildo: Massive Spanish below, delicate French above

Jackson Square: One of the great vistas of the New World

The Dueling Oak: Death in the shadows

Esplanade Avenue: For the Creoles, it was paradise

Broulatour Courtyard: Flagstones, arches, an air of repose

Carriageway and gate: The Orleanians wanted, above all, privacy

Cathedral alleyway: For sinners, saints and those between

St. Louis Hotel: The Creoles defied the Americans

St. Charles Hotel: But the Americans built a bigger one

Cornstalk fence: Anything you asked in ironwork

Or a grape pattern, if you wished

Old steamboat landing: All the world came to New Orleans

ix

PAGES 182-183

The front endpaper is *New Orleans, 1873,* by A. R. Waud. The back endpaper is *Comus Carnival parade, 1867, The Feast of Epicurus.*

The drawings and the map on pages 350-351 are by Tilden Landry.

QUEEN NEW ORLEANS

New Orleans Is a Lady

THE afternoon sunlight of New Orleans falls kindly across the mellowed face of the French quarter house, showing some of time's markings, but also all the fundamental strength of a place built for the centuries.

The smooth plaster covering, painted a warm peach shade, has broken here and there, to be repaired by friendly hands. At the corner a new segment has dropped, revealing a powdery brick. But the old building is still sturdy, and also beautiful in a way that no other kind of New World house is beautiful.

It is one in a line of similar structures, rising directly from the sidewalk, or *banquette*, as New Orleans calls it, each touching its neighbor, each an individual blue or pink or purple. There are small differences in the levels of the rooflines. And yet there is harmony, for each builder has fitted himself to the amiable climate, to the people, to New Orleans itself.

As we stand across the street, we see a façade dominated, as always, by tall galleries, two-storied and supported by a row of iron posts set into the curb. Of delicate ironwork, these galleries sketch a lacelike tracery of leaves and flowers against the stucco—waist-high railings, scrolled panels of filigree marking the lift of the higher posts, all topped by a final design against the sky.

Here, too, Nature has a tempering touch. In a shaft of

3

sunlight vines twist about the iron, merging with the filigree pattern. On each of the two upper levels dozens of containers hold plants, geraniums, wax flowers, ferns; and a big bird cage hangs on the lower one near a table and many chairs. Reaching across the banquette as they do, the galleries are deep enough to provide auxiliary living quarters for the family, for leisurely rest, visits, and meals in the open, à la Creole.

From one of the tall French windows opening on the lower gallery a Negro woman emerges, carrying a bucket, her head swathed in a white turban. In two swift motions she douses the wooden floor, then repeats the process. She is lavish, and why not? The Mississippi's full of water. It will wash away the dust and cool things for the hours of dusk.

Below, on ground level, is a pair of windows with neatly painted green shutters. Then at one end, the right, a short flight of steps leads to a formal doorway, paneled, set between half-columns under an arched fanlight. At the other end stands a larger entrance, a carriageway with heavy double doors. In one of the leaves a smaller opening is cut; New Orleans always believes in such conveniences.

From the smaller gate a girl now emerges, and we may enter, as visitors often do. The house is deep in proportion to its width, reaching far back to a large patio in the centre of the city square. The door slams behind us; ahead looms a tunnellike, flagstoned passage, cool and dim. Halfway back appears an arched opening into the carriageway, with a curved wooden stair that lifts in a swift, unsupported curve.

Upstairs waits the main story, in the continental style—a half-dozen rooms with a side hall. Sixteen feet high, the chambers have chandeliers, marble mantels, and several four-poster beds so large that they have stayed in the same spot for generations. In the curtained light of the afternoon there is the peace of settled age.

Below again, we move through a pair of high, scrolled iron gates that lead from the carriageway to the sun-splashed

greenery of the courtyard, the central garden-place toward
which the house faces. Flagstoned paths wind among raised
flower beds bordered by brick. At a weathered fountain a
bronze figure is sprayed by the jetting water. Near the metal
chairs, warmed by the sun, a dog is racing about a banana
tree, whose sheathlike leaves guard a bunch of unripened
fruit, green and bulbous. It is not a neat or a precise place,
this court; its beauty lies in its bounty and its casual grace.

The rear house wall is broken by a series of wide windows,
many-sectioned and topped with arches, with small balconies
before them. On the right, extending from the main building along the garden, is a narrow wing with double wooden
galleries. In older days it was occupied by younger men of
the family and by occasional guests, with servants quartered
on the ground floor. The last two sides of the courtyard are
high brick walls, giving shade during the hottest part of the
day, and also privacy.

Set close to the rear wall, a magnolia tree casts a circle of
shadow; among its burnished leather leaves appear cuplike
creamy blossoms. Birds fly around the fountain, and in a
corner a woman moves about, singing softly in her *gombo,*
the patois of New Orleans Negroes who served French families. A cat tugs at her apron. "Couri!" she cries, and he runs
off.

Over the court floats a pungent aroma, that of coffee dripping in a pot, and with it the incense of seafood in a well-
seasoned mixture. For a few minutes there is silence; then
from upstairs a woman's voice is raised in song. The dark
woman sets a table with a tray of cups, for the family will
gather a little later for sips of coffee before the meal.

The outer bell rings, and she walks quickly through the carriageway. As she opens the door, shrill noises break in on the
peace of house and garden. A bus rumbles along the street;
five or six passers-by burst into laughter over a joke; across
the street a group of small boys are jigging as they beat on
boxes and tin cans in the rhythm of one of New Orleans'

"spasm bands." So, through the centuries, much of the city has lived—clamor, easy-going gaiety outside; a timeless serenity in the shade within.

New Orleans is a lady—part American, part Spanish, more French than either in her essential viewpoint. She is intriguing in her swift changes of mood, *grande dame* one moment, *gamine* the next. She enjoys laughter, appreciates a show, relishes a quiet hour of happiness. By the unco guid she is considered a little shady, if not worse; she would be the first to admit she is no anemic Puritan. For she has seen a good deal in her day, and she doesn't shock easily.

It is generally admitted, however, that she has taste and judgment and poise unmistakable. To her have come glory and heartbreak, triumph and defeat, and she has profited from them all. She can look fate in the face and make the best of whatever befalls her. And above everything else she has her Gallic *joie de vivre*, her Latin appreciation of the generous intention, the gallant gesture.

Throughout her story New Orleans has remained faithful to herself, and to the river with which destiny joined her. In fat years and thin, she has stayed his Queen, now a consort in ornate halls, now a tired helpmate eating red beans and rice in her kitchen. With the Mississippi she will live to the end; and meanwhile she will go on as always, savoring, appreciating what the days bring.

A man once said that while in most of the United States business sometimes pauses for pleasure, in New Orleans pleasure sometimes pauses for business. Though, I hasten to add, not for long!

Over many generations America has looked on New Orleans as a place outside, hardly of its own kind. In a way, New Orleans is proud of that reputation, though she really doesn't care a great deal. At an early date she acquired tolerance, and she has been growing more tolerant ever since.

To her a shrug appears better than a frown, "taking things quietly" preferable to losing her temper. There aren't many things, she says, that justify a fit of indigestion.

Located on America's mightiest river, a hundred and ten winding miles above the Gulf of Mexico, New Orleans is a dry spot (geographically speaking) in a wet terrain; it is also a people subtly different from others; and it is an attitude. It has been American for a century and a half. Before that, for another century Louisiana belonged to France and to Spain. In mood, in philosophy, that first century was the more important. Despite all inroads of standardized "Americanization," much of the city's life seems closer to France than to New England, less akin to Chicago than to the Southern Europe of tradition.

For many decades people have come here to laugh and sigh, to be scornful and/or envious. The Puritan has termed it a hell-spot, dripping with scarlet wickedness. To this the Orleanian would retort that life is meant to be lived and that he cannot find it in himself to blame human beings for being— well, human. Yet only the most furious of bluenoses would call it a city without a conscience, for it is a place of countless churches and of faith continuously demonstrated. And none could term it placid, a scene to be painted in pastel shades. Past and present, it has seen unending struggle between man and man, and between man and Nature.

On the eve of Mardi Gras in 1699, the brothers Le Moyne —Pierre and Jean Baptiste—entered the forked mouth of the Mississippi on their way to a first sight of the spot. Days later they were staring at a vista of flat land inside a deep curve of the river, an Indian passage toward a narrow lake that gave rear entry to the Gulf itself.

Jean Baptiste Le Moyne, the Sieur de Bienville who was to become governor, never forgot this stretch, almost the only more or less dry area conveniently near the blue-green waters. By court order the first settlements were established along the sandy immensity of the Gulf; but Bienville repeatedly urged the need for a location on the great river itself, to be held for France. At last in 1718 came authority to establish La Nouvelle Orléans, christened after the profligate Duc d'Orléans, regent for the young Louis XV.

The general area was practically an island, bordered by lagoons, bayous, inlets, and low marshes. Wild birds haunted the meadowlike lowlands, and in shadowed swamps the brown water reflected the majesty of cypress trees. Nearby, workmen set out a walled rectangle, twelve squares along the river, seven in the other direction, and dug ditches to drain off the excess water. That parallelogram, the original French section, is still there, perhaps as little altered as any equivalent area in America.

The setting was one of blooming richness; strange birds winged in flights that shadowed the heavens. It seemed that the enthusiast was not far from right who said that the ground had only to be "tickled" to pour out wealth. The pioneers, however, found the spot less dry than they had supposed. Repeatedly the skies opened and tropical downpours turned New Orleans into a new lake. Then the river rose, and miserable soldiers, priests, and tavern-keepers struggled to spade up the first levees that were to grow like lines of giant caterpillars beside the Mississippi.

Thus began New Orleans' almost continuous fight with the environment. The city has been compelled almost literally to raise itself above its waters, and in the process has become a saucer-shaped expanse pierced by tranquil canals bearing boats, and drained by pumping stations as big as any in the world. The land lies only slightly above sea level in places, below it in others; to keep the town dry the pumps must often operate twenty-four hours of the day.

The levees produce a phenomenon that makes strangers doubt their eyes—the spectacle of ocean-going liners riding majestically higher than the town. During the spring crest, the river itself surges past above street level, restrained only

by the green mounds at its edge. Again, a passer-by turns a
corner to discover schooners riding along what seems to be
the edge of the street; canals still cut into the city. And until
recent years the Orleanian described the well-settled squares
as *îlets*, keeping the localism. When it rained, they were
precisely that. With all that it has had to fight, New Orleans'
survival has been a victory of ingenuity, of determination, of
adaptability.

Here the first warm-spirited Frenchmen lived an easy-going
existence, interrupted by occasional hearty fights. Visitors
detected an almost Caribbean flavor—slow hours in the glare,
rest in the blue shadows. There developed two styles: the
privileged elegance of the parlors for those whose black slaves
harvested the dark alluvial earth; and the simpler ways of plain
folk by the waterfront. For generations, too, a certain dual-
ism marked both these groups: rigid morality of family life
with sheltering care for Maman and the girls; at the same
time, in the cafés, saloons, and other establishments, a less
inhibited expression for the males. The pattern had a continental basis, of course, and New Orleans men seldom confused themselves with monks.

After some sixty-five years of French allegiance, Louisiana
was acquired by Spain, and New Orleans went right on being
itself. Let the Spaniards try to change that! But the town's
appearance altered, after successive fires and under changing
architectural influences. Some older, one-storied houses remained, with deep-hanging roofs, batten blinds and walls
briquetés entre poteaux (bricked between posts). More often
could be seen stuccoed houses with arches, scented courtyards, and ironwork of the simple wrought kind or of the
more elaborate cast variety. Behind this lacework Spaniards
courted Frenchwomen, and from their alliances emerged
a new designation—Creole. The New Orleans Creole is a
descendant of both elements, or of either, and the word de-
notes white, without admixture.

After forty years of Spain, Orleanians faced a truly shat-

tering change. In the intrigues of *haute politique*, Spain gave
the province back to France, which, astoundingly, sold it to
the United States—that incomprehensible place of uncultured,
troublesome backwoodsmen, said the Louisianians. The
Americans poured in. Beyond Canal Street, once the city's
dismal border, the newcomers built their own town on what
had been the old Jesuit plantation. For mile after mile they
took over territory along the river, giving it their own impress, introducing their codes and styles, and also buildings
in the more classic design. American and Creole clashed; but
with the "new people" arrived times of substantial wealth as
the town first awoke to the full potentialities of its location.

Days were golden. Cotton came into its own; steamboats
skimmed the Mississippi, and the richness of Ohio and the
river valley floated to New Orleans. Population doubled,
tripled. It was a roaring river port, a seaport, one of the
world's trading spots, cotton port of both hemispheres; and,
not least, part of the American frontier, the new "Southwest"
of Mexico and Texas, jumping-off place for hordes of adventurers. Everybody was heading for New Orleans to see
what it had for him.

Early and late it had been a melting pot into which tumbled
men of every nation, every color. And now came river boatman, farmer, plantation man, gambler, mulatto tradesman,
doctor, pirate, filibuster, land-schemer. Then and later, it
had a raffish, picaresque quality. To picture New Orleans in
more genteel fashion is to do it an injustice.

To the country at large New Orleans became a gaudy
name—streets thronging with wastrels, duels under the Oaks,
opera, quadroon mistresses for the wealthy, saloons, brawls,
and circuses. The disapproving called it a witch city, a wanton. Others dubbed it the Paris of the New World, or perhaps Marseille. The traveler Estwick Evans wrote with
acidity: "There is, perhaps, no place in the civilized world
where the influence of the gospel is more needed than New
Orleans." But none was more deeply shocked than Rachel,

wife of General Jackson of the Battle of New Orleans. Returning some years later, she wrote home: "Great Babylon is come up before me. Oh, the wickedness, the idolatry of this place! . . . Oh, farewell. Pray for your sister in a heathen land."

Despite Rachel or anyone else, the Orleanians pursued their good times, eating, drinking, and being merry. For mightn't they die or lose everything tomorrow or the next day if yellow fever arrived, or a flood, or a fall in cotton?

And New Orleans proved ever a beguiling spot. Those who came here might resent it at first, frown on it; before long they found themselves modifying their tone, even their disposition. They adopted the casual style, learned to sip coffee or harder stuff, developed a liking for what once had irritated them—the late-afternoon promenade. They were "Creolized." Many who had sniffed angrily ended by smiling and fanning themselves on the galleries. They might, I submit, have done worse.

Yet New Orleans was due for a fall. Linking itself with the Confederacy, it saw the river trade drop, the weeds push their way between the flagstones. The acid of poverty ate into the great homes; pillared doorways sagged, and ironwork rusted and broke apart.

Then, slowly, restoration, a near-miracle. Never a meek city, New Orleans fought back. In its struggle it found new resources within itself. Today it is vigorously on the way up again. At the same time it has maintained its ancient identity to a remarkable degree. There are those who claim that, if they were brought here by air, blindfolded, and set down on almost any street, they could identify the place instantly as New Orleans. A certain appearance, the "set" of a house, a sentence of speech—any of these is unmistakably *sui generis*.

The town spreads over a wide area, more than 350 square miles; only two other American cities cover a greater space.

The original town is but a fraction of the whole, though its philosophy dominates a great deal of the rest. This French quarter is today a conglomerate—some of it old, the rest not so old; French, American, Spanish, Italian, Filipino, Irish, German, Chinese, Greek—almost anything you mention. The quarter endured years of blighting ruin; yet for square after square, restoration has been at work here, too. Orleanians have "moved back," to repair, repaint, and refurbish houses in the earlier style, and to gather again in the evenings on the vine-hung galleries.

The old boundary streets are still there—Rampart, Esplanade, Canal, and also Orleans, the last the quarter's widest, opening at the garden behind St. Louis Cathedral and extending to Beauregard Square, where Negroes danced to the pound of African drums. The three-spired cathedral, standing where a church has stood during most of the city's existence, fronts the square at which soldiers drilled, monarchs proclaimed their will, and Creole youths met their girls under the eyes of chaperones.

At each side of the cathedral rise the heavy Spanish buildings of church and state, and the square is bordered also by great brick apartments—the Pontalba Buildings, about which the city has long talked. Just beyond is French Market, where Orleanians go, as did their great-grandmothers and great-grandfathers, to sample river shrimp, bayou crabs, vegetables, and spices. It is a many-flavored spot. . . . A few squares off is Royal, for generations the most fashionable of the original streets.

Beyond, the quarter shades into rows of houses once impressive, now forlorn, with clothes hanging behind iron scrolls that bear the monogram of long-dead owners. Bourbon, once the French Opera street, is now a glittering expanse of night clubs and saloons, strip-teases and a hundred other titillating spots. In its way Bourbon is now as famous as once-fabled Basin Street, where love was offered on a cash-and-carry basis. Only a few squares away, the ghosts of the madames moan in the semi-tropical evenings.

Esplanade Avenue, tree-bordered residential thoroughfare of later Creoles, is nearby, with lines of stuccoed houses showing touches of the classic. Old North Rampart, similarly, was once an aristocratic thoroughfare; a few homes hang on, next to garages and rooming-houses.

Canal, long the outer edge of town, is now the commercial centre, one of the widest of streets, almost endlessly decorated for holidays and special seasons. New Orleans is always having a festival, a parade, or a show of some kind. Into this hub of the town runs South Rampart, the street of Negroes, with hot-dog stands, pawnshops, and jazz—the city's great gift to millions of Americans.

From Canal, too, runs St. Charles Street, symbol of American influence. Higher up begins the Garden District, the homes of the Americans, made cheerful by the flower beds and by the birds in great oaks, pecan trees, and magnolias. . . . Beyond, for miles, stretch the wharves that line the Mississippi. Many smaller suburbs and municipalities that once existed along the river have been absorbed; at Carrollton the river turns and the city's expansion continues toward the lakefront, where old Milneburg was once a synonym for Joy. Into the lake goes winding Bayou St. John, with its plantation-style buildings, and nearby are Métairie, Gentilly, and other outlying sections with boundary lines of half-forgotten sugar estates among them.

Geographically, New Orleans surprises even Orleanians. Outside the French section, streets swerve with the Mississippi, or with the haphazard notions of bygone planners—curving, turning, returning. The river's bend leads, or misleads, the stranger to go long blocks out of his way, and even natives often discover short cuts they had never suspected. And almost always, a short distance off, there is water, the river, the lake, or one of the canals.

This town of some 600,000 people is a place of curious likes and dislikes, of assorted peculiarities. The Orleanian detests dimes: anybody who receives one immediately passes it to the next victim. Nobody says "porch" or "veranda"; to call a gallery by any other name reveals the speaker as an outlander. And Americans and Creoles alike spurn "sidewalk" in favor of that older word, banquette, from the French word for bench. (Originally the walks were low wooden structures over the mud.)

New Orleans has never been an apartment town; most natives prefer separate houses or half-houses. A few last old-timers, generally kindly ones, cling to the custom of *lagniappe*, the gift thrown in with a purchase, a sprig of green or a bit of candy. And nuns ride free on the busses and streetcars, because this is a strongly religious city and also because "the sisters" did so much to save the stricken population during successive epidemics.

New Orleans is a place of breadeaters, consuming more per capita than any other city in America. Orleanians refuse to give up their preference for long loaves of crisp French bread; and they render homage to the "poor boy sandwich," a half-loaf of that bread stuffed with meat, tomatoes, dressing, gravy—enough, perhaps, for a small family.

Daily more coffee is swallowed than anywhere else in the United States; regularly business is interrupted for the usual small cupful, and firms maintain continuous coffee service to keep employes, and also executives, happy. The natives, too, are certain—and, as one, I agree—that their strongly brewed kind is the world's finest, that what other sections offer is insipid stuff at best.

So strong is their liking for enthusiastically seasoned shrimp and crabs that families boil tubfuls and invite friends in for an evening of peeling and eating them. The oyster bar is also an institution; there are bars at which three generations of shuckers have served as many generations of customers. For years the New Orleans man who stays out late has hastened to a restaurant for a "wife pacifier"—a toasted, buttered loaf filled with golden-brown oysters. No wife, sniffing this, can stay mad for long.

In the French section, upstairs residents needing supplies attach ropes to baskets, call down to nearby merchants, and lower the baskets. Filled, they are drawn up again, and Madame has saved herself a round trip. Another labor-saver: You lock the downstairs door against intruders, but when a friend arrives you lean over the gallery, drop the key, and again eliminate exertion.

Today a few of the older Creoles stay, year in, year out, in their below-Canal-Street neighborhood. They are, however, not quite like the earlier residents who, as a matter of conscience, never set foot in enemy territory beyond the dividing line. Still, as one told me recently: "I went over Canal Street once. *Non*, two times. It was interesting. But I saw no reason to do it again."

And, despite the inroads of modern merchandising, black street criers still walk or ride about on wagons, offering figs, blackberries, and coal. Chimney sweeps, traveling in pairs, call "Raminay! Raminay!" They wear handed-down evening suits and high hats, and carry rope, straw, and palmetto to make the chimney draw. One I know makes a living as a theatre porter, earning three times what his chimneys bring; but frequently he calls a friend and goes to work with rope and palmetto. Why? "In ma blood," he guesses. "Papa, he done it before me. Never seen a bad fireplace, but he itch' to clean it out. Me, too." Many another Orleanian does what he does because it is "in ma blood."

It is a city that conceals much of itself from the too casual. Its moods vary; it is now cosmopolitan, again provincial; one part placid, almost pastoral, another white-hot in temper. It delights in gossip, yet its columnists print no impending divorces or births. It has some of the ripest slums in America, and in certain sections class lines harder than the ancient

ironwork. In general it is somewhat more tolerant toward
Negroes than most Southern cities; yet it has known more
than a few bloody riots against minorities.

Between upper St. Charles Avenue with its white houses
and palms, and Bourbon with its impudent and raffish air,
differences cut deep. The distance from the mirror-hung
plantation house on Bayou St. John to the French Market
coffee shop, where all the city meets after a Carnival ball or
a party, is a matter of far more than a few linear miles.

An artist group huddles cross-legged about an open fire in
a cubicle on Chartres Street, arguing economics, war, and
Freud. Next door two maidens of seventy sit in their courtyard beneath walls that their ancestor built long, long ago.
Fanning themselves, they talk sedately of *cousins* and *cou-
sines*, recalling what Monsieur le Gouverneur said to Grand-
père. Let the world change; they will never desert the great
shadowy house in which they occupy two of the eighteen
rooms.

A few squares away from that restful house, a black jazz
assembly seethes in an obscure shack, successor to Funky
Butt Hall of earlier, and redolent, fame. And a short way
from that, a group of light-skinned quadroons drink anisette,
that favorite liqueur of another day, and talk in French of
their mulatto ancestor shown in the wall frame, who had
slaves in his own name. . . .

Uptown, downtown, front of town, back of town, it is a
city of chance-taking. Gambling seems almost a folk thing.
In the town, or just outside (depending on the city politics
of the moment), it is provided for every taste: the plush
variety for those who like to go in evening dress; a middle-
class kind; and that for the poorer people—in big, brightly
lighted halls frequented by women in house aprons and coat-
less men, who ride out on a bus to gamble with the nickels
they have hoarded all week long.

A few steps from one of the loudest of such places lives a
group of quiet families whose existence is as staid as though

they lived in a community of five hundred. I once asked a member of such a family how she put up with the wild times at her elbow. "Oh," she twinkled, "I have *heard* of that place, yes. But I never go there myself. And so . . ." A great deal of New Orleans is like that. It has heard, but doesn't go, and so. . . .

I remember a remarkable bartender, Bussey of the one-time Press Club during Prohibition. Bussey liked his customers, and, careless in arithmetic, he often gave back too much change. Once when this was called to his attention he gave a wide grin. "What of it? It's all the same—six of one, fifty of the other!"

The lady that is New Orleans, too, often appears to smile and say: Six of one, fifty of the other.

PART I

Once a Creole,
Always a Creole

CHAPTER I

Largesse, Finesse, and l'Amour

THE richest young man in America and perhaps the most adventurous—such was the handsome Bernard Philippe de Marigny de Mandeville. Today, as in the nineteenth century, he is the Creole of Creoles, golden boy, symbol of gallantry and the engaging disposition that chuckles at anything. He laughed through a long career; what he did best, friends said, was enjoy himself.

Yet Bernard did more than that. As well as any man, he realized the heritage of his period and place—high Creole manner, zest, the ability to come to satisfactory terms with life. He wanted everyone around him to have a happy time, and he seemed almost too ready to make that possible. The open hand, the gesture of over-impulsive kindness . . . even his faults had grand style. He liked most things, particularly girls. If he had a main purpose, it was this: He would be good to the ladies. With Bernard it was *largesse, finesse,* and, above all, *l'amour.*

There had been Marignys in the New World before there was a Louisiana. In Canada one of them won letters-patent of nobility; another appeared early on the Gulf Coast with Governor Bienville. From the French court the Marignys took military posts and favors; then they aligned themselves with Spanish officialdom. In the late 1700s Pierre Philippe de

Marigny blossomed as New Orleans' biggest property owner; the colony could grow nowhere, upriver or down, without making him wealthier.

Below the town ramparts, fronting the river near what was to be the "Elysian Fields," Pierre Philippe erected his maison Marigny—a structure of heavy cypress, high-pitched roof covering a sweeping gallery. Brick piers supported tapering wooden posts, and before the house an avenue of grand oaks, moss-draped, thick with ivy, stretched to the levee. Grace King, in her *Creole Families of New Orleans*, described it as "a primitive sort of palace, remarkable chiefly for its size, which was that of two ordinary large mansions joined together."

Here Papa Marigny managed his land, sawmill, and canal and also sired a family of five, of whom the middle one, gay Bernard, outshone all the rest. Papa, Grand-père, and his other ancestors provided background; Bernard made the most of it. They had been Chevaliers of the Order of St. Louis and had achieved impressive interment inside the cathedral. But New Orleans would seldom recall them; all its talk would be of that engaging rascal Bernard.

From childhood he was the indulged favorite of his easy-going father and adoring mother. The men of the family praised his composure, his air of authority over his playmates; the women sighed over his dark locks and the grace with which he kissed their hands. The education and training given to the boy was what the Marigny tradition called "a gentleman's education": little book-learning, certainly no mental discipline, but thorough grounding in horsemanship, fencing, and the handling of firearms, with ease and skill in all the fashionable outdoor sports. Though he had a succession of tutors, studying interested him less than hunting. Bernard was always to find life itself an adequate substitute for any education beyond the three R's.

In 1798, when the boy was thirteen, New Orleans welcomed royalty-in-exile, the Duc d'Orléans (who would become King Louis Philippe) and his brothers; and to Papa Marigny fell the privilege of entertainment. With his elders, the precocious Bernard attended—and danced at—all the cotillions. At the Marigny home, with the attentive Bernard at their elbow, the princes blinked at crystal chandeliers, ponderous silver, suites of rosewood. They blinked again when Papa Marigny explained that he was thinking of moving to Cuba because there was more money there! So much impressed was the duke that, with some prefatory throat-clearing, he introduced a delicate topic: finances. Could he, might he . . . ? Papa understood. How much? The duke mentioned an almost staggering figure; without a murmur his host agreed to provide it. Then, the excited Bernard accompanying the visitors as far as the river mouth, they sailed away.

On the death of Maman and Papa, relatives were to look after the boy. But at seventeen Bernard had acquired skill in evading both guardians and chaperones. As long as he lived he would chase the girls, or the girls would chase him; in either case the hunt seldom flagged. Bernard's general self-possession was phenomenal. He rode a horse with style, tossing the reins negligently to a groom on reaching the theatre, waving to friends, making easy gifts to those in his circle. What he donned today, half the Creole youth imitated within a week. Yet he was no fop; he had the careless touch, the assurance that hardly bothered to straighten a cuff or push back a lock.

Not tall, about five feet seven, he was strongly built. The light-blue eyes looked out with a humor that showed also about the heavy lips. Ever an individualist, Bernard rejected the fashionable beard, to go smooth-shaven. Few joked about his lack of height or of facial hair, for he was a master duelist; it has been said that he fought fifteen men. Impulsive and capricious, he was far from vindictive. He never engaged in a match to the death. A spurt of blood—this satisfied him.

When one youth slapped him, Bernard sniffed: "He's a good fellow. I'll just give him a gash across the hand, so he won't forget the next time." For the day, this was a notably mild attitude.

The relative in whose charge the boy had been put was Ignace de Lino de Chalmette—about as bad a choice as could have been made. When he recognized his failure he turned the eighteen-year-old over to others. The family had business connections with the firm of Panton & Leslie in Pensacola, and thither went Bernard, smiling. It was hoped that, among strangers, the boy would improve; besides, Panton himself was both Scottish and rigidly puritanical.

Casually Bernard went to work in the firm's trading rooms. But little Pensacola, still under Spain, had night lights as bright as New Orleans'. Bernard turned strangers into friends, all too warm, and what he learned was not business. There developed an affair with a lady who did not regard her fifteen years' seniority as a handicap. Nor did Bernard. There were no women, he swore, to match these lovely Floridians. But when the rigid Mr. Panton heard of the affair he banged his ledger books, and Bernard left, still smiling.

So much for the efforts of the Pensacola partner; Chalmette would now try Leslie of London. That firm responded with something less than joy at the prospect, though this time Bernard made promises. Promptly he was embracing England and things English, nearby France and things French. But it was not long before George III's London bored him; his real delight was in a foray to Paris with its ballet and its ballerinas. There were no women, he swore, to match those lovely Parisiennes. . . .

Nor did the London experiment long endure. At the company's suggestion (if not outright demand), Bernard returned to New Orleans in 1803. Louisiana had learned that it was to be given back to France, and none was more overjoyed than Bernard. When the envoy Pierre de Laussat arrived, young Bernard entertained him, outdoing Papa with dinners, parties,

and fireworks at the house by the levee. The guest described
the scene: "The river shows itself here to the best advantage;
we are situated at a point in its crescent that dominates the
port. One hundred ships, some of France, some of Spain, but
mostly of Anglo-Americans, stretch out in the distance as
would a forest afloat, and offer a perspective worthy of the
busiest port in the world." Laussat objected to just one thing:
Often they had to retire as early as ten o'clock "to escape the
attacks of mosquitoes and gnats, which at sundown take possession of the air" and which are endurable "thanks only to
the acquired toughness of the natives' skin and their passion
for gambling."

The young man joined Laussat's staff as aide. But the
cession hung fire curiously; nobody knew exactly what was
happening. Then arrived shattering news: Napoleon had sold
Louisiana to the United States! Bernard didn't like this,
naturally, but he did not—as his friends did—recoil from the
newcomers. Others might forbid the use of the English
language in their homes; Bernard, who had learned that barbarous tongue, was willing to give anybody a chance, even
an *Américain*. His English never lost its accent, however, and
when he got mad he forgot every English word he knew.

Gold-braided to the teeth, Bernard went to the parties that
accompanied the double transfer, including one that began at
dusk, with card-playing, dinner, dancing, three-o'clock supper, and more dancing. He joined toasts to Spain, France,
and the United States, each with a salute of twenty-one guns;
and he was one of the last to leave when morning came. On
November 3, 1803, he stood with others in a steady rain at
the Place d'Armes as the Spanish banner dropped and the
Tricolor of France supplanted it; within three weeks he stood
there again as the Tricolor sank and the Stars and Stripes rose.

Now Bernard astonished his friends by volunteering as an
aide to General Wilkinson, the American Government's representative. For five years he was to remain in that capacity,
enjoying his place in the spotlight. How good a soldier he

made we do not know; but the Americans, anxious to enlist leading Creoles on their side, welcomed him. And soon he did another thing that demonstrated adaptability. Who do you think is getting married, Auguste? Bernard—and to a *demi-Américaine! Non*, it is not a joke.

The girl was little Mary Ann, daughter of Evan Jones, who had come from the East, served as American consul, and married Marie Verret, a Creole. In spite of her funny name ("Jones" sounded ridiculous in New Orleans), she spoke French and had a nickname, Pomponne. The gentle Pomponne was the best thing that ever happened to Bernard. A contemporary newspaper called her "good without ostentation." The bridegroom was buoyantly happy, and there were no more escapades. His friends beamed; a Pomponne was just what Bernard had needed.

They had a son, then another. Bernard applied to the legislature to be granted his majority even though he was not yet twenty-one, so that he might buy and sell property. For he had a great deal—indeed, he might have lived all his life on his income—and everybody regarded it as a good sign that he was showing serious interest in it. Then Pomponne fell seriously ill, and the young husband summoned a notary to draw up her will. She explained (so runs the pathetic contemporary record) that she wished to "anticipate the hour of death, which is always uncertain." She mentioned her children, and called Bernard "a good father, whose tenderness I so well know." Apparently doctors suggested a trip; a few months later Pomponne died in Philadelphia. When her body was brought home, he had a tomb built on the estate, so that he might have her near him still.

But he was so inconsolable that for a time he thought of leaving Louisiana. Relatives took over the care of the two boys, and Bernard sat alone in the big house. Friends, noting his lagging step, proposed a leisurely jaunt, and he rode over to Pensacola.

There Bernard accepted an invitation to a dance, where

his bored glance settled on a vivid nineteen-year-old brunette, and grew less bored. Hadn't he always said there was nothing like these Floridians? A friend frowned: "You'll get into trouble. Too many other persons are as interested as you are."

"Trouble? That's what I like. Take me over and introduce me!"

After his first dance, he asked for another. The girl was Anna Mathilda Morales, daughter of a former Spanish intendant at New Orleans; obviously Bernard was trying to improve American relations with Spain. As they danced he encountered bitter looks, and over coffee the next morning he flipped through a half-dozen challenges to duels. "Tell them I can hardly take them all on at once, *comme ça*," he yawned. "I'll meet them one by one, till I've finished."

Next day the first youth lay on the ground, and that stopped it. Having a clear field, Bernard ended by taking the dark-eyed girl home as his wife. The second Madame Marigny enjoyed the Marigny wealth and acquired a certain hauteur. Though she presented Bernard with one child after another until there were five, and regularly appeared beside him at the opera, whispers circulated that it was not an altogether happy marriage. They were to remain together for years, but Bernard had meanwhile amused himself in other directions.

Having conceived a scheme to turn the Marigny plantations into a new subdivision, Faubourg Marigny, he combined dalliance with business. Now he built cottages for his changing favorites. In a mood of recollection, he called a new street rue d'Amour. Later, observing the growing families about the cottages, he had an inspiration. With a chuckle he named the adjoining passage rue des Bons Enfants, "Good Children's Street." Another he called Bagatelle. Some say the title was taken from the familiar game. Others credit it to a convivial evening when Bernard lighted a banknote to find his way along a hall, and laughingly retorted to a friend's remonstrances: "It's only a bagatelle!" Members of the Cruzat family remember a story of how, when he once arrived at home in a gay mood, with two carriages full of fruits, cakes, and other gifts, Anna Mathilda asked where he had gotten them.

"Oh, the candies—from M—— . . . pretty thing! The cakes—from J——. That girl makes the best in New Orleans. Why, my dear, what's the matter?"

Anna Mathilda shook a trembling finger. "You have all the vices of—of—"

"Madame, I have all the vices of—of—a gentleman!"

A certain type of wife might have given Bernard a measure of understanding, have won him gradually from his ways. But Anna Mathilda was not that type. She had a Spanish temper, and moods to match. For the rest of her life she would feel sorry for herself, and throw things on the floor.

Bernard strolled through a city in which he knew almost everybody. He bought a flower from one of the dozens of *marchandes*, black or mulatto, who carried things ranging from fish to drygoods and candies. He stopped to sample a *cala*, a rich, sweet rice cake that was a Creole favorite, and for a few moments paused to joke with a *rabais* man. (A *rabais* was a "bargain," usually a cloth remnant bought by the frugal housewife.) At street corners he passed walls or posts bearing the fluttering notices by which the Creoles informed the district of deaths in their families; later in the day, formal invitations to the funeral would be sent.

On his way again, Bernard might be stopped by a dignified Negro, immaculately dressed and carrying a silver basket containing notices of a party. Deaths and soirées—Creoles were equally formal in each case. Since the servant could not read, he handed the basket to Bernard, who did what everyone else was doing that day—riffled through the cards to see who else was being invited. French New Orleans had few secrets.

Resuming his stroll, Bernard stopped in one café, then another, where friends sat drinking, smiling, arguing. At each place he signaled and the waiter took down from the shelf Monsieur Bernard's private drinking glass. Bernard bade a warm farewell to a young man who was about to make the grand tour of Europe. After that he and a pair of intimates rose, took a look at one of the circuses, at which a bear was pitted against a set of snapping dogs, then made a slow promenade past the parade ground of the military clubs, then to the slave pen near the levee, in which Negroes waited for sale.

Bernard's eye swept over a pair of demoiselles with their father on their way to the steamer. Three Spanish soldiers in tight jackets passed, whistling; behind them staggered an earringed man with a Levantine look, who almost collided with the two nuns going quietly along, beads swinging, white headdresses nodding. Bowing deeply, the stranger backed into an odd-looking fellow who carried a cage with a parrot screeching in an unidentifiable tongue. Bernard moved on, humming to himself. From the river edge, piled with merchandise, there rose a heavy, mixed fragrance suggestive of a dozen places—the sharp smell of fermenting molasses, the scent of rich spices from the Orient, the odor of overripe fruits, the penetrating aroma of West Indian rum. After a time Bernard said goodbye to his friends and started off for a night at the gaming tables.

More and more, gambling fascinated him; he would bet on anything. Though the sport of craps had long been known here, Bernard first made upper-class Creoles appreciate it. Soon he had friends bending with him over the cubes. The conservatives thought it undignified; Bernard said *Pouf* and went on playing. Eventually, after a losing streak, he selected a name for a new street. "Rue de Craps!" he shouted and Craps Street it became.

Now politics drew his eye. He hated regular hours; he liked the centre of the stage. What better than public office? He went to the territorial legislature, and to Louisiana's first

constitutional convention, as the youngest delegate. At
twenty-nine, as the British approached New Orleans and the
famous battle, he became chairman of the legislature's defense
committee. Leathery Andrew Jackson marched in, and Bernard looked forward to entertaining him, until rivals snagged
the prize. Bernard told how the mayor played a fool: "The
rain was pouring down; all present were wet, muddy, and
uncomfortable; but the mayor (given to singing madrigals
to persons in power) assured the general that the sun never
shone more brightly than when he was among them!"

Bernard pitched in, however, worked earnestly, and bore
no grudge. Eventually this lord of Louisiana came forward
as a red-hot Jacksonian, hurling epithets at his opponents:
"Aristocrats, minions of wealth!" Nor, when listeners
grinned, could he understand. Nevertheless he showed himself an advocate of extending the ballot and other democratic
movements of the day. As always, he fitted no mold.

A curious combination was Bernard de Marigny at this
stage, a combination of sophistication and a certain naïveté.
He believed himself to be the public man that Louisiana
needed, and he said so. Again, he used a highly original plea
in asking the voters to put him into a legislative office. His
opponents, he said lightly, were lawyers and notaries; if they
lost, they would still have their professions to support them.
He was neither lawyer nor notary, he added; if he lost the
election he wouldn't know what to do with his time! Always
he would be full-blooded, impractical, unpredictable. When
an American opponent poked scorn at Bernard's best-known
peccadilloes, Bernard conceded that he was a Lothario—but
since when had it been a crime to be a man? If this kept up,
ambitious Orleanians would have to suppress their taste for
l'amour. Did they want that? From a thousand lusty throats
came New Orleans' Non, non!

For years he was the Creoles' most fervent spokesman. He
loved shouting speeches. A contemporary observed: "With
all the trappings of the orator, it is really unfortunate that he

did not aspire more seriously to the glories of the rostrum. With a little more study, a little more method in fathoming matters . . ." Another, appraising his political writings, said: "He addresses his readers the way Napoleon used to speak to his soldiers." Nature had done a great deal for him; he had done less for himself.

Though he rose to high rank in Louisiana's House and Senate, he coveted still higher place—the governor's office—and ran for it repeatedly. Here he struck a new note; he hired bands, dancers, and singers and toured the state, putting on fine shows to woo the electorate. By nearly a hundred years he anticipated the devices of the modern Southern gubernatorial candidates who bake biscuits, croon their love of children, and call voters their Sunshine. The country people delighted in these shenanigans; they danced in the torchlight with their wives and girls. When Bernard left the platform to take a pretty hand and bestow a compliment, he sometimes lost a husband's vote. But after all, was politics everything?

He maintained a long friendship with his hero Jackson, sending frequent suggestions and advice. When President Jackson's undiplomatic remarks about the French threatened international trouble, Bernard wrote to the President and to the French court, urging a method of settlement. Whether or not he really had any influence, we may be sure that he took a firm tone with both.

His handsome face changed little with the years, and his charm became only more infectious. His children were growing up—the two boys by that first, happy marriage, and the three girls and two boys by the later one. Anna Mathilda was increasingly cold to him, apparently the only person in New Orleans who did not like him. He had a way of amusing the children by singing "broad" songs to them, and it infuriated his wife. "Now, *chérie*," he would remonstrate, tongue in cheek, "the children can't possibly understand those songs. Are you sure *you* do? A lady like you?"—which hardly calmed the lady.

In about 1829 Bernard de Marigny was ready to launch his greatest project. Beyond Lake Pontchartrain lay some finely elevated tracts, covering five thousand acres, which Bernard now acquired. The shore was lined with tall pines, interspersed with spruce, sweet gum, and the dramatic blooms of magnolias. At intervals rose gnarled oaks, and about them twisted slow bayous. In getting control of this land, Bernard had at first thought only of vacation quarters. He picked a wind-swept stretch; there was no single big house, but there was a pair of sprawling wooden ones with ample galleries. He had handsome parterres laid out, and planned roads and walks among the aromatic woods. Remembering his visits to France, he christened it Fontainebleau after the forest-bordered summer château of the kings.

Here he established a bachelor existence. Boatloads of friends came for week ends or longer, to follow Bernard at the thing in which he excelled, the pleasant use of leisure. At Fontainebleau-sur-Pontchartrain all hours were to be free. Did his guests like oysters? He would take them to nearby reefs. Ducks, wild geese? Guns were ready. Salt-water fishing? They would sail along the lake to the Gulf. Wine? The cellar was as well filled as that of Bernard's city home. Fontainebleau cream, butter, meats, chickens . . . and Bernard delighted in having it all brought out for picnics on the sunspotted green among the pines. And he added a final, regal touch. Over a low stream he had slaves build a drawbridge; before that could be lowered, a caller had to satisfy attendants. And if Anna Mathilda made one of her rare trips here, Bernard could delay her until he was ready to let her in!

Between amusements his ambitions expanded. Why not a town, a general vacation spot? He would invite the Creoles, combine the profits of an entrepreneur with the acquisition of pleasant neighbors. He cut more roadways and set out ornamental growths, and a sprightly toy town materialized, with market, town hall, and dock. He gave it part of his family name—Mandeville; it would be his, to reign over like a grand seigneur. When hotels appeared, he brought out great chefs from New Orleans, and for years Mandeville would be celebrated for its transcendent cuisine. He arranged for a ferry, and thousands flocked over. Bernard decided, however, that the place still lacked something, and he went to work to supply the lack. He liked gambling, and knew many others who did. With John ("Toto") Davis, theatre owner and gamester, he put up a small Monte Carlo with Marigny trimmings. Davis advertised other attractions, among them the sport of "pistol-shooting"—the targets live bats, released as participants took aim.

Meanwhile, unexpectedly, had come an opportunity that might have changed not Bernard's life only but also the history of New Orleans. When a group of American businessmen sought an appointment, Bernard pricked up his ears. His Faubourg Marigny grew only slowly; on the other side of Canal Street the Anglo-Saxons had not yet reached their stride. But he was surprised when Samuel J. Peters, their leader, made a quick offer: His group wanted to buy all of Bernard's suburb, develop it with a hotel, theatres, new industries. Even if there were not wharfage problems upriver, Faubourg Marigny offered better sites for the purpose. The man named the substantial sum the group were prepared to pay.

It could well be a major windfall; New Orleans would advance downtown rather than up—among the French element, Bernard's people. After a moment he agreed, documents were ordered, a day set for the transfer. On that morning Mr. Peters was greeted by Bernard, alone. The American knew that Madame de Marigny, too, must sign the papers. Bernard smiled: "I expect her in soon." A half-hour passed, then another. Bernard apologized. Would Mr. Peters come back Monday? A little coolly, the American agreed.

On Monday, the minutes again went slowly; again Bernard expressed regret: "Just a moment, Monsieur. I will make sure that she is in the house." But she was not. On the third attempt the caller was obviously impatient; his face darkened as the minutes went by with no sign of Madame. At last a servant brought word: Madame must be excused—she had to see her veil-maker. Peters' gorge rose; by this time he suspected that the Creole had instructed his wife to stay away. "I'll never forget this," he told Marigny hoarsely. "You'll live, by God, to see grass choking the gutters of this faubourg!"

The truth seems to have been that Anna Mathilda had decided to spite her husband or else that she did not trust his business judgment. In either case, she did not sign. So the Americans changed all their plans. Word of the situation spread, Bernard was blamed, and from then on his public fortunes declined. He shrugged, but he did make an effort to carry out the Americans' scheme in his own way. However, rich though he still was, he could not match their combined capital, nor did he employ such sharp guardians of operations as the Americans could. Time schedules and such? He couldn't bother over those things. With a grandiose gesture he ordered a wide central avenue—his Champs Élysées, with a superb "neutral" ground, handsomely landscaped, which was to become the choice residential boulevard of the city. But gradually the Americans won; he could not turn the tide.

By now he knew more personal sorrows. His favorite son of that first marriage, Gustave Adolphe, was much like him both in looks and in temperament. Who knew? If the boy put his heart to it, he yet might turn out a first-class rake! But he shared Papa's love of the duel, and it ended all hopes for him. One evening friends brought the boy home, his chest badly ripped, and in the big house on the river Bernard watched his first-born die. He had not suffered so much since the day of the news about little Pomponne.

Rosa, one of the daughters, married a Cuban revolutionary who took part in a Mexican uprising; the other side won, and he faced a firing squad. Then the other son of Bernard's first marriage died, and this had a bizarre sequel. (Wherever Marignys went, there would be humor or oddity.) The boy's widow took a second husband, Alexandre Grailhe, an elderly and foppish attorney. In spite of Anna Mathilda, Bernard always considered marriage a good institution, and he did not object this time. But he was shocked when he learned that the youthful widow had signed a wedding contract giving Grailhe full use of her property, about $180,000 worth. Bernard fumed that this "despoiled" the children by the first marriage.

What ensued is folklore. Here is the usual version: Bernard interfered, dueled with Grailhe, and quickly impaled him. Grailhe nearly died; then, slowly recovering, he could walk only if he bent forward. He would probably never straighten up; the surgeons were unable to reach a clot or abscess far back in the chest. As the story continues, Grailhe and Bernard quarreled again, and Grailhe insisted on a second duel; he couldn't use a sword any more, but he could manage a pistol. This time Bernard scored as quickly as before—in the same spot, and the bullet carried the abscess out through the man's back! Grailhe regained his health, but when he walked again, he found that instead of leaning forward, he tilted back. And jokesters offered bets on which way he would come out the next time.

But here is the true story: Grailhe had his first duel with another man and his second with Bernard's son Antoine James, known as "Mandeville." From the first duel Grailhe emerged tilted a little to the left, owing to a blood clot. In the second, young Marigny shot him in that same spot; but on recovering Grailhe still bent sideways—to the right!

Slowly the world grew less bright for Bernard. He had overextended himself, turned too much cash into land. He had seldom let such matters disturb him; money was too petty a thing to worry about, wasn't it? He mortgaged his Fontainebleau for some bank stock that looked good but wasn't. And always there continued the drain of his endless gifts and loans to friends and acquaintances. When little of this largesse came back to him, he shrugged. None could say of Bernard de Marigny, as they did of certain puritanical Americans in New Orleans, that he had ice water in his veins.

Banquets, drawbridges, speculations—all took their toll. The great 1837 panic hit the country; and at the demand of Bernard's creditors, financial men appraised his situation, to report that he still commanded $915,000, with debts of $320,000. His plantation needed considerable modernizing, and he made a fresh start with borrowed capital. Then he remembered something else. By now there was a new King of the French, Louis Philippe, once the guest of Bernard's father. Since that day—forty years ago—he had from time to time sent tokens of regard: a portrait in a diamond-studded frame, a dinner set bearing portraits of the royal household. Did he still, Bernard wondered now, remember the Marigny family and the money he had borrowed from its head? Bernard recalled Louis Philippe's earlier words: If ever he could make a return for that loan . . .

Bernard now wrote that he might soon be going to Europe, and presently there came an invitation to visit the "Citizen King." Arriving in France with his son Mandeville, Bernard hastened to the Tuileries, where they were made welcome at the royal receptions, balls, and outdoor parties. The king called Bernard "mon cher" and asked his opinions on American matters. When Louis Philippe mentioned Texas, Bernard at once informed him that he knew all about Texas and proceeded to demonstrate this at length. Never one for false modesty, our Bernard.

The Louisianian enjoyed the ceremonial splendor, the brilliant and friendly society; he was having perhaps the best time of his life. But there remained that matter of money. . . . Whenever an opportunity presented itself, he brought up Louis Philippe's visit years ago, with gentle emphasis on the Marigny hospitality, in a fashion that one would think even a king might understand. But nothing happened.

The king was cordial, but evidently the initiative would have to be Bernard's. Boldly, he became specific one day: he found himself in certain financial difficulties and had been hoping that Majesty would see its way . . . Majesty was all sympathy; of course Majesty would help—young Mandeville should be appointed a cadet at St. Cyr!

Swallowing his chagrin, Bernard nodded. Put not your trust in princes. . . . After he returned to Louisiana he winced whenever Louis Philippe's name was mentioned. As for young Mandeville, he stayed on in France for a few years as a cavalry lieutenant, but he missed the life behind the levee and he indulged in some hot quarreling. Presently he too decided to go home. As a parting gift from the king he received a handsome white mount. A horse—as repayment for what his grandfather had done for a duke.

Mandeville was troubled by the changes he found in Bernard. To keep afloat, Bernard had had to dispose of valuable properties, and this brought creditors buzzing about his ears. He was now sixty-two and—as described by an observer— "doubly burdened, by the accumulation of years and by his reverses of fortune. . . . He always acts busy, though as far as I know he has little to do." He was still "full of animation, merry and insouciant." Bernard wasn't beaten yet.

With the year 1850 came a break in the Mississippi levee that wiped out Marigny's crop. Well, next season's crop would be better. Then next season the levee gave way again, and ruin confronted him. Years ago Bernard had led fellow-legislators in creating the Citizens' Bank, which was to prove the agent of that ruin. His plantation would be seized unless he could sell it first; so he sold. Two years after this, at sixty-seven, he also lost his golden estate by the lake—his Fontainebleau—as well as his interest in the toy town of Mandeville. His summer house stood empty; to the latticed houses he had set up for al fresco dinners came only the wild birds.

By now, too, his Faubourg Marigny had declined badly.

His American competitor's angry prediction had come true: grass *was* growing in the streets. His Champs Élysées, so grandiloquently named, had been debased to a mere roadway, indistinguishable from its neighbors and used by the Pontchartrain Railroad whose engines spread billowing smoke over the area. High hopes had ended in smoke. . . .

He still owned the great house in which he had spent his life, and for a time he moved slowly about its echoing halls. Then this, too, had to go. He retained the furnishings—the carved tables, the desks inlaid with mother-of-pearl, the splendid rugs over which the great had walked; some he gave to friends, others he sold, and the few remaining pieces he took with him to a house on Frenchman Street, one of his last possessions. Here he would live in a bedchamber and a kitchen. He needed no more; few visitors came to see him nowadays, for his clique had evaporated.

The man who had once aspired to be governor now accepted a post whose irony he can hardly have missed—that of mortgage registrar. But it was soon coveted by the politicians, and the one-time prince of Fontainebleau had to issue a pamphlet defending his claim to it. Many years ago he had told the voters that they ought to give him an office because, if he lost, he wouldn't know what to do with his time. But there was no humor in what he told them now: If he were removed from *this* post he would have little left to live on. But he lost it, none the less.

From yet another quarter blew the winds of disaster. Anna Mathilda suddenly sued Bernard for full control of her remaining property. The two had long been estranged; both were approaching seventy, and she was almost bedridden. Most of the income that was now maintaining them was derived from her holdings, which Bernard managed. Now this function was to be taken from him—a step by which, cried his attorneys, Anna Mathilda might be condemning herself to "the same bed of straw to which she has, through this act, consigned her husband." Nevertheless, she won her main con-

tention, and for Bernard things had reached a low point indeed.

Within a year she was dead. He lived into his eighties,
through the war between North and South. Back in 1815, as
a young man he had joined in the successful defense of his
city against the British; now he watched it pass into hostile
hands. For several years after the war Bernard moved quietly
about the city that had spread wide as his own sphere shrank.
His health seemed excellent, his shoulders only slightly bowed.
His hair was still thick, and in these latter years he had let his
beard grow. But his light-blue eyes were the same as ever,
still sparkling when he spoke.

His walks took Bernard past many a place that had once
been his. Here was the site of the family's canal, long lost;
there had stood the sawmill, gone years ago. This was the rue
d'Amour—this the rue des Bons Enfants—and Bagatelle—and
Craps. Did the old man's fingers itch when he saw that last
name?

He never lost his practiced eye. No twenty-year-old could
rise more promptly to his feet and escort a lady to the dance
floor. On windy days the aged cavalier never hesitated to
halt when a breeze lifted a skirt about a slim ankle. A descendant in Paris tells me of this incident: Her grandmother, then
a young girl, was walking along one day with her parasol over
her head, when she heard two men whispering behind her.
She made out a sentence: "What a fine figure. Let's go around
her and see if she's pretty, too." The girl recognized Bernard's
voice. As he reached her, she turned around with a smile:
"Bon jour, Grand-père!" For once Grand-père could not
think of a quip.

February of the year 1868 brought cold weather. One
morning Bernard slipped on the banquette and fell, striking
his head. He was dead before passers-by could get him in-
doors. He was eighty-three. The news sped about the old
section. On the next afternoon, that of the funeral, New Or-

leans had its heaviest downpour in months. Nevertheless there were many present to mourn this representative of a bygone and almost forgotten era. Irony followed him to his grave: Though his will directed that he was to be buried at the side of his first wife—the Creole-American Pomponne—he lies instead beside Anna Mathilda Morales. Hers was the last laugh. . . .

Bernard Philippe de Marigny de Mandeville, last of the ancient Creoles, symbol of unchallenged wealth and pomp, can be read as a symbol of other things too. He stands for light-hearted folly, for *vanitas vanitatum;* but also for generosity and kindliness and zest. "Yes," says a Creole of today, "we have had greater men than Bernard de Marigny to represent us, but none that everybody liked so much!"

The great Marigny house by the river fell into the hands of an American to whom it seemed an anachronism only. In the eighteenth century it had dominated a wide and unsettled countryside. Now, hedged in by time and the mutability of events, it was destined to be torn down bit by bit. As for Bernard's place by the lake, it also changed owners and eventually disappeared. His Faubourg Marigny lost its very name; so did Love Street and Good Children, Bagatelle and Craps. The last one fell a victim to propriety. When a church was built on Craps Street the members balked at the ribald association; they petitioned the city, and the name vanished.

During recent years, however, Louisiana has recalled Bernard. Acquiring much of the land he had owned along the lake, the state has turned it into Fontainebleau Park. A plantation style of architecture has been revived for the park buildings in order to give a reminiscent flavor. It is, as it was long ago, a place of warm sands, deep running bayous, and aromatic pines. Among the palmettoes can be found remnants of brick walls, parts of sugar stacks, a half-underground chamber that may have been a wine cellar, and lines of trees planted by long-dead Marignys. The drawbridge by which Bernard sometimes held off Anna Mathilda? Gone, alas.

In New Orleans itself, the curious explorer may come upon a last piquant relic of the man. In a turn of Bourbon Street, at Number 1436, stands a stuccoed brick building of heavy timbers and ancient construction. The property, once a part of Bernard's estate, dates from the early 1800s; the original windows and door frames are there, and the Spanish tiles seem intact. In some respects it is an odd structure; it curves with the street, so that the hipped roof has five sides. This was Bernard's old gambling place, to which he took cronies and where—unsuspected by Anna Mathilda—they shot craps throughout the night. Is it significant that, of all the playboy's holdings, this one alone has survived? Perhaps his spirit laughs as it turns that corner and remembers.

CHAPTER 2

Bad Girl, Good Girl

WHOEVER would taste the true delights of love should come to New Orleans. Here it is that the tender passion holds sway, unruffled by self-interest, by jealousy, or by inconstancy." This florid compliment to the city, by a man who never went there, made thousands of Frenchmen sigh over the prodigal spot. For generations they frowned and smiled and cried when they read these words and others in the chronicle of Louisiana's first literary heroine, Manon Lescaut.

Who was Manon, what was she? Many have insisted she never existed save in the imaginings of her novelist-creator, the Abbé Prévost. Yet it appears that a Manon did live; and her story is in large part the story of early New Orleans.

The time was about 1720, when France entrusted its precarious finances to the Scottish visionary-speculator, John Law. So far, Louisiana had been a sorry disappointment to the French—all that land along the river and gulf, and no jewels, no precious metals such as the Spanish had found in Mexico, not even pearls from the water. Mistakes piled on mistakes; some years earlier, for instance, the colony had been turned over to a merchant who went practically bankrupt. Now, however, great affairs were in the wind; and the settlement of La Nouvelle Orléans, lying between river and lake, had become the core of it all.

Under John Law's wand a vivid fantasy was improvised. A

wild game had started; a bank was formed, and stock and
paper money rolled out as the Company of the West floated
its Mississippi Bubble. Clerks clustered around pictures plastered on the walls, gazing greedily at clean plump Indians
handing nuggets of gold to Frenchmen just as they stepped
from ship to prettily landscaped shore. Comely red-skinned
women smiled at the arrivals, clearly anxious to please any
settler from the old country. It must be true, Jacques—there
it is!

And La Nouvelle Orléans—a majestic metropolis, soaring
into the clouds; mansions and plumes, and jewels on everybody's coat; vast land grants for the highly placed, a chance
at excellent holdings for those below. . . . Yet the people did
not rush in as anticipated. It was all very fine, for the other
fellow.

John Law paused. He had promised to pour forth six thousand whites, and three thousand Negroes from the tropics.
Something had to be done; and so officialdom ordered a scraping process to fill the city and its environs. The "Mississippi
bandits" went to work in France, bandits whose name was to
be cursed for years by bitter men and women. A hunt was on:
the king's men after anybody who walked and seemed de-
fenseless, anybody it might pay to take. Whether they agreed
or not, they were dragged from streets, alleys, and hallways,
and shoved to the gangplanks. Bound for Louisiana!

A prison had a cellful of wretches; off with them! Here
stood a debtor, well-born, now only a consumer of jail fare;
he would do. There cringed a lout who had dared poach on
M'sieur's acres; the Mississippi waited. A merchant with a
rival, one not so powerful in elevated circles—what better
than removal across the ocean? Over at the inn—a likely serving wench, eh? Tomorrow she will be on her way. A son who
stands in the path of another, the black sheep of a family; a
girl who is an orphan or merely poor—these will do. And
there was issued many a mysterious *lettre de cachet*—this or
that person had offended a high minister, or the Regent him-

self. The reason? Does royalty need to give reasons? It all made up a grab bag of envy and trickery and malice.

For the women the prospect was the hardest—months of confinement on a lurching ship, an agony of heat and illness and overcrowding; and, at its end, wretched loneliness, without friends, without relatives. Some, shrieking, managed to escape; a few, less fortunate, killed themselves as the last resort. Early and late the number included girls who had gotten into trouble, beauties seeking a short cut to ease; or petty brawlers, women accused unjustly of minor offenses, victims of want and avarice.

Among these was Manon Lescaut, one of the "correction girls" scheduled for deportation.

The reader first meets Manon when the narrator, passing through Normandy, is drawn by the excitement of a crowd. Covered carts are lined up before an inn; an old woman emerges, wringing her hands over the cruelty of what she has seen inside. There, held together by chains around their waists, a dozen girls are waiting, among them one whose face and manner make her seem "a person of the highest rank." Despite her sorrow and the disarray of her costume, Manon is a beautiful creature.

Nearby stands a distraught youth who identifies himself to the narrator as the Chevalier des Grieux. Failing in his attempt to rescue his Manon, he has paid her amused captors to allow him to sit with her. But now his money is gone, and he is ready to sail for America—anything to stay with her. So the story unfolds.

They had met a few years earlier, this mismated couple; whatever happened, whatever friend or family said, they could not separate. Des Grieux' father would never approve, and so the two had slipped off quietly together. Untrained for any profession, Des Grieux drifted, became a card sharper; things went well for a time, then badly. Manon, who was weak, turned for help to other men. Yet somehow their love persisted. The moment arrived—so well known to opera-goers today—when Manon was confronted with want. This she could not endure; the Manons are not made for poverty. A wealthier prospect appeared, and Manon arranged to inform her lover's family of his whereabouts. He was taken from her, struggling. At the final moment, Manon sank weeping against the door.

Des Grieux became a student for the priesthood. Into his cell there suddenly entered a brilliant figure, jeweled and in the richest silks. It was Manon; together they left. Again they struggled for the luxury they wished; they knew easy months, then tenser ones. At last Manon was a marked woman, ordered transported to Louisiana. Des Grieux managed to board the vessel with her. On the way he learned that she, like the other girls, was to be given in marriage to one of the settlers. When Des Grieux claimed to be her husband, the officials believed them.

Now New Orleans appeared—and what a disappointment! A land of low wet earth, reeds, "a few trees stripped by the wind," a huddle of squalid houses. People rushed out to ask them endlessly about France. What was happening there, was there anyone here from Bordeaux, or Paris? The governor called forth the young men, each of whom had "languished in anticipation of a bride." The governor's nephew wanted the handsome Manon, but Des Grieux' story of the marriage was accepted.

Before the pair the drab landscape bloomed; here waited peace and happiness, and Des Grieux made his sweeping observation: "Whoever would taste the true delights of love should come to New Orleans. . . . Others have come to seek gold; they could not know that we found here a far greater treasure." So idyllic was their state that Des Grieux and Manon decided they should be married in fact; and by this decision they betrayed themselves. Asked to grant his permission, the governor was startled. No! In that case his nephew should have Manon!

Desperate, the couple managed to escape, cutting a path

through empty plains, fearful of Indians and animals. Finally, near the Gulf, Manon fell dying to the ground; and the broken-hearted chevalier "buried forever in the bosom of the earth the loveliest and most perfect creature that had yet adorned it."

Here was essentially the old story of the bad girl with heart of gold. The story-teller, the Abbé Prévost, had hitherto ranked only as a spinner of cheap and gaudy tales. But this new work of 1731 surpassed all his previous books; despite its lush plotting, it was a touching portrayal of two human beings. Though in its own day it shocked not a few—indeed was temporarily banned—its influence was felt for years; it has been termed "the first masterpiece of French literature which can properly be called a novel."

Was there a particular reason for the conviction that shone through the work? The subject, true, lay close to many readers' emotions, combining graphically the tragedy of a lost couple and the bitterness of forced transportation to Louisiana. But beyond these elements lurked one of autobiography: At more than one point the life of Des Grieux touched the Abbé's own. As a youth the latter had known a deep affection, involving a conflict long unresolved; he had studied for the priesthood; and he had left it for a lady.

Yet there was something else. The Abbé had made considerable inquiry into certain aspects of the Louisiana settlement. Official reports show that there was a Captain des Grieux who had taken his ship to Louisiana several times, and at least once he had carried a cargo of transported persons; and he may have told the Abbé a great deal about the "correction girls." Then, among French archival records of women taken to the colony from La Salpêtrière there appears the name of Manon Porcher.

Read the description of this Manon Porcher in the Archives of the Colonies. She had been "arrested for scandalous and public debauchery," and was scourged and branded after several thefts. Taken to the Salpêtrière for a fourth term, she used a razor to slash off two fingers of the arresting officer. In prison she set fire to her cell, got into a knife fight, kept watch to stab a nun, and plotted a rebellion involving the killing of guards. A heavy indictment; but it does not offer the other side—the defense that might have been offered by a girl at war with a society that had not been kind.

In 1716 the Governor of Louisiana wrote to the authorities in France: "I have the honor to inform you that a young man of rank called Avril de La Varenne, from Angers, has come here. . . . He brought with him a woman said to have been married. . . . She first took the name of Froget and at present bears that of Quantin, declaring herself married to the said Sieur de La Varenne." It has been suggested that the names "Froget" and "Porcher," pronounced similarly in French, might have been confused, and that the two were the same woman.

And now the lady's career further parallels that of the fictional Manon. Her chevalier, La Varenne, was sent up the Mississippi to trade by the director-general of the company, a man who desired her. The governor was complaining: "He has given her lodgings near his warehouse and employed her in selling there. He pays her such frequent visits that there is unfavorable talk." A later critic put it more ribaldly: "The lady knowing nothing of arithmetic, it was said that he devoted every evening behind closed doors and windows to teaching her the multiplication table."

The scandal grew; all at once one of the first Marignys became involved, and La Varenne, returning to the settlement, furiously accused Marigny of spreading false stories. Now he offered a new explanation. He and the lady had been married in France, but clandestinely; he had brought her here because of his family's opposition. Now he wanted to wed her again, to make everything certain. However, all the excitement had disturbed him, and he proposed to take her back to

France with him. Rather wearily, the governor commented that he supposed he could not stop it.

It seems clear, therefore, that there was a Manon all along; and, too, that in this far-off wilderness her beauty caused dissension. And there must have been other Manons, though not so named—some who did not die so soon, or go back to France, but who saw the beginning of a new hope in the colony. They became good mothers and watched their children earn a place denied them in the homeland. Such is always part of the story of a new land.

Next appears a girl of quite different character. Though a religious, a youthful novice, Madeleine Hachard was no dour, withdrawn person, but a brightly observant girl with a wit that stood her in good stead. No story demonstrates better than hers the adventure involved in a journey to New Orleans in the early eighteenth century. The Ursulines of France, the "Gray Sisters," had signed a contract to educate the young of distant Louisiana, and in 1726 a band of nuns and postulants was being gathered. Friends and relatives cried against the "folly" and "disaster" that awaited, and Madeleine Hachard's older brother remonstrated so strongly with her as to cast a shadow between them when she left. She had just passed seventeen; tiny, brisk, she had a well-filled mind and the knack of getting along with people.

Of good bourgeois family, Madeleine had four brothers and sisters in the religious life. It was hard to leave them all, but she forced herself to be cheerful as she set forth. Soon the stir of the affair caught her; she and her band were pioneers. First came a long, uncomfortable stagecoach trip across part of France. Word of their destination got out, and crowds waited hours for a glimpse of them. In the first of many spirited letters to her father, Madeleine was amused: "Probably you never thought your daughter would one day excite the curiosity of whole towns."

They passed through Versailles, and Madeleine was taken

by the beauties of the palace: "I was often tempted to shut my eyes in order to mortify myself." Another kind of mortification impended; at three one morning, their coach sank into a rutty road and oxen were required to help the horses pull it free. The nuns, walking ahead in icy night, waked an old woman and took refuge in her cottage, using straw to keep a fire going while a priest who accompanied them read his breviary till dawn.

"In spite of the fatigue," Madeleine continued, "we laughed often. From time to time there happened a little adventure which amused us." As was customary among the Gray Sisters, she was beginning to say "our" for "mine"; she could have no personal possessions. Once she discovered herself referring to "our nose!"

As she prepared to sail, she laughed less often. She wrote to the family: "It is only God, whose voice I hear and follow, who could separate me from parents whose tender love I have a thousand times felt." They were taking a Negro as a servant. "Dear father, be not scandalized," she begged; "it is the fashion of the country." They had also "a very pretty little cat who has wished to be one of our community, apparently supposing that in Louisiana as in France there are rats and mice." A problem arose; there were no gangplanks, and how would the modest nuns get aboard? Then the good-natured captain, "though little experienced in the handling of such merchandise," had them carried up in an armchair, one after another.

The nuns found their "apartment" eighteen feet by seven, their bunks in sets of three tiers each, so close together that they could not sit up. As the lightest, Madeleine drew a top tier. The cabin got hot and stuffy so quickly that only a few could stay there at a time, and they took turns at their rest.

Their ship, the *Gironde*, had hardly started when it struck a rock. Thrown to the floor, the Ursulines were certain the vessel was going down. However, though it leaked badly, they were spared. Almost at once violent winds buffeted them, throwing one against the other, sickening them and frightening the cat. At this, Madeleine managed a smile. But she did not smile when she learned that the storm had killed half their live-stock. Rations had to be cut; food became scanty, greasy, hard to swallow. As contrary winds held, it took fifteen days to make hardly more than the distance of three. After a forced stop at the island of Madeira, they set out again—and encountered pirates.

For this was the period when corsairs preyed on the lanes. The *Gironde's* officers grew agitated as a suspicious vessel made turns toward them; then they rapped out orders. All men, including priests, took up arms; three nonclerical women passengers donned male clothes and lined up with the crew, to help frighten the enemy from a distance. Below, the nuns held their beads. "We were not sad, thanks to the Lord," wrote Madeleine. "Not one of our company showed weakness. We were delighted to see the courage of our officers and passengers, who appeared ready to lay the enemy low at first charge." The young religious seemed almost to be enjoying it. And presently the other vessel, apparently daunted, slipped off.

Hard days, light days. Bad weather, when they had to tie themselves to their bunks. The ship crossed the equator, with the usual burlesques. Those who did not make payments were doused; the nun sighed that, so hot was the weather, this looked rather agreeable. Still, the restrictions of the holy life! . . . Santo Domingo loomed; at the island the planters poured out compliments. Couldn't the Ursulines put up a convent here, too; or stay and forget Louisiana, so that the growers would not have to send their children to France for an education? The nuns declined: New Orleans was their goal. Saying goodbye, the gentlemen gave them two barrels of sugar, three hundred pounds in each.

The *Gironde* floated becalmed, and weeks passed slowly. Would they ever see Louisiana? Without warning a new pirate threat, worse than before, broke upon them. A circling vessel halted, a boat was put down and a villainous crew rowed over on the pretense of buying wine. The ship's cannon was turned, ready to "send them to drink in the bottom of the sea." In her letter Madeleine almost growled; and the scoundrels sped off.

At last they were in the Gulf of Mexico and beheld an island not far from the Mississippi's mouth. More trouble. The ship shuddered and halted, caught on a sand bar, rapidly sank into the sand. Madeleine told her beads. Would their convent be established in the Gulf?

"Lighten her!" Over went the cannon, the barrels of sugar from the Indies, brandy, ballast. The nuns' clothing chests were to be next; they resigned themselves to "experience the greatest poverty." But the officers found less indispensable objects—cargo and supplies—and the Gray Sisters gave thanks. Meanwhile they were warned that the nearby island must be avoided; on it lived cannibals, who made victims drink the blood that poured from their hacked bodies!

Slowly the vessel moved; they were free. They proceeded a quarter league more, and felt a shattering new impact, the most terrible they had yet suffered. Men's faces whitened; it appeared certain that the battered ship was going to crack apart. The nuns sat in stiff terror, one clinging to their ever-present cat; several knelt at the knee of the Mother Superior, who quieted them with soft words. They dropped their heads in silent appeal—and the vessel moved again. Madeleine was certain there had been "good souls praying for us."

They were at the Mississippi's mouth. A brigantine approached, and they learned that the colonists had given them up for dead. Five months had passed since they boarded their ship. They moved to the Balize, outpost above the river's opening; on this muddy island in the greenlands of the lower Delta they enjoyed a week's respite, until smaller vessels arrived for them. One more long lap lay ahead, and the nuns re-embarked.

Crowded with their luggage in narrow shells—Louisiana

pirogues, or dugout canoes—Madeleine and her companions stared excitedly at the spread of grass on both sides, the salt marshes of Louisiana, retreat of long-legged blue herons and alligators that looked like logs along the bank until the pirogues approached and they dropped away. The Mississippi itself was a wide brown sea, tranquil to the eye; and yet, from stories that Madeleine heard, it was so deep, so swift and treacherous! The low sky, the eternal vegetation, alive with things that flew or crawled—it resembled nothing she had ever known.

Only gradually did the land rise and trees appear. A few were gray skeletons hung with drippings of moss, funereal to the stranger's eye; others were bursts of green, spreading in the air. . . . The winding trip took a week; and nothing that had happened so far could compare with the grimness of this passage. The sun poured down, burning faces and hands; the nuns' heavy garb, wet with perspiration, stuck to their skins. They sat nervously atop their baggage, praying that a shift of the load would not topple them from the delicately balanced vessel.

Each evening they stopped, to set up pallets along the ridge of river bank. Madeleine marveled at this phenomenon. The Mississippi, freighted with the silt of all its valley, left heavy deposits in spring flood, the greatest concentrations at its bank, thinner layers beyond. Thus the highest earth rose along the stream; drainage fell away from the river, not into it as in other places.

But Madeleine had scant time for speculations. They had to be in bed by sunset, well covered against a new enemy—Louisiana mosquitoes in thick clouds around them. These pests stung without mercy, without letup. The sailors had brought netlike covers, *baires*, which Louisianians were to use for two centuries to come. Thrusting wild cane into the ground, the men draped the baires around them; fully dressed, the nuns settled inside for the night.

This worked well enough, until Madeleine and the rest had

their first taste of the colony's hearty downpours. The baire was soaked, then mattress and nuns; their pallets nearly floated in the water. The Gray Sisters had colds, swollen faces and limbs, and another "more considerable malady." Even then Madeleine achieved a certain cheer: "These little troubles are trying at the time, but we are well rewarded by the pleasure in relating each her own adventure."

Nearing the last curve in the river, they learned how much they had been wanted. Plantations lined the stream, and to the levees ran men and women, overjoyed to see the nuns, competing to have them as guests. "Beyond our expectations, we found a number of good people who have come from France and Canada to establish themselves." These colonists had children they wished taught by the sisters; several tried to entrust them at once to the Ursulines.

It was five in the morning when the newcomers reached New Orleans, and few were up to see them. An imaginative artist showed an imposing group of officialdom near a superb oak (which would not have grown so near the river edge) extending an eloquent welcome, while amiable Indians, wearing seashells, looked on fascinated. Even the Ursulines' pioneer cat was in the picture; and one account described her as "the mother of all felines in Louisiana." It is not difficult to visualize Madeleine laughing at the foolishness of that remark.

What was this New Orleans like? Earlier arrivals had described it, in despair, as a damp and miserable spot, of rude shacks, reeking ditches, and nauseous swamp at the edges, a place of floods that swept over the low levee, of alligators and squalor. Madeleine, though unimpressed in some respects, found it far different from what she had been told. "Our town"—she was again prompt to use the plural pronoun—"is very beautiful, finely constructed and regularly built." The streets were large, straight, and wide; houses well constructed, "with upright joists filled with mortar between the interstices, and the exterior whitewashed with lime." She heard a song calling it as beautiful as Paris, but she would not go *that* far!

What she saw of the women shocked her. She had sharp words for them: "ignorant as to the means of securing their salvation, but very expert in displaying their beauty." They went about boldly in robes of velvet and damask, trimmed with expensive ribbon, while their families lived on hominy. "They use powder and rouge to hide the marks of time, and wear small beauty spots." Madeleine grew yet most positive: "The devil has a vast empire here, but that merely strengthens our hope of destroying it."

Again: "It does not seem that I am in America; there is as much magnificence and politeness as in France. Gold and velvet materials are common, though three times more expensive than at Rouen." On the other hand there was "not one devout person in all the country." There were many who would seem honest, good folk, but "in no place is there so little religious spirit." Just how Madeleine could ascertain that, she did not say.

On rather surer ground, she told of the magnificence of the fare: buffalo, wild geese, deer, turkeys, rabbits, chickens, pheasant, partridge, quail; "monstrous fish which I never knew in France," oysters, shrimp; that long-to-be-popular item, catfish; an array of fruits and vegetables, figs, watermelons, pecans, pumpkins. She described mixtures of hominy, meat, and fish which would later become celebrated New Orleans dishes; she told how all drank chocolate and coffee with warm milk. Once she observed that though wild ducks were cheap and plentiful, "we buy scarcely any; we do not wish to pamper ourselves."

She evoked the wonders of Louisiana sweet-potatoes, cooked "in the ashes, like chestnuts." ("I forgot to tell you, dear Papa," she interpolated here, "that when we were in great danger on *La Gironde*, I promised six Masses for the souls in Purgatory, on condition that you would have the goodness to have them said, knowing you would not refuse me.") She saw potential abundance on every side. "Here a man can work two days a week, plowing and sowing corn, and he will have harvest enough to feed himself for a year." Yet the greater part of the people lived idly—"apply themselves only to hunting and fishing." Such complaints were made by many another Orleanian of those days.

By now the nuns were taking boarding pupils and day students as well, holding a class for Negro and Indian girls; when their convent was built, they would nurse the sick. Officials also wanted them to assume charge of "the girls of bad conduct." And this brings us back to the Manon Lescauts.

From the colony's beginnings, women had been scarce. A few years after the arrival of the original settlers, the king ordered the dispatch of an assortment of girls—twenty-three from the correction houses; and in later years others were gathered, not always carefully. Once Governor Bienville sent an urgent request; he must have "wives for my Canadians; they are running into the woods after Indian girls." Yet, after a supply arrived in 1721, Bienville reported that out of the lot only a few were disposable. "Several were given to sailors who asked insistently for them; they could scarcely have been married off to good residents."

It was, however, a problem to strike a balance; or perhaps the colonists were hard to please. On another occasion a protest went to the ministry that of the dozen girls recently received, all were virtuous but also extremely unhandsome! After much effort authorities had persuaded two men to take them as wives; "it will be difficult to get rid of the rest." Certain sturdy Canadian *coureurs de bois* said they wanted "less virtue and more beauty." Still another kind of settler sent a brisk note to the council. Like his friends, he missed a "certain commodity" in Louisiana; but he would try to get along without it until officialdom sent ladies with at least an appearance of maidenly qualities.

Such was the background when, in the early 1720s, the

king ordered his ministers to send to New Orleans a supply of *filles à la cassette*—"casket girls"—of good character and trained to be housewives. A bishop was to make the choices; each girl would be given a chest or casket, with a set of clothes—a trousseau from His Majesty.

These proved ideal mates, and in great demand, though exactly how many shipments went to Louisiana is a question. For years a standard New Orleans joke declared that the "casket girls" were of a fantastic fecundity—so many, many families counted them as ancestors. But the "correction girls" obviously were all sterile—nobody at all was descended from them!

As Manon was the type of one kind of early arrival, Madeleine Hachard and the "casket girls" were another; between them, they made the city. It received all the kinds of settlers that have ever gone to colonies: officers of rank, younger sons turning to new fields, industrious merchants, farmers seeking a better chance, shopkeepers, doctors, thieves, the high and the low and those between. On most of them the alchemy of semitropic climate, river bank, and river water had its effect, making them over in a new mold, à la Louisiane.

They seem to have been hardly a docile lot. They were volatile people, and quarrels rose promptly over the way affairs were handled. For years at a time the colony was neglected by the court, needs ignored, foolish appointments made. Soon there developed a fixed habit of "writing home." Practically everybody sent dispatches, flaming attack and defense, charge, countercharge. Each side wanted its version to be available in far-off France, and each had the Gallic talent for controversy. Beyond this, there grew up a spirit of self-assertion, an independence that thrived as rapidly as cottonwood trees by the river. Whether or not they belonged to a king across the sea, the Orleanians wanted some things their own way; if not, they expected to be told why not!

Yet there was little of the puritanism that characterized certain of the colonial settlements along the Atlantic. The

Orleanians believed in letting the other fellow conduct his private affairs much as he wished. They liked the pleasant time, the good life, the casual rest after labor—a gay dance in the evening, a holiday procession, rounds of refreshment in the garden behind the house.

Here the Ursulines began Louisiana's first school, its first orphanage, its first educational programs for Indians and Negroes. The Gray Sisters have never left New Orleans. Turmoil broke about them—riots, fires, overnight changes in government; the Ursulines continued. When epidemics left orphans by the score, when need came for nurses, when Indians massacred families up the river, the Ursulines were called.

Madeleine Hachard and her companions saw the city fill, houses crowd the parallelogram along the levee. From a distance they beheld increasing shipments of Negroes from the West Indies and Africa—"brutes," the settlers termed them— sold on credit and paid for by installments. The Gray Sisters caught glimpses of heavy-framed Germans, some of them redemptioners, working for years to pay back the cost of their passage; and like other Orleanians the nuns shook their heads over the industry of the German farmer, who made the French appear indolent as he worked his vegetable gardens along the "German Coast" up the river.

The Ursulines watched a community life marked by extremes—poverty at one end, growing luxury at the other. Flavorsome foods, embroidered costumes, wines and delicacies . . . with these the high manner was not long in asserting itself. At the same time the nuns heard echoes of the violent excesses of soldiers and sailors who found chances for carousal in the taverns. At times it was a tough, raging settlement. There would long centre here an untamed element, men who made a living at the edges of the law, smugglers, quasi-pirates, fugitives from French and Canadian law. Like the priests, the nuns frowned at the general levity, the inclination of settlers to flout or ignore the church. But the Ursulines were at work with the women; and through them their influence spread enormously. Much of the development of the lower valley had its seeds inside the thick walls that sheltered the order.

The Ursulines first took temporary quarters near the city borders close to the plantation of Governor Bienville, at the modern Bienville and Chartres streets. Several years later they moved to a convent touching the present Ursulines and Chartres streets. This proved unsatisfactory, and in about 1750 they transferred to another in the same square, the building that has been called the oldest complete structure standing in the Mississippi Valley.

For three-quarters of a century the nuns moved about the walks and hallways of a massive plastered brick residence, two and a half stories high in the French Renaissance tradition, with a sloping tile roof. In the centre a pediment lifted a cross toward the sky; from the front extended a one-storied portico with a balustrade and finely carved fanlight doorways. Across front and back extended a series of deep windows, their batten shutters of blue-green, the lower openings grilled in iron. A line of neatly proportioned dormers stood like many eyes out of the roof. In all it had richness, almost elegance; by contrast the inside was plain, nearly primitive—massive timbers, heavy hinges, a staircase with iron railings.

The busy community covered four squares, with side buildings, rear ones, auxiliary structures. Nuns moved from classrooms to laundry, chapel to barns, chicken runs, vegetable plots; others took regular duties at the nearby royal hospital. Much of it was hidden behind a brick wall; at the front stood the *conciergerie* or door-keeper's lodge of brick and plaster, with a thick cypress gate, an ornamental knocker, and a peep-hole.

In 1824 the city needed further room, and the nuns moved several miles below; since then they have shifted again, higher uptown. Their old convent continued in use; enclosed in a smaller space, it became the archbishop's palace, then the parish house of St. Mary's Italian church after the church itself was built into the side of the old structure. It remains today, hardly less sturdy than when first erected, its walls a little worn, its stair treads hollowed in semicircular patterns by the thousands of feet that have trodden them through the centuries.

Entrance is through that same faded conciergerie with its slightly rusty hinges. A pathway leads to the portico, and on each side is a garden. Palm trees, taller than the building itself, sway lightly in the wind, and banana plants stand here and there. The place—"the old convent," as New Orleans still calls it—gives an effect of withdrawal, of agelessness, as of something that has felt many shifting currents, yet stayed firmly to itself, its strength and identity intact. And there is also something of Madeleine Hachard in the scene.

Madeleine served here from the day it opened until the end of her life. She gave thirty-five years to her order; she never saw her home again, never set foot on the soil of France. Under her gray robes she grew a little bent as she labored steadily through the years. The convent history tells of her great energy, her earnest work; the faded pages describe her work as secretary of the chapter and assistant directress of the "ladies of the congregation," the women who assisted the nuns.

Then, one morning in early August of 1760, she was missed at Mass. One of the nuns, thinking her ill, went to her narrow room; and there she was found, as the records of the Ursulines declare, "sleeping the long sleep of death."

She had smiled through her life; though some might not have used the expression, she had had her share of "little adventures," as she innocently termed her brushes with the world. Now she had come to the greatest adventure of all. . . .

CHAPTER 3

The Cannibal Widow

IT WAS about 1720, and the days were the drowsy ones of late summer, when a vessel rocked across the Gulf after a long voyage from France. Blue-green waters stretched far ahead as the ship felt its way close to the sandy, island-spotted shore. Evenings lengthened; captain and pilot studied the inlets and confusing curves of land. Then they halted, realizing they had made a bad mistake. Going too far to the west, they had missed the Mississippi's three-tongued entry to the sea.

By now they had reached a cool bay known eventually as St. Bernard. The men blessed themselves; from all descriptions this was the region inhabited by Attakapas Indians, reputed among the French as eaters of men. But the sailors saw no signs of red men, hostile or otherwise, and they needed fresh water. The captain gave the order: they would replenish their supplies. A boat was sent ashore, and with the crew went a group of five officers, anxious to stretch their legs. They were headed by Monsieur de Belle Isle, a full-blooded youth with stalwart frame and an eye for adventure. The party had a sixth member, Belle Isle's little dog; the master and his pet had been close companions on the journey.

Belle Isle reconnoitred about the heavily grown shore. Why not an hour or so of hunting? His friends, having brought their guns along, agreed. The crew would have to make several trips back and forth; the officers left word that the men were to await their return. The hunters followed a fringe of high ground, ending in salt marshes; the dog raced merrily at their side. They caught little, though they were impressed by the flights of wild birds and the splashings of unseen animals. They spent somewhat longer in their expedition than they had planned, and the sun was setting as they pushed through the vegetation to reach shore again. The bay was empty.

The errands finished, the captain had waited only a short time; and then (as a chronicler put it) he was "barbarous enough to weigh anchor and abandon the five officers to their fate." To Belle Isle came a sick realization. They were hundreds of miles from any other white people, and the cannibal Indians must be nearby. Beyond the shelf of earth lay a droning, water-threaded marsh, the still haunt of snakes and alligators—and mystery.

As dusk fell, mosquitoes converged upon them, and the black shadows held a hundred dim terrors. As best they could, the officers rested among the low bushes, taking turns at watch. The little dog, as nervous as the men, curled up with Belle Isle.

The next day and for days that followed, Belle Isle led the men in fitful wanderings along the shore, first in one direction, then another. Their eyes searched the sea; there was only the endless vacancy of water and sky. Ammunition gave out; they had no way to capture the birds and small beasts that rustled near them. Before long they were reduced to eating water insects and herbs, "not knowing which were good or bad"; and frequently they gagged over their diet.

They became gaunt, their reddened eyes staring from their sockets. The dog, scratching about the bushes, appeared at intervals with game for them; then even he grew lean. The men were steadily losing what spirit remained with them. When it rained they huddled miserably together under a tree, and often they woke at night to find the waters of this ever-moist area rising about them. Weeks passed; autumn was upon them, and they shivered under the driving winds.

They found less and less to eat. One day one of the men muttered: The dog! Belle Isle shook his head; he wouldn't allow it. The others turned away. They were growing weaker, fevered; their breath came in gasps. The same man went to Belle Isle: they had to eat, they had to take that dog!

This time Belle Isle could not object. The men staggered forward, and one grabbed at the animal. But by this time he was so weak he lost his hold. The dog, seeming to realize their intent, ran away and did not return. A day or so later one of the party was dead, and the others buried him. In quick succession went a second and then the two others. With half-convulsive effort Belle Isle dug a hole in the sand to cover the body of his last friend, "so that it would not become the prey of carnivorous animals."

Alone, Belle Isle stared helplessly. How far off was New Orleans, and in what direction? If the captain reported them missing, would someone by chance come to seek them? Yet he knew that was hopeless; they were given up now, all of them, for dead. Certainly he himself was all but dead!

Somehow he stayed alive. Perhaps it was his powerful physique, or his determination. Desperately he ate leaves, tore at rotten wood to dig out fat worms that he stuffed into his mouth. One day he blinked at a moving object. Yes, it was the dog, with a dark object in his mouth! The animal crawled closer, "fawning" in "a great demonstration of joy," and dropped the gift at the feet of his master. It was an opossum. Quickly Belle Isle tore it apart, and ate and ate. One source describes the opossum as the size of a suckling pig; he had enough food for several days, and he blessed his shaggy friend.

With the animal Belle Isle ranged farther and farther. But the autumn had deepened, and food was ever scarcer. Still, with the dog's help he survived. Every night he "made a little entrenchment at the foot of a tree," for a shelter against wild beasts. Early one morning, as he slept, a large shadow crept toward him. The dog, leaping forward, gave a warning that saved Belle Isle's life. It was a wildcat; the man managed to frighten it away, but the poor dog lay ripped and bleeding.

Now, "lest he turn mad," the master killed his faithful friend; and surely this must have been one of the hardest of Belle Isle's ordeals. Having done so, he did another thing he had never thought possible: He ate the dog.

The days were lonelier than ever. Would he ever see New Orleans? Finally Belle Isle reached a decision. Dropping to his knees, he thanked Almighty God for preserving him thus far. Hereafter he would resign himself and push steadily inland to search for any other man, red or white, that he might find. Days later he came upon footsteps, traced them to a low bank—and stared at a band of Indians, engaged in smoking meat.

The men and women ran forward, surrounding Belle Isle, shouting, pointing. His emaciated look, his whitened face alarmed them; for a moment they thought him a supernatural being. Then they prodded Belle Isle's flesh; they pulled off his shoes, his shirt, trousers, and underdrawers. The women and children stared at his nakedness. Heart pounding, Belle Isle wondered what would happen next. Despite their curiosity, he managed to retrieve a paper that he had been taught always to hold near him, his officer's commission.

After a few minutes he sensed that the Indians were puzzled, not certain how to treat him. He pointed to his mouth to indicate his hunger. A warrior handed him a hunk of meat. Belle Isle lifted it to his lips, then dropped it. It was human flesh, part of a leg! Then these, after all, were the Attakapans. . . . At this they gave him a fish, and, frightened though he was, he swallowed it hastily.

His hunger satisfied, Belle Isle went with the Indians to their camp. There one of the women walked forward. A widow, she is described in one account as "old," though another is silent on the point. In any case, she had an announcement to make. After peering over Belle Isle for several minutes, she decided she could use him as her dog ("an expression which signifies slave," says our informant). Apparently the lady was powerful in the tribe, and—though the men grumbled—it was decreed that Belle Isle would stay with her and under close surveillance until they decided just what was to be done about him.

Gradually Belle Isle regained his strength; his frame filled out; he recovered a small strip of his clothing, though no more than "sufficient to make his nakedness less indecent." "As Monsieur de Belle Isle was young and strong, he acquitted himself very well of his functions as a slave, and even gained the good graces of his mistress." Many must have been the times the Frenchman thanked Heaven he had captured the widow's interest. Nevertheless he remained sad, "constantly apprehending that his hosts would sacrifice him to false deities and afterward eat him." He found himself in a dilemma. The nonhuman food lay before him; would he be thereby chewing himself toward the grave, fattening himself for his own kill? Still, a man must eat. . . .

Continuing on a kind of probation, he was assigned unpleasant menial tasks; he even had to help look after the children. Then he saw busy movements that further alarmed him—preparations for battle. He was taken to a hut at the side, where the women guarded him while a fight took place. After it ended, Belle Isle was summoned. On the ground lay several prone figures, and he received his orders. Hereafter he would carry the corpses. That night he looked on, horrified, as the bodies were hacked apart and hung up for smoking; he shuddered as he watched them all, the widow included, gnawing at the breasts and loins.

He had one protection, the widow. It is indicated that Monsieur de Belle Isle made himself ever more agreeable to her. "She took him under her protection," and eventually "adopted him." The Indians, holding a final council, decreed that it would be cowardly to kill a man who had come to them, not in war but to seek hospitality. So he stayed at the widow's side, and the conditions of his enslavement were lightened.

By now Belle Isle was managing by pantomime and a few words to converse with the tribe. He learned to use the bow and arrow as well as did most of the warriors. More months passed, and they took him to war with them. In a spectacular episode, within sight of the tribe, he killed an enemy with his arrow. The Indians were delighted; from then on he was recognized as a true warrior, and could move about practically at will.

Two years went by. Ceasing to fear the cooking pot, Belle Isle could afford to let his frame thicken. He became more and more powerful, his skin bronzing, his health improving in this outdoor regimen, though with his features and hairy body he would never be mistaken for an Indian. According to two accounts, he also continued in the service of the Indian lady. Yet he was never really happy. Was this to go on for the rest of his life? Would he ever again see white men, and white women?

The Indians liked him, though one aspect of his behavior still puzzled them. On one memorable occasion, after skinning an animal he had helped catch, he asked casually for food. He paid no particular heed to what had been given him until, after he had eaten, he noticed that one of the red men appeared amused. Then the warrior told him: "You used to make trouble about it, but now you can eat man's flesh as easily as we do." At these words Monsieur de Belle Isle vomited all he had eaten, and the Indians shook their heads. How strange!

More months elapsed, and then one day Belle Isle's breath caught in his throat. Deputies arrived from another tribe to the east, with a calumet of peace. Curiously the newcomers gaped at his heavier body and odd face. Watching carefully and listening, Belle Isle made out that the visiting men were members of a tribe living in Spanish territory; but they had as a neighbor a white nation with which they got along well,

and it was French. They lived at an outpost called Natchitoches, in the present borders of Louisiana.

Though Belle Isle pretended to take little notice of the
conversation, he had determined to use this chance to return
to his people. Secretly he went to work. The precious
officer's commission, which he had never lost, was the only
paper he had. With a bird's wing quill, using soot for ink, he
printed a message telling where he was, begging rescue. Then
he called one of the visitors aside and struggled to make himself understood. This was a "speaking paper"; if the Indian
said nothing to the Attakapans and presented it to the chief
of the Frenchmen whom he knew, he would get great gifts.

Would the Indian agree? Belle Isle waited, heart thumping.
The man paused, as suspicion battled with avarice. He nodded;
he would do it. Happily Belle Isle saw him turn away; and
then arose complications. The Indian's companions learned of
the letter; they snatched at it, demanding that he show it to
them. In a sweat, Belle Isle watched the incident. Was everything lost?

But his Indian friend managed to run away from the others,
swimming over a stream to escape, holding the crumpled
paper in his teeth. The Attakapans, if they noticed the incident, did not connect it with Belle Isle; even the widow did
not know of it.

Now ensued months of apprehension, of alternating hope
and despair. Had the Indian changed his mind, or for one of
a dozen reasons failed to deliver the letter? Almost certainly these were the grimmest hours of his years in the wilds.
Then one morning the Attakapans were startled by a quick
thunder, a sound they had never heard before, coming not
from the sky where the gods spoke, but close at hand. Belle
Isle crept forward; he had recognized gunfire.

At the edge of a clearing his Indian friend waited with ten
companions on horseback. The red man had gone to the
French commander, who had been much affected, given him
presents, and sent the party back. They also carried several

shirts to cover Belle Isle's nakedness. . . . There followed a nervous pause. The Attakapans were close by; would they let him go?

His friend called to Belle Isle. He must get on this extra horse, quickly! The Attakapans chattered among themselves, but they were too amazed, at least for the moment, to offer resistance; and so Belle Isle raced off with the rest of them. One chronicler reports that the widow shed tears at the sight.

Belle Isle arrived in Natchitoches, the newly acquired shirt tails flapping about his sun-browned legs; then he struck out for New Orleans. There the people, on learning what had happened, were greatly excited. On his arrival Governor Bienville walked quickly forward, to embrace Belle Isle and ask the first of thousands of questions that would be put to him. Men and women crowded about, congratulating him, assuring him that le Bon Dieu must have watched over him. Presumably Belle Isle did not mention the widow's role in the matter, at least at that moment.

The governor looked Belle Isle over (he had found a pair of breeches by this time) and told him he seemed seedy; from His Excellency the newcomer accepted a suit. The officials thanked the Indians and gave them presents. Wishing to establish good relations with the distant Attakapans, Bienville sent gifts to them also, to reward them for letting Belle Isle go; after consultation with Belle Isle, the governor added a special one for the widow.

In return the man-eaters sent ambassadors to thank the Frenchmen, to make gifts of their own, and, perhaps, to get more gifts from the Frenchmen. Belle Isle and Bienville might well have been surprised when they beheld this new delegation. In the centre stood the widow herself! She must have worked hard to persuade the men to take her along. There were feasts and receptions all around; whether the widow wept when she parted again from her former "dog," we do not know.

Belle Isle proved himself of considerable value to the gov-

ernment. Few others understood so much about Indian customs. He taught Bienville what he knew of the language, and
for years remained in New Orleans in an official role. The
French drew up a treaty of alliance with the Attakapans; it
was asserted that at the desire of the white men the tribe "left
off the barbarous custom of eating human flesh." In time the
Attakapans appear to have softened their ways, and many
Louisianians moved near them. Today the Attakapas region,
in the bayou country, is one of the most sturdily French parts
of America. Might it be somewhat less so but for Belle Isle
and the widow?

There followed less happy relations with the Indians. All
too often arrogant appointees at the outposts goaded the
Indians to murderous fury. In about 1830 the pompous
Sieur de Chépart was assigned to the Natchez region along
the Mississippi, where dwelt a friendly tribe, advanced in
culture. Chépart cracked out haughty orders, growing ever
more dictatorial. When he seized their sacred tribal ground
for himself the Natchez Indians planned revenge. Working,
watching carefully until the proper moment arrived, they
trapped Chépart and most of the French settlers inside their
fort.

Knives flashed, fagots burned. Two hundred or more men
were killed, their heads piled up like oranges at a market.
Many were mutilated while alive, organs ripped out bit by
bit, faces pulled apart, arms and legs roasted slowly over the
fires. So detested was Chépart that the Natchezians did not
waste on him the efforts of a grown warrior; a stripling was
given a club and allowed to beat him to death. Pregnant
women were slashed in the middle and their babies torn from
them, to be caught on the tips of spears or tossed to the
dogs. Other women and children were spared, together with
at least two white men, a carpenter and a tailor. The latter
had to take the bloodied uniforms of the dead men and alter
them to fit the Indians.

The few French survivors raced to New Orleans. Panic filled the town, to be followed by cold rage. Reprisals began at once. Not far from the city lived a gentle, easy-going tribe, always on good terms with the French. A force of Negro slaves was sent against them, to wipe them out. Then the French captured four Natchez Indians and two of their women. The governor ordered a spectacle; the six were chained to stakes at the levee, just off the Place d'Armes in the town's centre. As the French subjects looked on in silence, the Indians were burned to death.

At Natchitoches, where Belle Isle had first emerged from his adventure, a large band of red men tried a ruse. To draw the whites from their post they offered to return a captive woman. The Frenchmen proving wily, the Indians dragged her to a nearby point and set her afire before the eyes of her countrymen. Her shrieks of agony rang through the clearing while the outnumbered Frenchmen prayed for her death to come quickly.

Warfare went on for years. The Natchez were surrounded, required to give up many of the captives, while part of their forces retreated to a hidden spot west of the Mississippi. The Louisiana governor proposed a truce to discuss peace; then, while discussions went on, the Frenchmen broke their word, caught the chiefs and threatened to kill them unless the rest surrendered. Most of them did, but again the French violated their promise. Various men were slain, and most of the others, women included, were sold into captivity in the West Indies. It is a wretched story altogether.

The fate of some of the French women and children at Natchez would never be known. For years distraught relatives, refusing to give up hope, ran to officials with reports from woodsmen that a white girl was living among the Indians or that a pale-skinned woman had been seen in a village far to the west. Could it be their daughter? Wouldn't the governor at least inquire? . . .

Gradually the colony recovered from its Indian terrors, and a fresh phase began. From France arrived a new governor, a scintillating figure who would introduce a greater, plumed splendor into the colony. In 1743 Pierre Rigaud, Marquis de Vaudreuil, set up a miniature court with rigid rules of elegant behavior, a haughty officer caste, and women's jeweled costumes *de rigueur*. At his side promenaded the Marquise, handsome, smiling, and hungry for cash. She utilized her official rank for making money, went into trade, forced soldiers and Indians to buy supplies from her shop. Nor was the Marquis himself above a measure of aristocratic corruption. He gave monopolies in return for payments of graft; he seized materials intended for the military, substituted sleazy supplies, and dropped the difference into his gold-laced pockets. Still, the eligible families had a charming time at the Vaudreuils' cotillions. Outside might be flooded walks and gutters odorous with hills of refuse; inside, the Marquis and his lady waved perfumed handkerchiefs and signaled to the musicians to start the evening's delights.

The Marquis' régime is notable for a final Indian episode, and its sequel. About 1753 a Choctaw insulted one of the Acolapissa Indians, who killed him and fled to New Orleans. The Choctaws followed, insisting that the Frenchmen give the man up. By now the guilty one had apparently escaped, and his father offered to surrender his life for his son's. To the Choctaws this was a fair thing, and understandable. The old warrior knelt beside a fallen tree, and died beneath the tomahawk.

An officer poet, Le Blanc de Villeneuve, was so impressed by the incident that he made it into a play in verse. The Vaudreuil drawing-room was turned into a theatre, the first in New Orleans, and a carefully rehearsed cast presented the tragedy to enthusiastic applause. Whatever its merits, *Le Père indien* is remembered as the first dramatic work to be offered in the city—a sympathetic treatment of a native American theme.

CHAPTER 4

One Was Fat, One Was Lean

IT WAS a decade or so after the dazzling Marquis and
Marquise left that a curious rumor began to be heard in
New Orleans. Louisiana well knew of France's loss of the
Seven Years' War, of the way she had had to cede Canada to
the British. And now came the story that Louis XV had also
turned Louisiana over to a new owner, his Bourbon cousin,
Charles III of Spain.

The Orleanians wouldn't believe it, couldn't. Spain, the
country they scorned and despised! Then official word arrived; the deed had been done nearly two years earlier—and
they hadn't been told. They had been passed around like a
dish of grapes. Resentment blazed through the town, up the
Mississippi, along the bayous.

Nothing definite happened immediately, however. Not altogether anxious to take possession of a place that had proved
a bad investment for France, Spain hesitated. Not until months
later, in 1766, did she send a representative. Possibly as peculiar a choice as might have been made, Don Antonio de Ulloa
was an icy astronomer who knew practically nothing about
government. With him rode a small band of soldiers, but he
was not yet ready to take over; he would watch and wait till
that day came. It was an anomalous situation, and New Orleans tempers rose.

Then the situation exploded. The colonials gathered for
mass meetings; men marched in from the country, and highly

charged words were shouted—independence, free trade, human rights, even that dangerous one, *Liberté!* Allegiance to France was one thing; but, if France didn't want them, they certainly didn't want Spain. There was even talk of setting up a republic, ten years or so before the uprisings on the Atlantic coast. Angry Louisianians forced the Superior Council to order Ulloa out, and happy cries rose as the vessel of that chill official floated downriver.

Gradually the excitement died down, to be followed again by uncertainty. How would Spain act now? New Orleans soon learned. His Hispanic Majesty crashed his fist upon Louisiana; toward the city sailed a bristling military force under command of Don Alejandro O'Reilly, Irishman in the Iberian service. The colony submitted; O'Reilly gave assurance there would be no reprisals—only justice. Then, without warning, he imprisoned the leaders of the movement and executed them. It was a black day, and the word "Bloody" would long be used when O'Reilly's name was mentioned in New Orleans.

Between Frenchmen and Spaniard hard looks passed, and sullen exchanges, hot words. But it was the collision of a pair of men that brought into clearest relief the differences between the two sides. One was plump and French, the other lank and Spanish. This is the story of Père Dagobert and Padre Cirillo, of the angry sounds that rose over the peal of the organ during somnolent afternoons, of the soul-searching that threatened to depopulate a city. It may also be the story of what happens when a fat philosophy encounters a thin one.

Père Dagobert . . . at his name New Orleans warmed with affection. Nobody was better liked than this superior of the Capuchin friars, vicar-general of the church. He had emigrated to the city a few years after its founding, as a good-looking youth of twenty-two, eager to fit himself to his assignment. The Père had grown with the town, in the atmosphere of the houses by the river, the open square before the church, the market place near the levee; and the process had been mellowing.

Reaching seventy, Père Dagobert might have been called Father Louisiana. White-haired, still handsome, he was smiling benignancy. Like his New Orleans, he would never be a fanatic. I doubt that he ever lost his temper. He was certain that things could be accomplished as well, or better, by persuasion, the calm way. Slowly, my children, slowly. Above all he knew his scene and people. Surely, if we appeal to man's better nature, give him time, *mes amis*. . . . It was said that Père Dagobert could do more with a sinner in quiet conversation than could someone else with a year's castigations.

There was understanding in his eyes, and compassion. Louisiana had always been high-spirited, hadn't it? Things must be tempered; gently he would lead. To drive—it was not in the friar's vocabulary. Instead he tried to fit himself to the requirements of this far-off, neglected spot.

He knew, they claimed, every secret of New Orleans. At one time he had christened or confessed nearly everyone, child of fifteen, silken matron of eighty, oyster fisherman, ancient beau with powdered wig, young gallant after his first fall from grace under the beguiling tropic sky. He was a guest in many homes, confidant of this merchant, mildly reproving friend of that bachelor.

As he trudged along Royal Street, he saw ahead of him the slow Monsieur Blanc, whom the Père had first met in his cradle; he had sprinkled water and given him his name, performed Monsieur's marriage ceremony, christened his six children, buried his wife. Now, alas, Monsieur was growing prematurely old. The Père would try to cheer him: "Come over today, Estève, for a glass of something good!"

As the two men halted to speak, Estève drew out his snuff box, and the Père reached for a touch of it. A sneeze, a soft sigh, and he was on his way. That night he would preside at a wedding at the home of Estève's ailing cousin. For a wedding no other priest would do. As for an anniversary: "Mais, bon

Père, would it be complete without you?" On such nights the Capuchin would talk with them all, and sit in an adjoining room while the younger ones danced.

A little wine for thy digestion's sake. New Orleans knew the Père as a judge of claret. This bottle, friend, it is good enough for Père Dagobert himself; that was no casual flattery. As for food, the Père understood it, savored it; he appreciated the art of its preparation, the leisurely enjoyment of a fragrant meal on a shaded gallery.

He was the ideal toastmaster; he liked a well-turned anecdote, the deft retelling of a ludicrous incident, even if it ended against him. "He mixed piety with joviality, as he mingled water with wine." His friends would ask: Need a man of God go about with face hanging to the ground? He loved to sing; when he intoned the Mass his rich, true notes soared triumphantly over the walk beside the church of St. Louis at the old Place d'Armes. Also, he favored processions. There's the Père again, with one of his long parades!

Easy-going as ever, the Capuchin friar had given signs of approval when the rebels rose against Spain. Then, as Spain arrived with a loud clank, Père Dagobert adapted himself again, leading a march to the river to greet the newcomers. The next governor, Don Luis de Unzaga, quickly grew fond of the Père, and things went well.

Then came 1772. Under France the Bishop of Quebec had jurisdiction over Louisiana; with Spain it would be the Bishop of Havana. Between the two, distinctions went beyond geography. From Havana came word that Padre Cirillo of that same Capuchin order was on his way with helpers, to inquire into the state of religion.

As before, Père Dagobert took his four assistants to the levee, embraced and welcomed the arrivals. Anything he could do, anything. . . . A long man, with a tight mouth and staring eyes that told nothing, introduced himself as Padre Cirillo. The Padre listened, nodded, and settled back to watch.

Days passed, and it became evident that a French Capuchin

and a Spanish Capuchin were hardly the same. The Spaniard sniffed. *Madre de Dios,* what was this Dagobert doing? Smiles, bows in all directions—and jokes! In Çuba the Orleanian had won repute as a churchman "holy and influential." But the Spaniard saw nothing holy here. How could a man of God be so round?

As one commentator declared: "Father Dagobert was the thorn upon which the newly arrived piety of austere Spain unexpectedly sat down." Promptly Padre Cirillo was writing his bishop the first of many letters which give, unwittingly, a self-portrait. At first he contented himself with hints. The people were "in general religiously disposed," profoundly silent during services; he noted "small things," though time would probably remedy these.

Then the Padre discovered that Governor Unzaga, friendly to Dagobert, had recommended his continuance as vicar-general. Feeling his way, the Padre agreed that the Père deserved consideration. Yet he could not, he informed the bishop, pass over the deportment of the French monks, "those . . . how shall I designate them? For certainly I cannot call Capuchins those I consider unworthy of that holy name." He saw no austerity: "In their dress, shirts, breeches, stockings and shoes, they resemble the laity. They say they have a dispensation from the Pope; but of what nature? I have not seen it."

Assuredly, he went on, no dispensation would permit them to possess watches with fine fobs, clocks "striking the hours" in their rooms, another in the refectory that cost nearly three hundred dollars; or to have "so many silver spoons and forks that it is doubtful your Grace owns the like." The Padre spluttered: "Not only silver spoons of ordinary size, but small ones to take coffee with!" He would not speak of the furniture, or the luxuries of the table, reputedly the best in the city. "Very often they even eat in their rooms." Truly Padre Cirillo had sat on a thorn.

The gimlet-eyed monk warmed further to his subject.

Sermons were not delivered every Sunday. And, though con-
fessionals were better constructed than in Spain, the friars
did not hold confessions in them but in the vestry itself,
"where they sit in an armchair, by which the penitent kneels."
The heat was blamed. Still, the Spaniard fumed, *he* stood the
heat.

Someone had whispered that the French Capuchins went to
balls. This he conceded to be improbable; the youngest of
them was fifty. However, they frequently attended dinner
parties, especially when performing marriages; and he protested vehemently that too many weddings were taking place
in homes rather than church. He would, if he had anything
to say, forbid the friars ever to take dinner with their parishioners!

The pen ripped on. He had smelled scandal! The French
Capuchins had, as waitresses, "young mulattresses or negresses
who are not married." The Padre, it developed, was not above
spying on these servants: "I felt so much solicitude that I
arranged matters so that I was one day enabled to see—at
four o'clock in the morning—a white man sallying out of the
chamber of one of them." He had a harsh solution. Require
the Negro women to marry Negro men; expel the others to
the plantations, or sell them.

With his next remarks, the Padre allowed another side of
himself, his ambition, to peep forth: The bishop might post-
pone the naming of a vicar-general, giving *both Dagobert and
Cirillo* the direction of affairs. He went further: "Should it
become my lot to organize and reform this mission, I would
do the work with the most careful precision." But he did "en-
treat Your Grace, in all sincerity," not to make him vicar-
general. Oh, he was not afraid he would suffer the fate of
St. Benoît, murdered by monks whom he ruled! (A fantastic
thought, this, in connection with the good-tempered Dagobert and his associates.) "But I think my abilities unequal to
the task." Here was a highly revealing document.

Meanwhile Governor Unzaga had written to the Bishop of

Cuba, siding not with his fellow Spaniard Padre Cirillo, but with the French Capuchin. The governor had learned much in Louisiana, and most of it inclined him toward plump Dagobert. Things were not really in a bad state, he said, though he admitted some laxities, growing partly out of circumstances, partly out of the amiability of the French friars. All were excellent men, zealous and thoroughly familiar with local needs. As for home marriages, these were infrequent. Regarding the Negro servants, they had been born on Capuchin property and remained through "the excessive kindness of Father Dagobert. They are a set of people whom he reared and kept about him from the cradle." If changes were required, "the prudence of Your Grace will know how to cure this distemper without cauterizing the patient."

The bishop took the governor's advice, and Père Dagobert continued as vicar-general. Promptly, however, Padre Cirillo wrote again, not one but two letters, and now the pages all but smoked. *Charge:* Dagobert had really sided with the French rebels against Spain; the man "aimed at nothing but power." *Charge:* Dagobert forgot to tell the people of the approach of Ember Week. His attention called to it, he simply transferred the observance to the next week. When the Spaniard protested, Dagobert replied: "Very well, you may fast this week if you please, but the public will do it next." *Charge:* There were gnats in the religious vessels, so many that Cirillo had to throw out the contents! "So great is this detestable negligence that I think these men are disciples of Luther or Calvin." *Charge:* During intervals in services the French Capuchins "demean themselves, stuffing their noses with tobacco, crossing one leg on top of the other, staring round in every direction, scandalizing the people, and moving the very angels to wrath." *Charge:* "He [Père Dagobert] rises at six, says or does not say Mass (such Mass as he says!), preparing himself in this way for duties of the day. He then goes to church, hardly makes the proper genuflection, claps on his bonnet, says his Mass, which does not last a quarter-hour, without any of the prescribed ceremonies, uncovers his head, makes another genuflection as for grace, and, taking his three-cornered hat, which is a very superfluous and unworthy appendage for a Capuchin, he goes to a somewhat suspicious house, where he idles until the dinner hour."

With each accusation the Spaniard became more frenzied. He had a solution. Drive the French Capuchins "out of the land." Let the bishop dispatch someone here to take over, or—and here the Padre showed his hand again—"invest me with the powers to perform the work of reform."

Meanwhile the amiable, white-haired Père Dagobert went sadly about town. Whatever he did, whatever he didn't do, how he shrugged, what he appeared to be thinking—all was grist to the Spaniard's mill. The town stirred to his defense, but the Père as always counseled moderation. Let us wait, children, let us see. He modified one practice, discontinued another. So far as I know, however, he did not give up his good wine, and I have faith enough in the doughty friar to believe he never did.

Still things became worse, and one day Père Dagobert stood before the governor, his stout face creased. Monsieur, would it not be best for him and his assistants to give up, go home to France? At this the governor stiffened. There'd be fury in the colony if that happened. He saw hundreds packing up, telling Spain it could keep its New Orleans. Overnight the governor took the initiative, writing the bishop that, while he concurred in some of the new and stricter regulations, Spain's own interests would suffer if Cirillo got his way. Under France the colony had had "the fullest liberty. . . . Your Grace will readily understand that it is not always that the laws made for one region can be safely adapted to another."

But the governor had gone too far for his own good. The bishop turned furiously on him because *he* seemed too lax, too much like Dagobert! Was it the Louisiana air that did such things to Capuchins, to Spanish governors? The matter widened; into it the bishop brought the Governor of Cuba, the Captain-General of Cuba; the problem bubbled up to the court of Spain itself, to a minister with the mighty title of Bailiff de Arriaga.

At this climax Governor Unzaga argued earnestly for compassion, for a philosophy of government adjusted to Louisiana: "The people will remain quiet as long as they are gently treated. But the use of the rod would produce confusion and ruin. Their dispositions are the result of the happy state of liberty to which they have been accustomed from the cradle, and in which they ought to be maintained so far as is consistent with laws of the kingdom."

These were strange words for a Spaniard. He thrust home his meaning: "An enlightened prudence and a good deal of toleration are necessary here." After all, the Louisianians were still "French at heart," with "that spirit of independence which arouses resistance to oppressive laws." With that the governor revealed a small secret, another source of the Spaniards' annoyance at the French friars: "What is it to the king, for instance, whether the French Capuchins consider the teal duck amphibious and eat it on fast days?"

And this view prevailed. The king's minister sent out letters, sought opinions; then he let matters rest, with good Père Dagobert still in authority. In effect Spain, realizing the unwisdom of the rigid Padre Cirillo, gave in. Père Dagobert's ways, slightly modified, continued; and the years that followed found him again peaceful and serenely happy. Padre Cirillo fumed helplessly, then subsided. The Padre even gave way somewhat as time went by; eventually he was seen in quiet conversation, now and then, with his once arch enemy. (Though not, of course, over a bottle of sherry.)

Père Dagobert remained as vicar-general for three more years. At his death in the spring of 1776 (he was seventy-five) he ended pacifically, gently, fifty-three years of continuous service in the humid outpost of Louisiana. On a May morning the roll of bells drew thousands to the parish church of St.

Louis, to fill the seats and aisles and form dense lines across the banquette outside. The priest of the occasion? It was Padre Cirillo himself; and it is said that he delivered a generous sermon, eloquent and understanding!

Thus, having awaited his turn, the Padre finally stepped into Père Dagobert's shoes. He never became quite a mellow man; this would have been too much of a miracle. He got into certain difficulties with successive governors. But never again did he fulminate. Was there something, after all, in this atmosphere of New Orleans?

In general, then, this was the course of Spanish rule in New Orleans: harsh threats—readjustment—modification. Spain sent her officials with braid and scarlet uniform and files of soldiers. Rigid form was followed; but usually it would be form only. Quietly, the Orleanians did much as their fathers had done, and stayed as thoroughly French as ever.

Comparatively few Spaniards came over; throughout the colony, one local official after another had to be chosen from the Creoles. Quickly, too, the Spaniards intermarried with the French. Governors, military commanders, subofficials . . . the list of such alliances is long. As has often happened, the conquered people conquered its conquerors; the French, as always, were a pervasive and persuasive race. (Many a great Creole family has a Spanish great-grandmother, and to this day an occasional member whose black hair and eyes are Iberian rather than Gallic.) During quiet evenings, in the shadow of wide-galleried houses, the Spanish newcomers learned to enjoy the New Orleans style. A fountain tinkled in the distance; a Spaniard made a gallant remark, and the Creoles reflected that after all the French and the Spanish were cousins, much the same people, *n'est-ce pas?*

His Majesty sent a series of rather popular governors, notably one Gálvez, an adventurous youth who appealed to Orleanians as much by his behavior in the parlor as on the public platform. Under Gálvez, a strong soldier, the Creoles drilled happily. The American Revolution broke out, and when Spain wished to aid the Atlantic coast colonies against Britain, the Louisianians co-operated with pleasure. Taking up arms, they attacked Pensacola, upriver Baton Rouge, and other English holdings in the South. Thus many a Creole could say that, though a subject of Spain, he had fought in the American Revolution, and on the right side. (Whether or not they admired the Americans, any side that opposed Britain was the right side!)

In trade the Spanish colony had a mixed experience. The rigid trade rules were modified or winked at. Though legally the port could deal with only a limited number of Spanish points, smuggling thrived with the West Indies and other places; it was during this phase that there grew up the custom of illicit trading which was to attain near-phenomenal proportions.

The swampy, marshy land below New Orleans was threaded by thousands of meandering bayous. To patrol it effectively—Señor, this would have required all of Spain's navy! Through that labyrinth of streams moved vessels with ever-increasing loads—goods for every taste, cheaper than could be purchased in any other way. This district was a heaven for smugglers, toward whom the easy-going Orleanians developed a casual tolerance. From time to time, of course, unhappy "accidents" occurred. Impulsive or careless privateers destroyed ships in the Gulf, sending them down with all hands aboard, though the more sentimental might let some of the crews and passengers float away in skiffs, to be picked up if lucky. Orleanians frowned when they heard of such cases. How sad! But, after all, it didn't happen often—and they went on dealing with the smugglers.

Not unsusceptible to graft, the Spaniards were frequently willing to look the other way, especially if the graft were large. It was in petty matters that the law's majesty was more scrupulously respected. At one time—so the story goes—

the Spaniards devised a scheme for curbing lesser violators. Since vessels bearing contraband might not come all the way into New Orleans, they ran in as far as the bayou or river edge, where they met carts to which the goods were shifted for the run into town. Now the Spaniards adopted a fresh regulation: The wheels of these carts must never be greased, but must by their grinding squeaks proclaim their presence in advance. To be caught with a greased vehicle would be good evidence of the intent to smuggle, and the cart could be confiscated.

But the Spaniards had reckoned without the native ingenuity. What the smugglers did was to ride along at each side of the creaking cart, letting water drip on its hubs from the containers they carried, with the result that there was no noise at all. If the Spaniards did find the cart, there was no evidence of grease!

As the eighteenth century advanced, most of the new faces seen in the city were not Spanish but American. A sizable band of businessmen—adventurers, dealers in a hundred kinds of merchandise—was drawn here by increasing opportunities. A less prosperous breed also appeared—brawny river boatmen, floating their goods from Ohio and the upper Mississippi, the "West" of that day. Spain did not seem to know quite what to do about these bold new Americans; it opened the river to them, closed it, opened it again. For years the governors were plagued by the American "problem."

In the 1790s a yet more pressing question arose, a far more dramatic surge of population, as thousands of French refugees fled before the slave uprisings in Santo Domingo. New Orleans was the nearest place in which they might find sympathy, and New Orleans was glad to have them. They gave a further exotic flavoring to the city, a new infusion of Gallicism and an added culture. The islanders brought the town's first professional dramatic troupe, its first newspaper. They brought blacks and mulattoes, too, and these were strong believers in Voodoo, incantations, chicken-feather charms, snake-pot mysteries—and had a tendency to use poison among themselves. Among these darker people, Voodoo "kings" and "queens" operated quietly, though none the less effectively. New Orleans' mixtures were thickening.

The greatest impress that Spain left was architectural, and this came about partly by an accident, or two of them. On Good Friday of 1788, when all pious natives lighted candles, a breeze lifted the altar hangings of a house on Chartres Street, near the levee. Quickly New Orleans blazed, and in less than five hours its houses, largely of wood or the old half-timbered kind, were swept away; more than eight hundred and fifty disappeared, nearly four-fifths of the town. Then, six years later, a second great fire came to destroy over two hundred structures, among them the vital shops and warehouses missed before. Thousands, left homeless and poverty-racked, went to plantations upriver or along nearby Bayou St. John, or set up tents in the Place d'Armes.

By this time most of the old French town had disappeared. It had been succeeded by a Spanish city of heavily walled brick houses, two-storied, tile-roofed, with wide arches, fan-lights, and Spanish-style courtyards. But the new houses had certain French elements as well. And almost everywhere was seen the gallery of cast or wrought iron across the front.

It was in these days that the ironwork—perhaps the most distinctive mark of the city's architecture—appeared. At least some of it, as Stanley Arthur noted, came from Southern Spain; designs and measurements were drawn up here, and sailing vessels brought back the finished product, in simple wrought patterns. Gradually, however, New Orleans produced its own *forgerons,* sometimes slaves, again free men, who created the more ornate cast iron of brilliant variety—patterns of flowers, leaves, acorns, arrows, trees, vines—and of a striking delicacy despite the use of heavy metal.

For a long time supplies of iron were difficult to obtain

here; and yet, oddly, the craft flourished as in no other part of the United States. The explanation may be that the Spanish introduced the ironwork, and the Orleanians came to like it—and have never stopped liking it.

Stuccoed in most cases, the houses were tinted pale yellow or green or peach-color, providing a rich panorama of hues. Though each was individual in design, in color, in roofline, they yet shared a basic identity. The gallery became indispensable; it permitted the family to "take the air" in the afternoon, it protected the house from the heat, it provided shelter from the rain. Flush with the banquette, the houses stood close together, one wall against the next. For space was at a premium; and, in addition, the French have ever been friendly among themselves. The Creole generally liked his neighbor. High walls gave privacy, but neighbors could always call across the gallery or the courtyard, couldn't they? . . . In a sense, those disastrous fires were good for New Orleans, since their ultimate consequence was to endow it with a new uniformity and to make it a city without parallel in America.

Here and there among the new places a few of the earlier single-storied houses continued, ancient and honorable, fading a bit with each year but maintaining their integrity. More rarely might be found an example of a plantation style that survived in spite of everything. By almost a miracle, one such structure remains—the oddly named "Madame John's Legacy" at 632 Dumaine Street, simple, doughty, veteran of veterans. Back in the days when Père Dagobert took his pleasant rambles, there rose here a single-storied wooden house of unpretentious lines; old maps show it on this square. Then, in about 1775, part of a family property was sold, and apparently the house was moved a short distance; a brick first floor was built and the wooden structure was lifted upon this. What resulted was the kind of smaller residence that planters constructed along the river and bayous. Curiously, it lasted while others went—a magnificent anachronism.

The first floor of Madame John's Legacy was now of stuccoed brick; the second of the original aged cypress. A deep porch cut into the house, with a long hipped roof reaching toward the banquette line, marked by seven wooden colonnettes and wooden railings. Beneath the gallery the basement floor opened directly upon the banquette; above it all rose a pair of fine dormers. At the back was another gallery, and windows and doors showed the early type of French design—small, simple, with slightly arched tops.

The site had originally been owned by a ship's captain from Provence, Jean Pascal. In the days of the Company of the West he had acquired it on coming to New Orleans; and on it he built, in about 1726, the one-storied house mentioned above. Then, three years later, he went upriver to Natchez, where he became one of the scores of victims decapitated in the bloody Indian uprising. Though his family survived him, the house went to others. In the 1770s it fell to René Béluche, captain and busy contrabandist in the bayou area below New Orleans. His ship was appropriately called the *Spy*.

The house lay directly in the path of the first great New Orleans fire, but the flames halted just before reaching it. During the next century it passed through many hands until, in the 1920s, it was acquired by Mrs. I. I. Lemann, who preserved it. Recently the state has made it a museum. Its name, "Madame John's Legacy," is a fictional one, bestowed after George W. Cable wrote " 'Tite Poulette." According to this story, John was a gay-spirited youth, member of the "Good Children's Social Club." Dying, he left the house to the quadroon Zalli, who had been his mistress, "Madame John," and her daughter 'Tite Poulette. Sadly Zalli sold her legacy and put the money in a bank—which failed. The lank Padre Cirillo, could he have heard this story, would have disapproved severely. But Père Dagobert would have sighed a fat man's sigh, taken a pinch of snuff, and sauntered on his way, musing over human frailties.

The eighteenth century closed; world diplomacy shifted, and Louisiana (again "like a dish of grapes") went suddenly from Spain back to France, then—still more startlingly—from France to the United States. Whether the city liked it or not, its American days had arrived and with them a future of which nobody had dreamed.

Jackson tips his hat as he rides past the cathedral

New Orleans Item

Ursuline Convent: Centuries have mellowed the walls

Dan S. Leyrer

Marigny "Casino": The gay Bernard was good to all the ladies

Eugene Delcroix

Pontalba Buildings: The red-headed baroness had temper and taste

Claiborne Courtyard: The fanlight is studied grace

Guy F. Berna[

Cabildo: Massive Spanish below, delicate French above

Jackson Square: One of the great vistas of the New World

The Dancing Oak: Death in the Landscape

Dan S. Leyrer

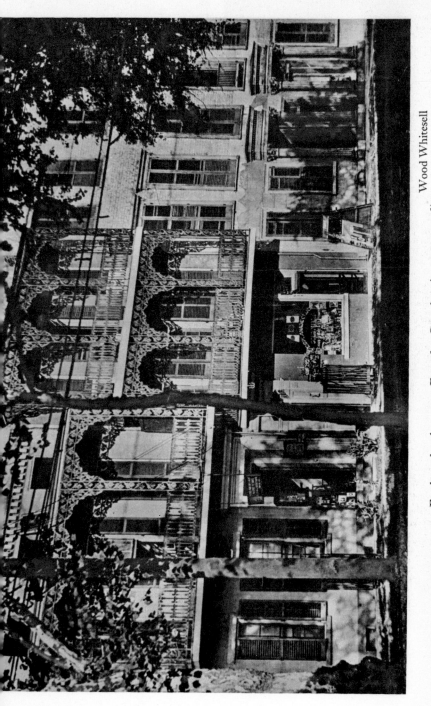

Esplanade Avenue: For the Creoles, it was paradise

Wood Whitesell

Broulatour Courtyard: Flagstones, arches, an air of repose

Carriageway and gate: The Orleanians wanted, above all, privacy

Dan S. Leyrer

Cathedral alleyway: For sinners, saints and those between

St. Louis Hotel: The Creoles defied the Americans

St. Charles Hotel: But the Americans built a bigger one

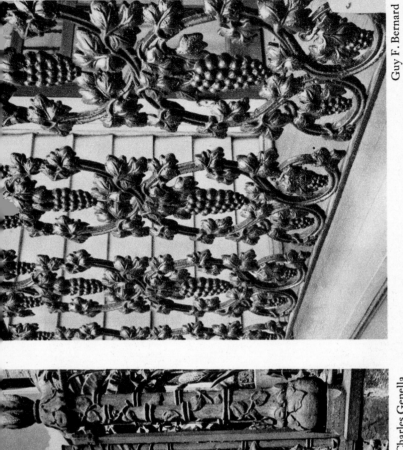

Charles Genella

Cornstalk fence: Anything you asked in ironwork

Guy F. Bernard

Or a grape pattern, if you wished

Dan S. Leyre.

Old steamboat landing: All the world came to New Orleans

Everybody Dance American!

FOR its first American governor Louisiana might have had that remarkable man, the Marquis de Lafayette. President Thomas Jefferson offered the place to the warmhearted old soldier-nobleman, already made an honorary American citizen for his services in the Revolution. But Lafayette said No.

Meanwhile an application for the job had been made by a no less remarkable man—the sandy-haired young Tennessee politician named Andrew Jackson. (We may smile at the vision of Jackson, who seldom hesitated to use sword or fist to get what he wanted, presiding over the fiery Creoles.) This time it was Jefferson who said No. He was not, of course, to foresee that within a few years Jackson would be going to New Orleans under different circumstances—to make war on the British. Had Jefferson given him the river city when he first asked for it, Jackson might not have found himself in arms when the battles of 1814-15 broke; and in that case, almost certainly, he would not have reached the White House.

In Jackson's place the President turned to a mild-mannered young man of twenty-eight. When the Creoles heard of the choice, they groaned. A gambler of 1803 would have hesitated to take a risk on the future of William Charles Cole Claiborne. From New Orleans' point of view, Mr. Claiborne had practically everything wrong with him. He wasn't an

Orleanian, nor even a Frenchman from France; he was that sad thing, an *Américain*. Worse, he spoke only that peculiar grunt of a language, English. How is this man to know a banquette from a mosquito baire, will you tell me?

Meeting Mr. Claiborne, the Creoles hardly changed their minds. Though pleasant-faced and with regular features, he seemed to lack dramatic force or frowning vigor. A painting shows Claiborne with short hair slightly disarrayed above a high forehead, a hint of growing plumpness under the chin, and looking a trifle uncomfortable in a barbarously tight collar. He was destined to be uncomfortable for years to follow. Any man in his place would have developed insomnia and indigestion at least. Yet on further study the portrait reveals a certain candor and, around the bright eyes, a hint of fixed purpose. These qualities would not be long in revealing themselves.

William C. C. Claiborne came of a Virginia family, with an ancestor who had arrived in 1621. Though William's father lost his means, the boy had an education. Almost a prodigy, at fifteen he was valedictorian of his class. With a few dollars in his pocket, he pushed ahead, took a place as minor assistant in the national House, and attracted Thomas Jefferson's eye. The Tennessee territorial delegate advised him to try that thriving area. William did, moved about in politics, became Tennessee Supreme Court judge at twenty-two. After two more years he was in Congress, though under the legally required age.

There, when Jefferson and Aaron Burr were tied for the Presidency, the serious-minded youth joined in the voting between the two. A single shift would have won for Burr, and, as the balloting went on and on, the Burrites reportedly made rich offers to William. But he stayed firmly with his fellow-Virginian—and for this act alone his country might be grateful to him. Also Claiborne was a strong believer in Jefferson's liberal, anti-aristocratic beliefs, and demonstrated his faith throughout his life. A little later, when Mississippi was admitted as a territory, Jefferson made him governor; doing well, Claiborne then received Louisiana. Here in truth was a success story, though many predicted that the young man had now reached a place in which he would stub his toe.

With a handsome wife and their young baby, Claiborne arrived quietly at the end of 1803, to find New Orleans in ferment. These first months were startling, even harrowing. The Creoles were bitterly dissatisfied. They had been sold down the river, tragically, to a horde of barbarians! To make it worse, a considerable part of the United States showed no less firmly that it did not want Louisiana.

Jefferson had not been altogether certain of the legality of his Purchase. This "greatest real-estate deal in history" brought in more land than all the rest of the United States, and it was simply too much acreage, shouted his opponents; it would be cut up into too many new states in order to outweigh the older ones. The thing, sir, was—was against the Constitution! These Americans quivered when they thought of the Louisianians. "A hotchpotch, a mixed race of Anglo-Hispano-Gallo-Americans who bask on the sands at the mouth of the Mississippi"—so the invectives went; not fitten to be American citizens, at least not for a long time to come. Nobody at all was happy about the change.

To say that Claiborne's position was curious is grossly to understate. A thorough democrat, he found himself with dictatorial powers. For a time he would be executive, legislative, and judicial branches combined. He had vague instructions: He was to fit French and Spanish laws (which he could not read) into an American system. Yet when he talked to Orleanians about American legal principles, they blinked. Common law, unwritten law? How can it be a law and not in writing? Then, when Claiborne introduced trial by jury, the new Americans grimaced. All those strangers prying into a man's affairs! What business was it of theirs?

Daily Claiborne had to analyze, interpret, administer. The Orleanians complained that they appeared before him, eloquent and devastating in their logic; and the man just sat there, his face as expressionless as an oyster, not understanding a syllable of their civilized tongue. More than that, he was bringing in English-speaking assistants to run their affairs, issuing proclamations in terms nobody understood. What do these crazy words mean, Alphonse?

Grievances multiplied, and the Creoles had a number of plausible ones. They had been promised that Louisiana would be admitted promptly to the Union; instead, they were being kept on probation. Worse: Congress cut their land up, and "Louisiana" would be only a fragment. They had been assured that their rights would be maintained; and here were laws to prohibit the introduction of new slaves. This, they cried, was treachery.

But Claiborne was worrying about actual treachery. For Louisiana contained numerous partisans of Spain, and His Hispanic Majesty had been greatly concerned when France sold the vast territory to the United States. Now there were those who muttered that Napoleon, in making the sale, had violated the treaty with Spain that had given him Louisiana. You watch—Spain will move on New Orleans and take it. There was Spanish power nearby—in Mexico and in West Florida, which included points only a short distance upriver from New Orleans. Repeatedly couriers ran to William Claiborne with alarming reports. The Spanish forces were making mysterious marches, and there seemed to be substantial basis for those reports. And still another element felt sure that it was France who would return. According to them, Napoleon had merely gone through the motions of selling Louisiana. Let him but finish off the English, and the glorious Tricolor would float once more at the Place d'Armes!

New Orleans was a kind of international frontier. Spain, France, England, each had a finger here. Neither the French nor the Spanish officials would go home. By agreement these forces were to leave within three months; sixteen would pass before the first departed, and others would delay and delay.

Spanish soldiers refused to give up the official barracks, and, though this was now the United States, the Americans had to sleep in tents. In all these delicate foreign matters, Claiborne knew he had to move slowly.

The main barb in the governor's side was the Spanish representative, the Marquis de Casa Calvo, who had acquired an embracing love of Louisiana. The Marquis went beaming along, adroit, a social favorite, making gifts right and left, dropping poison in the well of Spanish and American relations. Claiborne had him watched; the man showed a marked scientific interest in American military installations and had an uncanny way of prying out facts about them. However, though Claiborne tried everything he could think of, he could never get the fellow to leave Louisiana.

Wherever he looked, the governor met surprises. He encountered Negroes with large slave holdings, gamblers on a monumental scale, adventurers of a hundred varieties, rank outlaws, fugitives, speculators, manipulators, men with filibustering schemes against Latin countries. Enigmatic persons plotted Mexican ventures, planning to fight here, there, anywhere, gathering equipment and funds, violating laws at every turn; and nobody seemed concerned about it. As one man has said, a visitor to New Orleans in that day could find anything, even a band of followers to join him in colonizing hell.

In the country districts, something like civil war broke out among rival families. The Spaniards stirred up Indians and Negroes; hundreds of escaping blacks took Spanish uniforms and went off shouting Hurrah for the King. To add to the tension, enemies tried several times to burn the city down. Stories spread of a Negro uprising. Placards were regularly slapped on the walls, calling for general defiance of the cursed *Américains*. In the lantern light, crowds roared happily over the words; when police tried to pull the signs down, mobs halted them.

In part, of course, all this was just the confusion and excitement that normally attended the formation of new American territories. That it was happening in New Orleans, however, made it different—more gaudy, more involved, more explosive. In his dealings Claiborne had no guides, no rules of action; he had to improvise as he went along. By now, though, the natives were beginning to realize that this man's quiet manner had fooled some of them. He would try to placate and adjust, he would give in, up to a certain point; beyond that point he stood fast. Washington officials considered him overfussy, but none ever questioned his integrity. His conciliatory policy may itself have been the thing needed most at this troubled spot, and in all essential matters he continued to hold a steady course.

A major problem was that of the public balls. Louise Livingston Hunt has told how a dance was once disturbed by a thunderlike sound, a mild earth shock. At this an elderly gentleman cried: "Ce n'était pas du temps des espagnols et des français que le plaisir des dames était ainsi troublé!" (In the Spanish and the French days, the ladies' pleasure hadn't been interfered with like that!)

Not long after his arrival Claiborne attended a ball. As usual in French New Orleans, quadrilles were in order. As the music began, a group of Creoles formed a quadrille. Then, unexpectedly, a circle of newcomers started an American dance. Tempers broke; an American army surgeon, shouting to the musicians to play as he wished, raised his cane to hit one of them. A flash of rage ran through the audience. Calmly, Claiborne stepped in and argued persuasively with the American, who presently gave way, and the French quadrilles were resumed. Then another American demanded an American dance. An ardent native cried that the women there would never dance it if they had a single drop of French blood—at which the ladies left in a body, and the evening was spoiled. Some of the Spaniards tried to draw Claiborne into making some sharp comment, but he declined to be provoked. Yes, he said, New Orleans loved France a great deal; he saw it every day!

At another ball General Wilkinson, commander of the American forces, rose with his staff to sing "Hail, Columbia." Automatically the French bristled, and one began to sing, *"Allons, enfants de la patrie!"* That, Messieurs, was *their* anthem! Men's anger rose, women shrilled, each group trying to yell down the other. It remained for Claiborne to intervene and end the fracas.

The Creole looked at the American and saw a hog. The American called the Creole a peacock, or worse. One eyed the other and gave up trying to understand him; a Claiborne and a Marigny were as different as noon and midnight. There were many kinds of Americans, but the Creoles divided them into just two: river boatman and businessman.

The river men were the first Americans that the average Orleanian ever saw—and one sight was enough. The belching, hell-roaring Westerners were there to get rid of their produce, then drink anything in sight and take any woman who came within reach. Unlettered, adventurous, they snorted at whatever looked foreign, which meant all of New Orleans. In grimy trousers and ragged jackets through which their muscles bulged, they strode about the city, punched, brawled, got sick on the street. A sunburned face, hair growing out of ears, eyes bloodshot from last night's frolic—and there was the flatboat bully. He might hail from any one of the "Western" states, but the Creoles, staring down their noses, lumped him with all his friends under one word, "Kaintuck." The term implied something you turned over, carefully, with your toe.

Next to the river man, the Creoles disliked the American higher in the economic scale—a "Yankee," no matter what his place of origin. He wore clean shirts and he did not spit on the floor, but in Creole eyes he was no less a barbarian. As a trader, he was known to be a sharp dealer . . . his squint-eyed concentration, his speed as he raced along the street . . . the Creoles looked in the other direction.

The native Orleanian was usually a person of careful manners, of punctilio even. There were correct ways of doing business—the leisurely meeting, the soft inquiries about a dozen matters, the discreet question that launched the business discussion, the delicate probing of possibilities. Another cup of coffee, Monsieur, with brandy this time? And you say you will be here for only a week? None of this did the American trader understand. It made him squirm. All he wanted was to get this deal settled and move on to the next one.

Nor—being often somewhat puritanical—did he go for all this drinking, this liquor with everything, even in the food. And dancing and music all the time, too; you couldn't walk a yard but you'd find somebody playing music, or run into a band, or hear songs coming through an open window. And there were further shocks. On the waterfront, along the main streets—everywhere, I swear—these folks *gamble*. Why, they tell me thousands of dollars pass across those tables every night! Even on the streets, people take bets. . . .

As for the Creole, when he watched the Americans scurrying along, he shrugged. What did these people want out of life—a pain in the back of the head? *La vie*, it was to be smiled at, laughed with, gaily coaxed—a feast day. But these Americans behaved as though it were merely one big market place.

The Creole loved birthdays, anniversaries, family gatherings, evenings at the opera. The American looked with suspicion at this sort of thing. Why so many parties and dances? They only produced a headache next morning. How could a man attend to business? At this, the Creole would lift an eyebrow; let business go, then. For the most part the American was stolid, methodical; the Creole was mercurial, volatile, a man of zest rather than determination. The American expected to live in the way he had always lived. But the Orleanian had adapted his way to the thermometer, to the slumbrous afternoons when only a light breeze drifted from the river and bare existence demanded slow movement in the shade.

Each was intolerant of the other. The newcomers stalked about, lording it over the town. The future was theirs, their eyes said. They saw French signs displayed, French and Spanish names on the stores, but they made no effort either to understand or to pronounce the words. This is the United States; let these foreigners learn American! And let them, also, give up those funny gestures and ways of walking, grinning, jabbering in every tongue, and sashaying around, doing nothing, with coffee on the side. . . . By the same token, the Creoles tossed away even the official proclamations in English. *Mon Dieu,* such gibberish.

The Americans shook their heads at the Spanish stuccoed walls and the spiked ironwork like a fan against a line of tall windows. And right smack *on* the sidewalk, these places were, with no lawns or gardens. When the new arrivals learned that the Creole house faces its inner courtyard and turns its back to the street, they stared. What for? Right offish, that. . . . As they passed the carriageways with their ornamental iron gates and caught glimpses of figures in the patios, the Americans might wonder. What was the place really like inside? And some of the Creoles grew similarly curious about *ces Américains.* That couple, they looked pleasant; were they altogether bad? Years must pass before either side got its answer.

Meanwhile the courts that William Claiborne supervised were becoming bilingual. Everything had to be translated and retranslated. Difficulties arose when a witness spoke no English and the attorney who was questioning him spoke no French; to make it worse, the lawyer for the other side might not understand English. The first lawyer's questions had to be translated for the witness; the witness's answer had to be translated for *him;* and the second attorney had to be kept informed of what was happening. Then somebody would protest that one of the versions had been inaccurate—and the whole thing would start over again. The next witness would prove to speak and understand only Spanish, which complicated matters in still a new way.

In the selection of a jury the attorneys struggled furiously. The Frenchman wanted as many Creoles as possible; the lawyer with an American client demanded a maximum of Americans. When it came to the attorneys' final arguments, the jury operated in shifts. As a lawyer began to speak in French, the Americans went out to smoke. Then they returned, and, as the next attorney launched into English, the Creoles left. When they all got together in the jury room, half of them could not understand the other half. The French were sure they had heard the correct version, the Americans that only the English argument could be right.

In the legislature, too, curious scenes were staged. In one instance a Creole stood up, with gestures and spluttering energy, to make a verbal assault on an American member sitting nearby. The American, understanding not a word, twiddled his thumbs. When the Creole resumed his seat, the interpreter explained to the American, who straightened up, flushed, and bit his moustache. Then he rose and ripped out with a black attack on the Creole, who slouched quietly back —only to rage in his turn a few minutes later!

It was Étienne Mazureau who best demonstrated the three-way language situation. Addressing a mass meeting, he declared: "I see three nations before me. Americans, I'll speak to you first; Frenchmen, you next; and to you, my Spanish friends, last. I'll take two hours with each. It will be the same speech every time, so none of you will miss anything." It took six hours, but M. Mazureau knew he had reached them all. And the new Governor Claiborne watched it all from a distance. Virginia was never like this.

Through these early days William Claiborne had the reassuring presence of his young wife, Eliza, and their baby.

But they had been here less than ten months when yellow fever made its appearance. Husband, wife, and child were all stricken. Claiborne himself slowly improved, but Eliza and their little girl died on the same day. For a time things would be harder than ever for the Governor of Louisiana.

Now the newspapers were printing baseless attacks on him, and fellow Americans suggested he do something to suppress the outbursts. He declined; one difference between autocratic Spain and the democratic United States, he observed, was that freedom of the press was an American right. One of these newspaper campaigns, however, brought William Claiborne his next taste of tragedy. Less than six months after the deaths of his wife and baby, he wrote to Thomas Jefferson about it.

Already a "licentious press" had persecuted him; "every circumstance, as well of a private nature as of my official conduct, that calumny could torture into an accusation against me, has been brought to public view and exhibited in every shape that malignant wit could devise." But worse had now come. One newspaper exacerbated its attack by bringing in Mrs. Claiborne's name, printing a poem that described her ghost as moaning at night outside their house while the governor caroused inside. It was a cheap fabrication, of course. Claiborne's secretary and brother-in-law, Micajah Lewis, found out who had written the poem and—without letting William know—challenged the writer to a duel. At the first fire Lewis got a bullet in his heart. Claiborne's cup of sorrow was filling up.

At the same time, church troubles were exploding in his face. New Orleans had come under the authority of the American Bishop of Baltimore, who named as vicar-general an Irishman, Father Patrick Walsh of the Capuchins. The pastor of the Church of St. Louis was a Spaniard known to the Creoles as Père Antoine, an easy-going and widely popular priest. Irish and Spanish temperaments clashed. The Spaniard defied his superior; in a curious episode, the parishioners held a public meeting and with shouts and hurrahs

"elected" Père Antoine their priest. One element among the
Creoles had been infected by the spirit of the French Revolution, and now—though they insisted they were good
Catholics—they rebelled violently against the church authorities. Nativist feeling was spreading; Orleanians objected to
"foreign" influences even in religious matters, and announced
that they would run these as they wished! The Irish vicar-
general went to court and, in a remarkable step, interdicted
the church, declaring its ceremonies to be profanations. Next
he appealed to Governor Claiborne for support, placing that
unhappy man squarely on the spot.

Carefully Claiborne declared he could not take sides. Had
he done so, he would have been the target of violent assaults
from both directions. Yet he himself had been growing
alarmed over Père Antoine, who was altogether too close to
the Spanish representative, Casa Calvo, that man who would
not go home. Within a few swift hours Claiborne summoned
the priest and, in the presence of witnesses, made him swear
allegiance to the United States. Since that time, evidence has
come to light strongly indicating that the Père was really a
secret agent of Spain. . . . For some years a holy war raged,
with fisticuffs on the street and shouted interruptions of
church services.

For Claiborne, the year 1806 was unusually eventful—first
a time of personal tragedy, then of widening happiness. For a
long while hate had simmered between him and a flamboyant
Irishman who had arrived in the Spanish days. Daniel Clark
was an engaging, slightly questionable merchant with large
ambitions. Working assiduously, he often made Claiborne
squirm. (Clark is now remembered primarily as the father of
a girl, Myra, who fought the longest and most romantic court
suit in America to prove herself Clark's legitimate daughter.)
In these troubles, as in others, Claiborne had kept firm command of his emotions. But there came a time when he could
no longer control himself. The city pricked up its ears when
it heard he had delivered a stiff challenge. Ho! This Claiborne,

who had been talking so much about the need to reduce dueling . . .

To get beyond the limits of Louisiana law, Claiborne rode across the territory for his meeting with Clark on that July day. The sheriff, setting out in pursuit, missed him, and the two men faced each other. On the signal they fired at the same second; Claiborne staggered, seriously though not fatally wounded. In this particular trouble, however, many of the Creoles (who considered Daniel Clark rather shady) sympathized with the governor.

A brighter day arrived when at last he received authority from the city of Washington to tell the procrastinating Marquis de Casa Calvo to pack up. The Marquis professed astonishment; it was an insult to the king. Ah, no, Claiborne retorted; the fact that he had been allowed to stay so long showed how much the United States respected His Majesty. Scratch off one worry!

Then a yet more joyous occasion. With each month additional Orleanians found themselves liking this governor. Oh, we would never vote for him, but he does dance well, and hasn't he lost some of that Yankee stiffness? At a party he met young Clarisse Duralde, of impeccable New Orleans standing, her father a Spaniard who had served at the Attakapas post, her mother a Frenchwoman from Quebec. The young widower saw Clarisse several times, then paid a formal call on the family; and the couple were married before a gathering of Creoles and Americans.

With his Creole wife the governor began to follow Creole customs. On holidays he walked about the Place d'Armes, stopping at the corner to buy flowers from a *marchande;* and, like every old Orleanian, he went with Madame occasionally to the French Market to buy supplies for the family.

It was to the site of this market, everybody said, that the Indians had paddled when it was a convenient trading post. A few animal trappers had followed them, and then Germans came from upriver with their fine vegetables. In the 1790s the Spanish officials put up a roofed place on the site, and the market thereafter expanded rapidly.

Along an arcade of heavy pillars, the Claibornes inspected fish with gray-blue bodies shining in the sun; wriggling craw-fish, tiny things with belligerent claws; somnolent crabs; piles of eggs wrapped in Spanish moss. When Madame Claiborne hesitated before the eggs, the seller broke one at the curb to prove it was fresh, then tossed it negligently into the gutter. They moved on to the fruit and vegetable section, with prickly pineapples warming in the sun, and piles of golden bananas. Over there clustered the meat dealers; next a huddle of flower sellers, and a group of bayou hunters with wild ducks and geese, the birds' iridescent feathers gleaming in the morning light. One man held a great turtle, its dragonlike claws helpless as it awaited a purchaser and executioner; another offered a trussed-up alligator, and the governor wondered what anybody could do with that.

All around them was noise. Hens squawked, parrots screamed. A dozen languages were being shouted on every side, all of them in the modified New Orleans forms. Negroes cried out in their French patois—the "gombo" that Claiborne had such difficulty in understanding. Indians in gaudy blankets squatted before woven baskets, waiting silently for what the day would bring. . . . New Orleans was a pleasant place, now and then an exciting place, and William Claiborne found he liked it, after all.

That same year of 1806 saw the first observance of Independence Day in New Orleans. On July 4—undoubtedly at Claiborne's bidding—stores were closed, fireworks set off, a ball was held, and (typical New Orleans touch) a High Mass and Te Deum were sung. Since the Irish-American vicar-general was fighting with the Spanish pastor of the church, the city had two separate services, and the governor, "always unwilling to give offense to any party, politely held a candle at both ceremonies." That night an audience applauded a new play, *Washington, or The Liberty of the New World*, which Claiborne described as a "tragedy."

It was in this year, too, that New Orleans entertained a scintillating figure—Aaron Burr, whom Claiborne had voted to keep from the Presidency. The visitor waved a jeweled hand; his deep eyes were meaningful, and he talked grandiloquently. Though none as yet knew precisely what Burr was planning, the country buzzed with rumors of a plot against Texas and Mexico, some scheme for an "Empire in the West." The idea seemed to fascinate the Creoles, and there were whispers that the city would join whatever machinations Burr was up to.

Like many around him, Claiborne felt alarm. Would the Creoles stay loyal to the United States? Then Burr left the city. But not long afterward the whole country was excited —Burr had headed for New Orleans, to seize power! Martial law was declared in the city, men were arrested right and left. Then the whole thing collapsed. Burr, sailing downriver with a tiny band, was arrested near Natchez; and no Creole lifted a finger against the American flag. Another crisis had passed for the Virginian-turned-Orleanian.

His Creole wife gave William Claiborne a son, and for a year or so the couple enjoyed a genuine happiness. Then, on a visit to the bayou country, Clarisse died, and again William faced the loneliness of a widower's life. Four years later he married again, once more to a Creole, Suzette Bosque. Hers was a sprightly family, and a proud one. And Mademoiselle Bosque's father, a well-to-do merchant, had given the old town a showy object that nobody else ever matched—a gallery of galleries.

At the present 617 Chartres Street stands a neat example of stuccoed construction with superior ironwork, and it is in the iron balcony that one sees Monsieur Bosque's individuality. The Creoles often had their initials worked into the balcony design; and in the later days of the Spaniards, Papa Bosque did the same thing. But apparently he was thinking of himself rather than of the passers-by. Most Orleanians had their letters facing the banquette. Not Papa Bosque; the "B. B." faced *him,* so that he could sit there and admire his initials by the hour!

Little Suzette had her father's engaging and unconventional directness. It was while she was still in school, about to graduate, that she met the governor. A bright girl, she had won the highest honors in her class, and she had just finished writing and memorizing her valedictory speech for delivery before the governor. Then, however, she misbehaved in some trifling way, and the principal spoke firmly to her: The speech would be delivered by another girl! But because only a few hours now remained before the ceremonies, the other girl would have no time to memorize it and would therefore read it.

Suzette set her lips, went on stage with her class, faced the audience, and waited. Now the other girl rose, turned toward the governor, and opened her mouth. At that moment Suzette darted forward, bowed, and told Claiborne, breathlessly: "That's *my* speech, Monsieur! I wrote it, and I don't have to *read* it." And as her rival stood by with crimson face, Suzette proceeded to prove what she had claimed.

The governor, intrigued, hid his smiles behind his hand. Afterward he reproved Suzette gently, and she said she was contrite—though nobody thought she showed it. Soon he found opportunity to call on her parents, and now he did not conceal his smiles. Eventually he put his question to Monsieur, and was accepted. The ceremony, interestingly, was performed by Père Antoine. With Suzette the governor's days were never tedious. Those who had found him a trifle stodgy decided that Suzette had put a bit of French gusto into him. And when one of their daughters eventually married a son of Bernard de Marigny, the union of an American family with the Creoles could be considered complete.

In at least one respect Claiborne still differed with the Creoles. It was in the matter of the smugglers and pirates, who were getting bolder with each year. By now they centred about the Barataria region of the Gulf; when in New Orleans they swaggered through the streets in brilliant attire, patronized by persons of every rank, protected by wealthy businessmen, lawyers, and legislators. They defied American law by flooding the town with "black ivory"—smuggled slaves. Normal commerce suffered because the Baratarians could provide anything at a cheaper rate. When Claiborne proclaimed a five-hundred-dollar reward for the person of the leader, Jean Laffite, that cocky magnate retaliated by issuing his own proclamation, offering fifteen hundred dollars for the governor! New Orleans thought it funny, but Claiborne didn't.

All the town knew that Maspero's Exchange (now at 440 Chartres Street) was a favorite resort of the Baratarians. In an upstairs room they held conferences with the respectables, planning new deals, new routes; one of the chief rendezvous of established business was a pirates' hang-out—and Claiborne could do little about it.

Then, late in 1814, William Claiborne met the most spectacular crisis of his career. With his fellow Louisianians he awaited the approach of the hostile British fleet that would almost certainly conquer New Orleans; at the same time they awaited the coming of General Andrew Jackson, who would defend the city. Up rose all New Orleans—grand seigneur and river fisherman, Livaudais and Jones, Creole, Anglo-Saxon, Italian, German, Greek, Indian. Down swarmed Tennessee frontiersmen in coonskin caps, howling flatboatmen, and red-faced farmers of the valley.

Though he and the dynamic Jackson did not hit it off any too cordially, Claiborne took a militia command and emerged creditably from the struggle. Throughout the episode he served as a buffer between the excitable Jackson and the no less excitable population. Several times he had to defend the

Orleanians against Old Hickory's criticism, steadily avowing their loyalty.

In this moment of trial the Baratarians, enemies of American law, made a choice. The Laffite brothers, Jean and Pierre, received offers from the British—shining rewards if they would only transfer their allegiance. At the same time the American government was at last turning its armed forces on them, blasting out their hideaways. Still the Baratarians parried for time. They sent copies of the British letters to New Orleans—ironically enough, through their respectable friend Jean Blanque, businessman, legislator, and associate in trade. If they were pardoned, they said, they would fight on the American side. At first Jackson rejected them, calling them "hellish banditti." Then he relented; and now, beside the others, were fighting the Dominick Yous, the Chighizolas, and the rest of the swarthy, earringed crew that Claiborne had once sworn to send to prison or the gallows.

The scene of the major clash, in January 1815, was the field of Chalmette, just below the city, property of Ignace de Lino de Chalmette, young Bernard de Marigny's guardian. Toward this spot the men marched in ragged files. Over their balconies women threw flowers, and from their lips issued two songs: "Hail, Columbia" and "La Marseillaise." The Creoles among them cried and begged for an American victory, and as they did they sang "Allons, enfants de la patrie." At the Ursuline convent, women fell to their knees and prayed with the nuns while gunfire boomed in their ears.

On the ground of Chalmette the British moved in overwhelming array, red coats gleaming beside the river bank; and there they died in overwhelming array, under the guns of French Orleanian and Kaintuck, buccaneer and river rat. A courier clattered up and shouted the word: The British had lost! In the convent chapel the successors of Madeleine Hachard wept with the other women and sank to the floor again in prayers of thanks. The battle had been fought after peace had been agreed on at Ghent, but New Orleans would never forget the occasion. Afterward came the time for wine and fireworks, for cheers and laurel wreaths. William Claiborne and his Creole wife stood next to Andrew Jackson and the bishop, near dandy and river rowdy. Did the governor reflect on the fate that had brought him so far from his home to bizarre New Orleans?

He now had only a short time to live. He had been in charge of Louisiana's affairs for thirteen years; first as provisional governor; then as appointed executive; and finally—when Louisiana became a state—he received what many said he could never achieve, popular election to the same office. Re-elected, he served briefly, and was then chosen for the United States Senate. Preparing to start for the Washington he had known as a hopeful youth, he fell sick and died in 1817. As a token of their feeling, the managers of the St. Louis Cathedral cemetery on Basin Street allowed this Protestant's body to be placed in a yard reserved for Catholics, though it had to be enclosed by an iron fence.

William Claiborne had confounded the odds-givers, succeeding where none had expected. He had proved the value of tolerance, the soft answer, the generous approach of a man of good will. He had been attacked as weak, bumbling; seldom had he used the stern power at his command. By just such means he had, perhaps, succeeded at his task of reconciling, in the main, two nearly irreconcilable peoples.

CHAPTER 6

The Baroness Had Red Hair

OR most of its days, the life of New Orleans has had
as its centre the Place d'Armes. The old, green square
—parade ground and assembly place—came into being
with the city itself. Here occurred the ceremonial happenings;
here began or ended the great events of conquest and victory,
heartbreak and loss, the pageantry of centuries. Old buildings
have disappeared, new ones have gone up; but for the past
hundred years there has been little change in the picture—the
symmetrical plantings of grass and shrubbery in the centre;
on one side the thrust of the aging cathedral, flanked by the
massive house of state and house of the church; and, forming
two other sides, long twin buildings of brick with stately
galleries like black lace thrown over a crimson shawl.

This has always been the heart of New Orleans; for many
it will always be the heart. In the soft evenings the area is
dimly illuminated: flickering points from the church's windows and half-open doors, a dull glow from inside the
adjoining structures, and the blink of lights in the stretch of
buildings that make up the second and third sides. And here
stroll the couples, the single figures, the crowds as they have
always strolled in the night. Beyond, across the wharves, lies
the river.

Though it grew out of no single plan or design, this tableau
was the work of a man and a woman, father and daughter,

about whom New Orleans speculated through all their lives and beyond. In their day each was described as controversial. They lived life on their own terms and never underestimated themselves.

Don Andrés Almonester y Roxas and his daughter Micaela shared a talent for dramatic disagreement with those around them. Was it a matter of vigorous temperament, or plain hotheadedness? Whatever it was, the Almonesters usually had their way. Through all their experiences they adjusted the world to themselves, not themselves to it. And if that is the standard of happiness, then Don Andrés and Micaela should have been the happiest of beings. Yet those close to them wondered if they had so truly satisfying a life as, say, the Indian squaw at the French Market or the cotton loader by the levees. And when Micaela became the lurid central figure in a Parisian scandal of the nineteenth century, they wondered even more. . . .

Not much is known of Don Andrés of Andalusia before he arrived in New Orleans in the train of the Spanish conqueror, "Bloody" O'Reilly, in 1768-69. It would appear that he had no large means at the time; he began here as an *escribano* or notary. He was forty-four, a childless widower. For most men this would have seemed late to start a career in a new land. But times were in flux. In Spanish Louisiana, privilege bred privilege.

As a notary, the Don managed to handle a considerable amount of official business. He became friend of the great, and also *alferez real*, a lifelong government rank whose chief duty was the bearing of a banner on ceremonial occasions. But with this went an important privilege, a seat as alcalde in the governing body or Cabildo. In time he also stepped forth as a building contractor. Politics helped construction work; construction helped politics. Organizing his business like a modern operator, the Don used a nucleus of several score slaves—all his own, none hired or employed on a temporary basis as in most such cases. Putting up his own kilns, he took over swamp land thick with the best of lumber; he trained corps of specialists in wood-carving, ironwork, plastering; and none could deny he did excellent work.

Yet New Orleans has always had two opinions of the Don. One element has held him to be, all things considered, a generous man; another termed him chill opportunist. The truth probably lies between the two. The fact remains that hardly anyone greatly liked the man. In contemporary comments he is given credit for various deeds, but few omit to point derisively at his motive. This may be set down to the jealousy of the less successful, or the Don may have gone about things rather too directly. Starting out late as he did, the man *had* to run!

Before long he branched out further. The best-situated land in New Orleans bordered the Place d'Armes, which everybody frequented. Until this time all of it had been public property—the king's; and in his name O'Reilly had ceded to the city two large and valuable parcels of nearly 700-foot frontage. These, Don Andrés now acquired on perpetual lease. For those who had eyes to see, it was evident that this Almonester would ultimately be one of the colony's richest men.

Ten years after his arrival New Orleans suffered a shattering storm, during which its hospital was wiped out. Don Andrés, who had hitherto kept a firm hand over his pocket, came forth now with a generous offer to rebuild the hospital at his own expense. The town applauded, and the sound was good in the Don's ears. Soon he was promising a handsome chapel for the Ursulines. When the disastrous fire of 1788 razed the old town church, he made a munificent proposal to erect a bigger one.

Presently, however, the Don got into squabbles over his benefactions. He delayed starting the church, and delayed again. The Cabildo asked if he would "kindly state whether or not he had decided to rebuild"; if not, the Cabildo itself would proceed. At that moment his reappointment as alcalde was hanging fire, and it has been suggested that the Don was bargaining to continue in the post—perhaps even to be made something better. In a few hours, he was reappointed alcalde. At this he announced he would go ahead with the church; and promptly he was chosen Perpetual Commissioner and Royal Ensign of the Cabildo!

The Don gave a building for a school, land for a leper hospital. But the officials were soon fuming again: He had built the promised hospital—yes; but he was also trying to run it. Don Andrés pointed to the rank of "patron" granted him for his beneficence; this, he snapped, gave him the right to appoint the staff and handle all monies. Even the governor collided with the ambitious Spaniard; Don Andrés, complained that official, was trying to do more than even the governor was allowed.

The matter went to King Philip III himself, who responded with a whacking vindication of Don Andrés. The Don could appoint everybody at the hospital—doctors, chaplains, nurses; he need account for his funds to nobody, governor included. In future he must be treated with "deferential regard as one who has found grace near My royal person through achieving his great works." Let the Don's enemies put that in their pipes and smoke it!

The Don's ideas expanded. He studied the new church, rising to dominate the square. Why not a house of state at one side, a house of church at the other? At the northern end, where the Capuchins' quarters had stood, he began the religious structure, only to fall into a dispute with the friars. At this point the second great fire, in 1794, wiped out the old government building, and the Cabildo contracted with Almonester to hasten a replacement on the opposite side. Lacking funds, it borrowed from him; as a result, the Don by this time had a finger in everything important in town.

The new state building or Cabildo became a rich example of Spanish construction. It was of brick stuccoed to provide a solid mass. Along the first floor thick columns were connected by arches; above, the walls were broken by fanlighted windows with Creole wrought-iron balconies, providing delicacy in contrast with the base. A pediment bore the royal arms of Spain, and a balustrade topped it all. Some years later the church house, almost a duplicate, would be completed. In the middle stood the church (now the cathedral), finished in 1794, a firmly built Spanish structure with a pair of bell-shaped towers. It was an impressive whole.

Now, at sixty-two, the Don decided that the hour for romance had come. As in everything, he reached high. He could not have set his eye on a better-placed *parti*, as the Creoles used the word, than Louise de La Ronde.* Louison—such was her *petit nom* or nickname—counted twenty-nine years, well past the Creole matrimonial age; and a family connection, the Baron de Pontalba, described her as pettish and sullen. Yet it was apparently a successful marriage. Don Andrés could give Louison any jewel, any gown she wished; one account says he presented her with rubies the size of marbles.

If Don Andrés hoped for a male heir, he was disappointed. A daughter arrived; and, after a time, a second daughter— Micaela. Since the Don was then seventy-one, here was another feat of which he could boast. The first child died, and upon Micaela would eventually descend the father's wealth. How would the girl turn out? New Orleans wondered.

Meanwhile the old father appeared in new splendor; he was made Knight of the Order of Charles III. It was the highest point of his life. The Baron de Pontalba (who was unimpressed) describes the ceremonial thus: "He was covered

---

* Louise's father is remembered for the superb double line of fifty-two great oaks near the crumbling walls of the family estate below New Orleans. A tourist story claims that the father had been one of Catherine the Great's lovers, that she had once told him that his fifty-two predecessors had all been better men than he, and that his planting of this number of oaks was an expression of pique.

by a great mantle and his train carried by three lackeys in red. An immense crowd followed as he went in state from the cathedral to his house. He placed himself, in his mantle, at the door of his drawing-room, where he affectionately kissed on both cheeks all who approached to greet him, to the number of more than three hundred." Then the Don sent up a balloon from the centre of the square, with "a small display of fireworks." Sweets were passed around, and guests played cards until ten o'clock. As for Louison, she was indulging one of her sulks.

Pontalba adds a sharp comment: "That poor fellow is never satisfied. As soon as he gets one thing, he strives for another." Though the Don's forte was not military, he had a rank as colonel of militia; now he yearned for the title of brigadier. A portrait shows him as he looked at this period—pipe-legged, stomach bulging, brilliantly clad. His wig is powdered; one plump hand grips his sword, while the other is pushed into his vest. Three-cornered hat, embroidered suit, elaborate vest, wrist ruffles—altogether he is a man pleased with himself and his world.

Don Andrés enjoyed his knighthood for but two years, dying suddenly at seventy-three. It is said that he had asked to be buried in the parish churchyard; after a year or so, however, his body was brought inside the cathedral and placed in a tomb before an altar. Over him went a slab recounting his charitable acts; and, as he had requested, every Saturday thereafter priests intoned prayers for his soul.

A few years passed and Louisiana went into American hands. All at once the Creole friends of the family were frowning: the widow Louison, forty-six, was behaving skittishly, twittering at Jean Baptiste Castillon, the French consul, a dark and handsome youth. She had been married before to a man old enough to be her father; this one was young enough to be her son. The grandes dames twitched in their chairs. Louison told them, in effect, that they could go on twitching. She married her boy.

What resulted is Louisiana history. For generations New Orleans had enjoyed charivaris, rough-house serenades to taunt oddly mated brides and grooms. If a trembling ancient reached for a convent miss, if a crone hankered after a school-boy . . . ah, they would get a charivari. But the town never had one like this, and there were several reasons. One was the couple's prominence; another was Monsieur Castillon's manner. Born poor, he was showing himself a prig, walking about as though he disdained the very smell of New Orleans. To shake the Almonester tree for that shriveling peach, and then put on airs!

After the wedding, Louison and her youth proceeded to the fine house left her by Don Andrés. The lights had hardly gone off upstairs when from every direction came men, galloping on horses or mules, in carriages or carts, on foot. They carried buckets, spoons, drums, horns, anything to make a noise. A signal rang out, and thousands started a raucous yelling, screaming, and banging.

At the window the bride clutched the curtain. All New Orleans was running toward her house, to howl and point and throw things. It was but the beginning. Hours passed, and the crowd only increased. An eye-witness wrote: "Every-body looks waggish, merry and pleased. . . . All civil author-ity seems suspended."

A wise couple usually accepted the inevitable, opened the doors, and invited the mob in to refreshments. Not Louison. *Canaille!* She'd show them. If the youthful Castillon had anything to say, we do not know of it. The new Madame Castillon sat through it, all that night, and the next day and night. The police were helpless; the crowd refused to dis-perse. Men appeared in shifts, going home, returning to take the place of friends who needed rest. On the third night Louison and her young bridegroom jumped into a carriage; the big gates at the side of the house swung open and they rode out.

Free! But they only thought so. After them galloped horsemen, blowing horns, screaming to passers-by to look at the old lady and the boy; and the comment became specifically anatomical. Louison directed the coachman toward the levee, back again, below town, above. At last, half-weeping, she ordered the carriage turned homeward.

There, soon after they arrived, a lighted cart rumbled by. In the name of Dieu Seigneur, what was that? A black coffin with a wax figure in it; in the flickering light she made out the name on the scarlet costume—Don Andrés, Knight of Charles III! Then she saw worse—a half-naked man in woman's attire, with bulging false breasts, and a bridal veil, bearing a sign: Louison. She screamed and collapsed. Reviving, she asked what they wanted. The answer was prompt: a fine gift to charity and food for everybody—and her assent, as she sank back exhausted, cost her three thousand dollars. Not long afterward she went to France to live for a time. She had only a few years with her Jean Baptiste Castillon; he proved less lasting than she. Now twice widowed, Louison returned to New Orleans, money and temper intact.

By now the daughter Micaela was approaching her teens, a pupil at the Ursuline convent. Within a short time the girl had taken over the family spotlight. She was a sharp minx, with a large measure of self-admiration and self-will. "Just like her father," said some. "Like her mother, yes!" remarked others even less friendly. Whether she could have been called handsome is a question; there are portraits of her only as an older woman, by which time she was not quite a beauty. She had red hair, her eyes were wise, and her lips could be hard. With all that fortune, to be sure, what need had she for looks? Every calculating *mère* in New Orleans picked her as a potential daughter-in-law.

In spite of the nuns' care, Micaela was thoroughly spoiled. It was not long before she was leading her elders a dance. She was only fifteen when there were rumors of engagements; the Creoles still say that she once cast her eyes at least temporarily on a youth neither very rich nor (worse) of French descent. If so, it ended promptly; the Almonesters were angling for bigger fish. Louison, no less querulous than before, had resolved that Micaela was to make a glittering alliance; and the girl was not unwilling. As matters stood, however, New Orleans had nothing quite high enough. Then there entered that Baron de Pontalba already cited. He had thought little of old Don Andrés but had no objections to the Don's well-dowered daughter as a mate for his son.

The first Pontalba had come to Louisiana in the French days, and the present baron—duelist, man of the army and of the world—had moved between the colony and the home country. Returning to France as Napoleon's star rose, he had cast his lot with the First Consul. He married a relative of the celebrated Marshal Ney's wife. Before long Napoleon made Pontalba a nobleman, master of the château of Mont l'Evêque, Department of the Oise, an establishment in the grandiose style. In everything the aging baron was both shrewd and proud—a little like red-haired Micaela herself; and in her tangled affairs was presently to play a prominent role.

The Pontalbas had one son, Célestin, to whom they gave the affection that an only son always gets. "Tin-Tin," they called him, giving it the nasal French pronunciation. Tin-Tin became page to the emperor, then cavalry lieutenant under his relative Marshal Ney. A miniature presents him as wavy-haired, soigné, a candy-box type of young man, whom people thought pretty. Cavalry service or not, Tin-Tin remained spiritually close to Maman and Papa.

Now, though the young couple had never seen each other, a marriage was arranged. Micaela's mother showed herself almost overanxious. Letters were exchanged; they were cousins, but a dispensation was obtained. The portrait of Tin-Tin was sent across the sea, and Micaela is said to have sighed over it. (The only time I know of Micaela's doing so weakly feminine a thing as sigh.)

Eventually Louison wrote the baron: "I see with sorrow

that my young cousin [Tin-Tin] has not yet arrived. . . .
Send him to us soon. If he pleases my daughter, I will take
charge, and ask nothing of you. Micaela has asked me to beg
you to send him as soon as you can. What a pity if such a
fine match were to fail, as they seem made for one another.
. . . If your son were a long time in coming over, I should
have a hard task trying to prevent my daughter from marrying. You will realize that at fifteen, pretty and rich, she is
not without admirers."

Curly Tin-Tin, getting leave from his cavalry post, came
to Louisiana with his mother. (Through most of his life,
Maman was nearby.) Micaela gave Tin-Tin a searching look;
Tin-Tin smiled charmingly, deferentially. Was it the defer-
ence that won Micaela? He would do. . . . Louison had her
lawyers draw up a marriage contract.

The result was the most glittering union New Orleans had
ever seen. From the family house on the Place d'Armes the
procession moved to Don Andrés' church. The crowd caught
the swish of silks, the shimmer of diamonds, the fragrance of
massed flowers. On behalf of Marshal Ney, Bernard de
Marigny gave away the bride. She was sixteen, Tin-Tin
twenty.

In the light of the candles, Micaela retained her cool poise.
What woman in New Orleans wouldn't have traded places
with her; what man wouldn't have liked to be Tin-Tin?
With the two Mamans, the couple set sail for Europe. At the
castlelike Mont l'Evêque, Micaela spent several quiet years
with Tin-Tin and the elders, who included two admiring
aunts. Maman Louison moved about, living sometimes with
Micaela, again by herself at her town house in Paris. In rapid
succession three sons were born; and, so far as New Orleans
heard, things were going well with the young Pontalbas. Two
years after the marriage Tin-Tin resigned from the army, to
try the life of a countryman on his broad acres.

Tin-Tin was a home body who liked the family circle,
the evenings by the fire, the pastoral hours. Slowly, however,

it became clear that Micaela was bored. The children were very nice, but she had other interests. She looked at all that grass and yawned. Worse, she yawned at Tin-Tin. He behaved pleasantly, altogether too pleasantly; one would guess that Micaela preferred strong feeling. He was always going to Papa with requests for help in running the properties, and the masterful old man was ready with advice. Micaela was not long in acquiring a thorough dislike of her father-in-law.

One particularly disturbing fact eventually emerged: Tin-Tin embroidered, spent hours making scarves and screens which he presented to Micaela. And this was not quite what the red-headed young matron wanted from a husband.

Most difficult of all was the matter of money, that Almonester money. When the old baron looked at the marriage contract, he asked innumerable questions that neither Tin-Tin nor his wife could answer. Louison had originally written: "I will take charge and will ask nothing of you"— but she (or her lawyers) had taken a great deal. The baron's eye hit on a property valued, supposedly, at 125,000 francs. Why, he grumbled, the purchase price would not have to be paid for years; and what was this trifling amount that Micaela was supposed to get out of her father's estate, while Louison had inherited many times as much? A widow had to protect herself, of course, but . . . Worst of all, a final provision gave Micaela the right to handle a great block of revenues in her own name, even though she was Tin-Tin's wife. The further the baron investigated, the more upset he became.

Thus the family relationship grew strained. Louison was on bad terms with the Pontalbas, though she and Micaela remained friendly enough. More and more the baron was irked by his daughter-in-law. As the Pontalbas put it later, they did try to keep her happy; there were jewels, there were trips to Paris. But none of this was enough. Emancipated at eighteen, she wanted to extend her sway, be queen not only of the Pontalba ménage but of the fashionable outside world too, with servants, livery, crowds of callers.

For a time, though the baron was cold to the idea, Tin-Tin provided these. Then, alas, the cupboard was nearly bare. Everybody got angry; the baron came out with his resentment over the wedding contract; Tin-Tin fretted; Micaela lost her temper, threatening to sue her mother for a larger share of Don Andrés' estate. These recriminations died down when a new settlement was drawn, giving Micaela the valuable New Orleans properties fronting the Place d'Armes. For several years there were fresh funds, fresh means of self-expression, gifts for everybody, including dazzling toys for the children. Micaela ordered and spent, spent and ordered. Even with her increased resources, her debts multiplied. If Tin-Tin objected, she waved a hand: "A fortune, *mon cher*, demands that one play the part!" A rich woman should help the arts, patronize music, lead the fashion. Money wasn't meant to be kept in strong-boxes!

But Tin-Tin was increasingly restive now that Micaela had the whip-hand; and presently there came a morning—the two were on a trip—when she awoke to discover that her husband had left her to go home to his father. The letter he sent from the château explained that he had found it too much to endure; Micaela had gained the ascendancy, had ceased either to love or to respect him. Now he was going to try to overcome his weakness; henceforth *he* would be master! In this shrill letter there is a pathos that indicates something of Micaela's problem.

She replied, and there was a reunion. She had a suggestion. Why not start all over again in their own house in Paris, away from Tin-Tin's Maman, his Papa, his aunts? Getting her way, she now set up splendidly in the rue du Houssaye— a house whose rooms were full of mirrors and inlaid woods, its ménage including a maître d'hôtel and numerous servants —and proceeded to win fame for the brilliance of her receptions and the ingenuity of the entertainments she devised.

Soon, however, Tin-Tin resumed his laments: he had become "a stranger in his own house" and felt ill at ease at her affairs, to which his old friends no longer came; while Micaela played queen of the ball, he acted as mother to her children; he was only his wife's cashier, and far too much money was being dropped into a bottomless pit. For a time he got her into the country, but, inviting her gay friends there, she put up a theatre and acted in it with a troupe brought from Paris. Micaela, of course, took only leading roles, and her audience is described as "politely indulgent." Presently, however, the singing of the birds got on her nerves and she took Tin-Tin back to Paris.

Some years passed. In 1826 the tired Maman Louison died, leaving everything to Micaela, so hedging it around as to prevent the Pontalbas from touching it. For once Tin-Tin grew hot: "We shall break that will, Madame!" Other tempers flared, and tangled finances became further tangled. The Pontalbas called Micaela extravagant; she retorted that they were hungry for her money. Eventually a delicate settlement was reached that involved payments, promises of payments, new arrangements. Thus were sown the seeds of still more bitterness. Inextricably intertwined were the principals—Micaela, pretty Tin-Tin, and rigid father. Nobody could be quite sure whose rights were whose; she controlled some of the properties, they others, and everybody distrusted everybody else.

For something less than a year the couple lived together once more. Then Tin-Tin started off on a trip from which he did not return to his Micaela. He went home to Papa again. Not long afterward, Orleanians learned that somebody in Paris had suddenly grown interested in the value of Place d'Armes properties. Then New Orleans was favored by a visit from Tin-Tin himself. He had come to check up on the maintenance of these properties. He was followed shortly by Micaela, on the same errand. But she went further, calling on attorneys and demanding control of all her mother's possessions. More—she wanted a divorce; and when the Pontalbas heard this last they appealed to the French government. The

French minister in Washington pointed out that Micaela was a French subject—and the divorce idea collapsed.

Over in France the Pontalbas seized other properties of Micaela's, and Tin-Tin, calling himself a deserted husband, won a court order bidding Micaela come home. Ignoring this, she took a leisurely junket around the New World. Showing up in Washington, she got herself introduced to Andrew Jackson, and forever after insisted she was a "Jackson Democrat," even though she owned three châteaux in France and ruled scores of servants. The Pontalbas' fury was boundless. Politics on top of everything else! On questioning some of Micaela's friends, they charged that she was leading a "vagabond" life. When eventually she returned to Paris she found her house padlocked against her. According to what she told the court, she then went to Tin-Tin at Mont l'Evêque, only to be relegated to a smaller château reserved for visitors. When she joined the family table an icy curtain of disdain descended between the family and herself. This time, for once, it was Micaela who left Tin-Tin.

The years went by until 1834, nearly a quarter-century since that shimmering marriage. The three boys were grown, and problems developed about one of them. Late one evening Micaela went to Mont l'Evêque to discuss these with Tin-Tin, and the stage was set for tragedy. The two talked for hours. At the end it was too late for Micaela to return to her house and she stayed at the château. In the morning, when she was preparing to leave, her maid encountered the old baron as she went down the stairs. Brushing her aside, he climbed to Micaela's room. Entering, he locked the door and quietly approached his daughter-in-law.

She whirled around; from his pockets the baron took two pistols. "Don't make a sound, or you're dead!" The faded eyes were frenzied.

"What do you want?" (Probably he meant only to frighten her?)

"Sit down!"

Micaela obeyed, folding her arms. "Well, what?"

"Prepare yourself to go! I'll give you a few minutes—" But his trigger finger quivered and he fired. Micaela fell back, bleeding at the shoulder. She staggered toward an alcove. The baron followed.

"Please," she cried. "I'll—"

As he fired again, she raised her hand to her heart; the top of one finger was shot off, others were torn. Screaming, she struggled to another alcove. Another bullet went wild. Before her was the locked door. In agony, crying for help, Micaela worked with the key, but couldn't make it turn. The baron was almost on her when at last she gave a savage twist and succeeded. As she stumbled down the stairs, her maid caught her. Tin-Tin ran in. A few minutes later another shot echoed through the building. Tin-Tin found his father in a chair; he had blown out his brains.

This was the kind of scandal that Paris loved, and for weeks the gazettes ran details. New Orleans talked of it for years, of course. Gradually Micaela recovered, though one bullet would never be removed from her breast, and she fell into faints from time to time. Though she never went back to Mont l'Evêque—the separation was now final—she developed, strangely, a mild liking for Tin-Tin. He occasionally appeared at one of her parties, smiling amiably.

With the old baron out of the way, Micaela resumed her bright social life, beguiling, bejeweled, and still red-headed. She bought a palace originally put up by Louis XIV for the Duc du Maine. It contained some three hundred and eighty-five rooms, too many even for a Creole baroness. She tore it down, reserving the chandeliers and fixtures for use in a new house. This one, copied from a yet older château, was much smaller—only a hundred rooms.

The year 1848 brought revolution in Paris, and Micaela fled to England. There she found only ennui. Why not see New Orleans again? It was this visit by the fifty-four-year-old Micaela that left on her native city the chief impress of her personality. She observed the surging growth of New Orleans, the way the French section was losing to the American—for uptown the Americans were erecting neat, impressive stores and houses. All this denoted a decline in the value of her Place d'Armes properties. She drew a good income from them (she was probably the biggest single taxpayer in the city), but her buildings were once described as "very mean . . . covered with dreadful tile roofs, partly white, partly red and black, with narrow galleries in the second story, the posts of which are mere unpainted sticks; but they let at enormous rents."

How to influence the tide of city change, help her French New Orleans and also her fortune? As usual Micaela thought in large terms. First she planned an imposing arcade along both sides of the square, with "granite pillars running the length of the building," making it "a combination of the Place Vendôme and the Arcade Tivoli." Then she went further: she would put up whole new buildings on each side.

Losing no time, Micaela called on James Gallier, most distinguished of New Orleans architects. She asked city officials, as a contribution to a civic enterprise, to do something for her—make her properties tax-exempt for twenty years! Though the proposal shocked some, the baroness, who had friends, carried the day. After a time the city claimed she had not complied with a portion of her agreement, and the exemption was withdrawn. By then, however, the older buildings had been torn down, and Micaela went ahead anyway.

The baroness was domineering. She could deal with any man, pit her wits against attorneys, financiers, agents. As always she demanded every penny of her rights. One story says that as her new structures went up, she sat in a nearby house watching through a spyglass; and it is often asserted that when the upper bricks were being placed she bade a workman help her climb up three stories by precarious ladders, so that she could make sure the best bricks were being used.

By early 1851 Micaela was ready to open her two buildings.

They were unusual examples of brick construction in Renaissance style, with uninterrupted stretches of ironwork reaching to the tall third story. She knew just how she wanted the buildings occupied. The first floors were to be used for select shops, after the Continental plan; above these were the family dwelling units, the most magnificent apartments of their type in America. The leases she drew included strict provisions barring cafés, cabarets, fruit stands, and boardinghouses. She worked hard at publicizing the facilities provided. In a number of interviews she invited leading Creoles to live in the buildings, and she asked visiting celebrities to occupy the finest apartments. And she succeeded to the extent that several of the old families moved back to the site.

Meanwhile Micaela had looked over the Place d'Armes itself. It was bedraggled; why not a Parisian park, with formal plantings and curving walks? She summoned officials; ready to spend her own money on the project, she had her way. Though many protested when she had century-old trees chopped down, she made the spot all she promised. Next, she added politics to esthetics; recalling her old fondness for Andrew Jackson, she reminded New Orleans of its debt to the dead warrior. Why not rename the square for him? Again she won.

But Micaela had still another ambition: she wanted a memorial to Jackson. For years informed Orleanians had been grinning over the great feat and the bad art of the sculptor Clark Mills, another who cherished Old Hickory's memory. There had been a competition for a Jackson statue to be placed in Washington. Although Mills had scant knowledge of either sculpture or horses, the plaster model he submitted showed an equestrian figure. It impressed Congressmen as uninformed as he, and got him the contract. Among competent authorities there was gnashing of teeth over the model. Mills had the animal rearing on its hind legs in an unnatural pose; how would this bronze oddity be made to stand? Such works usually had stumps or props at strategic points. Mills only scowled and stuck to his task. The result went up in Washington; patriotic folk and Jackson-fanciers touched handkerchief to eye, while people who knew art called it one of the damnedest things they had ever seen.

But the baroness approved it, and so did Jackson's other New Orleans admirers. Together they had a thirty-thousand-dollar duplicate of Mr. Mills' statue erected in Jackson Square. The experts were wrong in one respect; Mills' Jackson was sturdier, more adequately balanced, than he appeared. He has stayed there for nearly a hundred years, through hurricanes, rumbling carts, booming cannons.

In time, the situation in France grew easier for the nobility, and Micaela went back to Paris. She lived until 1874, energetic and party-loving until she breathed her last when she was seventy-nine. Her pretty Tin-Tin clung to life even longer. Now and then the couple had continued to meet at her parties; their conversations must have been diverting.

It was on her native New Orleans that the baroness left her most notable mark. The Pontalba Buildings have been described as the first (or among the first) large-scale apartment structures in America. They show the Renaissance style adapted to the Creole locale. Originally each building contained sixteen apartments with thick walls, deep doors and windows, and folding doors to permit wide rooms to be turned into wider ones; chandeliers, marble fireplaces of unusual splendor, and furniture of the rosewood so much liked by the Creoles. Interior courts gave entrance to rear apartments, smaller and wooden-galleried, at right angles to the main ones.

The front balconies extended the full length of two floors and the width of the banquette, with regular repetitions of designs in cast iron of the entwined letters—A for Almonester, P for Pontalba. (Today's tourists often take them for the initials of a nationally known tea company.) The fourth floor, originally attics for the servants, has cast-iron window grilles. The galleries curve at the corners of the buildings; and the colors of the exterior are the softened red of brick, black of iron, green of shutters, and cream-white of woodwork.

The baroness and her father could well be proud of the eventual ensemble—that line of three gray structures facing the river: the cathedral in the middle flanked by the Cabildo (the state building) and the Presbytère (the church building); the Pontalba Buildings enclosing two other sides of the square; and in the centre of the greenery General Andrew Jackson, eternally tipping his cocked hat to New Orleans—or to Micaela.

About 1850 the cathedral was extensively remodeled, with steeples to replace the former bell towers. Three years before, the Orleanians had added a new floor and mansard roofs to both the Cabildo and the Presbytère, sacrificing something of their Spanish integrity. Time, however, has softened the effect, as it has softened the harshness of Jackson and his rearing horse. And on a spring afternoon of the present century, a young girl walks quickly by, her feet tapping the banquette; a black man ambles, humming softly to himself; a nun leads an orphan by the hand, her dark skirts rustling slightly. As dusk falls it is not difficult to imagine that this is the earlier New Orleans. A horn sounds from the river beyond, and from the park rises the fragrance of unseen flowers.

PART II

Prodigal Days

CHAPTER 7

Destiny in the Wind

UPON New Orleans of the 1830s there rolled such wealth as it had never before known. There was destiny in the very wind—a wind heavy with the ultra-sweet odor of molasses, the pungency of mixed spices, and flecked with wisps of cotton floating off the bales piled on the levee. New Orleans—the richest city in America, cried the enthusiasts; and indications were indeed multiplying that it had the country's greatest per capita wealth. None could question that for nearly a decade its banking capital soared higher than New York City's. Its port competed with that of New York as the nation's biggest; and in exports, pouring from the heart of the nation, it frequently ran ahead of its eastern rival.

The land along the river was packed with people; New Orleans ranked third or fourth in population among American cities. As for Chicago, St. Louis, and several others—the town looked on these as mere frontier outposts. In a single decade her population doubled, and still they came, men and women from East and North and South, New Orleans-bound. To much of America, this meant prosperity-bound.

As for the future, why, this would be the metropolis of the world, beyond London, Paris, New York! As Thomas Jefferson had declared: "The position of New Orleans certainly destines it to be the greatest city the world has ever seen." It was to be "forever the mighty mart of the merchandise brought from more than a thousand rivers, leaving the emporia of the Eastern world far behind." A less famous American put it more simply: "Kick a barrel of flour at Minneapolis, and it will roll to the Gulf."

Cotton was king, a more powerful king with each passing year, and sugar came close after it. The New Orleans waterfront was one of America's sights—"the master street of the world." For four or five miles the levee bustled with ships and men and goods; nowhere else—not even in London itself, they said—could be found so dense a compression of people and things. The line of craft, curving with the river, lay two and three deep; for much of the distance a man might step from boat to boat without once touching shore.

Vessels crowded in from everywhere, vessels of all sizes, shapes, and colors. Grandest were the steam-packets, white and arrogant, at their landing along Canal Street, that old outlying waste now burgeoning as a commercial centre. On one side, in front of the earlier French section, rode ocean-going ships, gray sails furled, gangplanks turning out sailors in the garbs of a dozen nations. On the other side, up into the American town, huddled flatboats, keelboats, smaller river craft, floating stores presided over by Westerners, ready for a sale or a fight, and somewhat inclined toward the latter.

Here were tobacco, hemp, animal skins, salted meats, kegs of pork, barrels full of pickled foods, rum, tar, coffee with its unmistakable scent, and always cotton. Bales towered on the open wharves; not for years would New Orleans bother to cover these places of deposit. What if millions were lost in spoilage? There was so much more around, coming downriver by the hour.

Now and then the biggest vessels churned in, every discernible foot of space piled with the bales. The market was high; en route the captain had felt the temptation to add a few more, then more, until the boat threatened to go under with the first strong wave. But pass up cotton? No, siree.

Brisk Yankees from New Hampshire, their faces showing a

deceptive amiability, moved by with ambling Carolinians;
Kentuckians talked horses and liquor; Georgians gaped at
each new sight. Stevedores scurried; men ran to clear the
holds. Tin-roofed shanties lined the passageways, with stores
that sold sailors' trinkets. For miles, grogshops were crowded
with customers; new arrivals waited in lines outside. Here
and there was an oyster stand, with a native lifting his delectable wares from their shells. Blind men played fiddles,
children jigged for pennies, Spaniards hawked flowers, and
black women waddled by, bearing coffeepots in their baskets,
ready to pour a cup for any who wished.

The din was everywhere, unending. "All is hurry, jostling
and confusion; the very drums of the ears ache with the
eternal jargon, with the cursing, swearing, whooping, hal-
looing, cavilling, laughing, crying, cheating and stealing."
Most of the noise came from the drays. For New Orleans was
a city of drays, heavy clattering vehicles, each with two mules
that ran tandem through the streets. The city had more drays
than any other vehicles, and they sped ahead in swift files.
When a tie-up occurred, they stood in block-long lines as
the drivers shouted and threatened. At other times they swept
by, missing the edges of fruit stands by inches, making men
jump back, colliding with others racing in the same direction.

Their objectives were the steamboats whose double stacks
towered over their surroundings, pennants fluttering, paddle
wheels reflected in the still water at the levee. On they rolled
to New Orleans in a continuous parade of ornamented white
wood, lights blazing at night like those of a castle aglow.
From the levee two hundred or more people rushed aboard
each of the larger ones, milling about velvet-hung saloons
ornamented with greens and statuary. Bars stretched yards
long, with bartenders capable of producing drinks of subtle
potency. Some vessels had their own orchestras, processions
of mulatto maids, cabins whose appointments matched those
of the best hotels. And the cuisine could equal that of nearly

any place in America, though not, said Orleanians, the restaurants of the Creole town itself.

As the engines steamed and the vessels slid away, their saloons filled with men at cards—wide-hatted, wide-gesturing planters and quieter professionals with soft voices and hard eyes. Fast ladies swept along, and disapproving matrons drew skirts aside. Couples moved about the ballroom to violin music. On the decks sprawled river boatmen, swapping jokes and whisky; having sold their produce in New Orleans, they were riding free on the upriver trip in return for loading the vessel when it stopped for wood.

And from the reaches of the vessel, during moments of quiet, came the sad notes of the Negroes, throaty, muted, the beginnings of the blues and jazz that would eventually rouse so many Americans to enthusiasm. For the blacks there was laughter in Memphis, a dice game in Natchez or Vicksburg, a quick-stepping girl in St. Louis; but there was also the ageless desire for a thing known as freedom. . . . Everybody going to or from New Orleans, everything big, everything rushing. One caller confessed: "I shall want a microscope when I return to England, so miserably small and petty will seem . . . all its features." After New Orleans most things looked small and drab.

The city was growing in four directions: upriver and down; across it to a stretch named Algiers; and then, unexpectedly, toward its back entranceway, Lake Pontchartrain. The ancients shook their heads. Everybody knew that the original town occupied the only dependable land in the vicinity. They'd never dry out that swamp, those low stretches all around. Watch and see.

Especially did the old-timers disapprove the talk about the lake area. There they were opposed not by a newcomer but by one of the city's most aged men, shrunken Alexander Milne, a tiny fellow already in his eighties. Until he was thirty-one, Alex had spent his life in a Scottish community. Of plain birth, he had taken service as a footman to an easy-going duke. Now Alex Milne's hair was a bright yellow-red, and he was monstrously proud of it. When, therefore, his Scottish master suddenly ordered his servants to powder their hair, Alex retorted that he would powder for no man, and left the duke's service.

In New Orleans Alexander Milne did well, winning the respect accorded to the successful businessman, until he decided that the city was going to expand far out toward Lake Pontchartrain. People felt sorry when Alex packed up, moved out there, and sank every dollar into adjoining land; the poor fellow was potty. He became a hermit, seldom leaving his beloved lakeshore. When he built a small reproduction of the old castle in Scotland, New Orleans wrote him off as a pathetic loss. He reached eighty, and eighty-five; the city had nearly forgotten him. Then the unexpected happened.

From the beginning there had been a certain amount of commerce between lake and city, along curving Bayou St. John and a canal built by the Spanish. Now merchants decided the city needed a quicker connection; why not one of those new railroads? The year was 1828, an early one in the nation's railway development, and the promoters were scorned. Why, the route they proposed, from the end of Marigny's Elysian Fields, was nothing but swamp. A railroad would sink in it like a spoon in hot oatmeal.

The builders went ahead, however—though occasionally wondering whether the skeptics weren't right. As fast as they piled up earth it sank away. They kept on piling, and at last it stayed firm and dry. The cost was high, and the work took three years, but they showed that the job could be done. The Pontchartrain Railroad, finished at last, was four and a half miles long—the first in the South, the first west of the Alleghenies; and the only one, I think, to be equipped with sails as auxiliary power! For when the steam engine gave trouble or actually failed, which was often, the engineers put up sails and the wind sent the locomotive skimming along.

New Orleans called it "Smoky Mary," and the line remained in uninterrupted existence probably longer than any other in America, a hundred and two years.

To take full advantage of their schemes, the original promoters needed land along the lakefront, and they found that it all belonged to old Alex Milne. Of course he'd sell? He wouldn't. He would only lease; and, at that, he had a condition: they must call their terminal "Milneburg." They had no choice, and in one stroke Alexander Milne achieved vindication, fame, and a fortune. "Out to Milneburg on Sunday" became a byword for all-day picnicking, dancing, and eating at lake-edge restaurants with a distinctive seafood cuisine. It catered to varied tastes; the élite put up the Elkin Club, an establishment purveying vintage wines and vintage dishes, while nearby were middle-class locations as well as actual dives.

All along the lake developed pleasure spots: Spanish Fort, West End, Little Woods, and others, with parks, gardens, hotels, fishing camps, theatres, and saloons. It was the city's great recreational spot. And it all happened because the young Alexander Milne had admired the color of his own hair. Meanwhile, did the old Alex relax in satisfaction, and die? He did not. He lived to be ninety, to approach ninety-five. Only then did he drop away. In death, years later, he was (as we shall see) to find further fame through the medium of something Mr. Milne never heard of: *le jazz hot.*

Up in the American section, during these 1830s, businessmen decided that they must have their own connection with the lake—a deep canal to outshine the railroad on the other side. To this end a bank charter was obtained. In the New Orleans of this speculative period, you opened a bank if you wanted to start a gas company, a theatre, or anything else. The canal would be cut through the low, swampy area, presumably by local labor. But what labor? It would be hard to procure the thousands of slaves needed to cut a six-mile ditch. Besides, this would be dangerous work, under a killing sun, and Negroes were too valuable to be risked thus. Then use free labor! ("Free" would apply in another sense, too.) But New Orleans' supply of white labor was badly limited. Well, why not use the Irish? Life in Ireland was hard, famine-ridden, and plenty of Irish were eager to emigrate. Soon ship after ship was bringing ruddy men to New Orleans in search of a better life.

The actor Tyrone Power (great-grandfather of today's player of that name), who came to Louisiana at this time, left a vivid picture of working conditions there. He saw his countrymen laboring under a sun "at times insufferably fierce, and amidst a pestilential swamp whose exhalations were fetid to a degree scarcely endurable even for a few minutes . . . wading amongst stumps of trees, mid-deep in black mud, clearing the spaces pumped out by powerful steam-engines." They were paid very little, while contractors wrung their profits "from the men's blood." Noticing women who looked as haggard as their husbands, he thought they were remembering old Ireland, where things had been bad, but the valleys were green and the brooks sparkling.

The onerous working conditions were not the worst, however. In 1833 and several subsequent years New Orleans was struck by epidemics of yellow fever and cholera. Along the canal thousands died; bodies were thrown into wheelbarrows and dropped into hastily dug ditches, to be covered with a thin layer of mud. Some rotted in the sun; unmarked remains lined the banks for hundreds of yards. Work stopped, started, stopped; predictions were made that the bloody ditch would never be finished.

But it was. After nearly seven years, New Orleans saw the opening of its New Basin Canal. It became a dreamy waterway for melon schooners from Mobile, charcoal vessels, boats with colored sails and cargoes of wine and fruit. The canal was paralleled by the Shell Road, a highway along which speedsters raced carriages at fifteen, even a daredevil twenty, miles an hour. To defy time and death by hurtling into space . . . New Orleans called this truly living!

Their work over, the Irish stayed, thousands congregating near the American waterfront, giving their name and customs to the "Irish Channel." The men served the river, the cotton presses, and related industries. They took over cabs and drays, and at least one visitor jumped when a red-faced cabman, taking his directions, told him "Oui, yer honor." Also, as they did everywhere, the Irish went into politics. Thus was added to the New Orleans gumbo a new and lively flavor.

The Irish maintained a hot independence, a love of their own people, a tendency to occasional moodiness. They liked strongly, they hated strongly; they shared good and bad with one another. The city came out to watch the great annual marches of the "screwmen"—those who packed or screwed cotton into the vessels. And, every year, there was the St. Patrick's Day parade. Often it rained, and the city was turned into a gray lake; but the Sons of Erin laid a line of boards down the middle of the street and walked right on; not even New Orleans' drainage could stop the Irish and their hawthorn sticks.

The Channel was crowded, friendly, easy-going in the main. But the Irish were explosive in both humor and temper, and there was many a fight. Let the Creoles use the rapier; the Irish preferred fist and brickbat. The women sat on steps along the sidewalks that they learned to call banquettes; the men rocked and passed the beer. But what the Channel really lived for was the wakes—glorious evenings (sometimes three in a row) of keening and talking, drinking and eating. Sorrow in the front room, food for everybody in the kitchen; sad stories, and jokes. Warnings, too. When a black bird flies around that way, trouble's coming. And be sure to turn every mirror to the wall. But don't tell Father Albert at Redemptorists. He'll say you shouldn't believe them things. Still, I know, *me!*

It wasn't long before some of the Irish, like some of the Creoles, were using a firm "me" for emphasis; if they didn't add "me," you knew they didn't mean it. And the Irish even began to shrug and gesture a bit as if they were taking in French ways along with the air they breathed.

At the waterfront, clusters of Italians appeared, to handle oysters and vegetables. Below the city Sicilians took a share in the dredging of shellfish. At the market near the Place d'Armes, and in cobwebbed, fragrant shops near the square itself Slavonians were setting up fruit stands. The Germans, too, came in increasing numbers—political refugees, liberals in flight, craftsmen seeking opportunity. These settled along the river in part of the uptown Irish district, and downtown below the French section. They became metal workers, brewers, shoemakers, and they put up beer gardens with brass bands and pavilions, about which the stout burghers moved decorously with their stouter wives. Along the river were the settlements of the poorer French—the Gascons. In these newer, plainer sections eventually appeared dwellings distinctive of a phase of New Orleans—narrow-fronted, wooden "shotgun houses," so-called because the rooms extended in a single line, and a bullet would cut through all of them from front to back. The city was growing ever more complex, its colors ever more variegated.

It still had more Creoles than Americans in its governing body, and the former naturally favored their own section—which did not please the Americans. All that money for levee work and new streets downtown, and none in our sections! As long as the Americans only shouted, they got nowhere. When, however, they rose in a body, it was to embark on one of the strangest ventures in American city government. In 1836 they went to the legislature and had New Orleans split into three towns or "municipalities": the original French quarter;

the American faubourg; and the less settled sections below the French centre—each "municipality" having its own officials, taxes, and ordinances. Here was a kind of states' rights movement carried to a lunatic conclusion.

The consequence of this division was confusion, uncertainty; as a whole, New Orleans suffered. But it also speeded up American victory in the conflict between the two elements. For Samuel J. Peters, the entrepreneur whom we met earlier, had taken a legislator to the boggy American area and promised that, if the man would vote for the separation bill, Peters would make that spot The City of New Orleans. Now he proceeded to make good on his promise. The Americans raced to take advantage of their chances, launching all the improvements they had hoped for, the projects they had envisioned. They voted street paving (cobblestones to replace the mud) and loans to encourage cotton warehouses to move uptown. When the Creoles tried to emulate them, the battle of prestige was on.

For sixteen years this battle raged about the issue of hotels. Which would build a better hotel, the Americans or the French? Out of this rivalry came what were perhaps the most splendid caravansaries the country had ever seen, as well as a type of hotel life uniquely Orleanian. The Americans put up their St. Charles Hotel, the Creoles their St. Louis. Each cost close to a million dollars, and each was a monument to human vanity, a symbol of ambition—and of heartbreak.

Both used European-born architects. The Americans turned to the Irishman Gallier, designer of the Pontalba Buildings, and their St. Charles was completed first. Its site was that of the present hotel of the name, two squares above Canal Street; and the whole country talked of it. The New York politician Oakey Hall spluttered: "Set the St. Charles down in St. Petersburg, and you would think it a palace; in Boston, and ten to one you would christen it a college; in London, and it would remind you of an exchange. In New Orleans it is all three." To Joseph Silk Buckingham it appeared "not only the largest and handsomest hotel in the United States, but the largest and handsomest hotel in the world."

The façade had a projecting portico of fourteen Corinthian columns topped by a lofty pediment. Above, a circular colonnade of heavy marble supported a shining white dome topped by an open turret that dominated the terrain. Highest object in the city, the turret could be sighted for miles. To it led a curving staircase which visitors climbed for an incomparable view—the close-packed French quarter on one side, the widespreading American on the other, with yellow river, marshes, and lake gleaming in the distance.

The hotel's second wonder, its oval barroom seventy feet across and twenty feet high, was reached by a double flight of stairs. Like everything else at this old St. Charles, the consumption of liquor, by day and by night, was continuous and prodigious. Indeed, the whole hotel interior had "astonishingly grand style," according to an experienced and traveled foreign observer. The draperies in the great parlors were unmatched elsewhere, the lobby as big as many an entire hotel. The management set up a custom of reserving certain rooms for celebrities. In the men's dining-room, five hundred could be fed at once; but the critical sniffed that the grates in the rooms were made only a foot wide, to save fuel!

"After dinner," reported the overwhelmed Charles Mackay, "the drawing rooms offer a scene to which no city in the world affords a parallel. It is the very court of Queen Mab." Planters' daughters sparkled in silks and diamonds, even at breakfast. The elegant swung by, and the awkward, the awed, the supercilious; and everybody talked, exclaimed, waved hands. It reminded Mr. Mackay of the Paris Bourse when traders "roar and scream and gesticulate like maniacs." He shuddered at the vast task, the skills required "to rule such a hotel as this in all its departments, from the kitchen and wine cellar to the treasury and reception rooms, with all its multifarious array of servants, black and white, bond and free, male and female; to maintain order and regularity, enforce obedience, extrude or circumvent plunderers, interlopers and cheats, and above all, to keep a strict watch and guard over that terrible enemy who is always to be dreaded in America—fire."

The wonders of the St. Charles had their influence on the street itself. Its neighbors—lesser hotels, restaurants, and gambling halls—sought to borrow some of its glittering elegance. For several squares the passer-by saw nothing except such places; anything else would perish. One Orleanian set up a "literary exchange." Business proving nonexistent, he installed a bar sixty feet long, and flourished.

A year later the Creoles had their answer to the St. Charles: their City Exchange, eventually the St. Louis Hotel. It was to have occupied a full square, at Royal and St. Louis streets, until the 1837 depression cut the space to half of that. Though it was not so massive as the American establishment, those who understood buildings pronounced it in many ways the better structure. Its architect, Jacques Nicholas de Pouilly, had designed no outthrust portico but a line of six graceful columns; in the New Orleans tradition, ironwork galleries opened before outer rooms. It was the rotunda, however, that became the hotel's marvel.

The authority Nathaniel C. Curtis has termed the rotunda and dome "an outstanding achievement in the annals of American architecture." Set closer to the ground than the St. Charles', the dome had to be structurally firm, yet of almost impossible lightness; the builder resorted to a device seldom used since the time of early Italian churches. It consisted of thousands of hollow earthenware pots—shells graduated to the curve of the whole. Experts were to admire it for generations.

At once the Creole hotel was hailed as the centre of the city's French business, entertainment, and culture. As a point of honor the Creoles clustered here rather than at the St.

Charles; and French was the language that rose above everything else. Every night, throngs attended the *bals de société*,
subscription affairs given by the Creoles. The flippant caller,
Oakey Hall, siding with the Americans, described it as
"headquarters of Creole loaferism," but this was mere Anglo-
Saxon envy and prejudice.

The two hotels shared a sight that made certain visitors,
Southern as well as Northern, wince. Here stood blocks on
which human beings were auctioned. From one point of view
it was merely a sale of property, no different from that of a
horse or a table. From another—but let us watch such an
event as eyewitnesses reported it.

An elderly dark woman, sunken-chested, is helped up to
stand on the block. The auctioneer starts briskly: "Now,
gentlemen, here's Mary. Clever house-servant, excellent cook.
Only one fault, shamming sick. Nothing wrong with her
any more than with me. Put her up, gentlemen. A hundred
dollars to begin?"

Several men reach over and prod Mary in the ribs. "Are
you well?" one asks.

"No, very sick." The words are strained. "Bad cough, pain
in my side, suh."

The auctioneer interrupts: "Gentlemen, I told you she's a
shammer. Damn her humbug! Give her a touch or two of
the cowhide, and she'll do your work. Speak, gentlemen.
Seventy dollars only? Going, going, gone!"

Nobody is much interested. "Lot of skin and bone," a
younger man comments, and his neighbor chuckles loudly:
"Guess that 'ere woman will soon be food for the land crabs."
Amid general laughter, the sick slave is led away.

A bright-eyed youth steps up. The auctioneer praises his
intelligence. Neither he nor any of the others would be for
sale, the man says, if their master were not in financial trouble.
Several growers escort the boy to a side room to strip him
for sores or other imperfections. A high price. Next!

A smile on her lips, a pert mulattress glides over. A stout

man opens her mouth to examine the gums. He and several others make a motion to the auctioneer and take her away, as in the previous case, for private examination. A yet higher bid, a lively raising of it while the girl's smile widens proudly. Sold!

A middle-aged woman takes the block, her eyes sombre, in her arms a sleeping child. "How much?" The auctioneer describes her training at length. Not once does she raise her eyes from her baby. He tells of her experience, what her masters have said of her dependability. She still stares down. Sold! Next. . . .

The planters stroll about, bored. "Not much left, eh?"

"Have to hurry home, anyway."

They throw on their top coats. Tonight they will be back, a few feet from this spot, sipping wine, dancing. And the cadence of the music will rise where Negro men and women have been whispering together, and the dancers' feet will slide across a polished floor where slave people shuffled to the block and off it again.

Within a few years the hazard which Mr. Mackay mentioned in his comments on the St. Charles struck the rival hotel; in 1841 the Creoles' building burned down. The French Orleanians pressed their lips together, and rebuilt it in identical style. Ten years later the St. Charles itself went up in a blaze. It, too, was replaced, and would be replaced yet again.

But by now the three-part division of New Orleans had ended. The Americans were triumphing, and the city could be reconsolidated. As a symbol of the victory, the seat of government was shifted in 1852 from the Cabildo at Jackson Square to the new City Hall of the Americans. It was the exact spot to which the promoter Samuel Peters had taken his friend that day when he promised that the new section would become New Orleans.

At least in a material sense, it had happened as Peters said. . . . The soul of the original city would continue, perhaps, in the French section, but its physical growth would develop elsewhere. In any case New Orleans had a City Hall which—still in use—is perhaps the finest example of Ionic architecture in the United States.

Higher up the river spread the American residential movement. Scattered suburbs emerged—Lafayette, Livaudais, and others (usually named after a former plantation), swallowed up by the new population, by dairies, warehouses, and merchants' quarters. About Lafayette Square, Julia Street, Annunciation, and other nearby thoroughfares, well-to-do Americans erected homes of their own, ranging from delicate Georgian to pillared Greek Revival, in brick or wood, with porches and paneled doorways. The rooms were adapted to the New Orleans climate, sixteen or eighteen feet high, with folding doors to be thrown open, long windows, wide doorways. Ironwork galleries were added in the style of those below Canal Street, and occasionally an adaptation of the French courtyard at the back. Inside were carved stairways, marble mantels, and touches of the Creole in ornamentation. And always, before the door, stood a marble carriage block.

The Americans were creating their own social world with distinct rules and traditions. Families were smaller than their Creole counterparts, customs rather less formal. The Americans held dances in their parlors, balls at the St. Charles; they rode briskly over the Shell Road to the lakefront, and they were raising clubhouses at outlying points, pavilions, and picnic grounds, all *à l'Américain*. And above all they were building the Garden District, their answer to the French quarter below Canal.

Some twenty years earlier, the Mississippi itself had given the impetus for this predominantly Anglo-Saxon residential area. The planter François Livaudais had owned an estate above the Canal Street dividing line. It had once been part of the Marigny properties; then it had passed to Bernard's handsome sister, Marie Celeste, La Perle, who married a Livaudais. On a spring morning in 1816, the river broke a nearby levee.

M. Livaudais shielded his eyes at the first sight of the inunda-
tion. His big new house, not yet finished, was half-lost in the
rushing flow; lakes covered his fields, and he lost his crop.
The residence was never completed, but remained there, a
place of many whispers, the haunted house of the neighborhood. Eventually, however, the flood waters trickled away,
and M. Livaudais realized that the Mississippi had left, everywhere, several feet of light brown earth, the cream of
America's valley soil. The plantation would be more fertile
than ever, and it would be higher, better drained.

Other Orleanians saw more than plantation uses in the scene.
Members of a syndicate called on M. Livaudais; they would
like all of his property, for division into a residential area.
Soon there appeared elaborate new homes, some of the
largest New Orleans had yet seen, in the middle of broad
lawns with plantings of shrubs and flowers. Thick oaks trailed
branches over iron railings; vines grew up the ironwork, outlined against the white wood of the houses. Magnolias were
planted, and pecans and palms, and then gardeners went to
work. Crêpe myrtles held clusters of pink blossoms against
the sides of the gardens, with sweet olives and figs among
the rose bushes that grew magnificently in this enriched soil.
Among the hedges stood marble figures, with sundials and
wide flagstone walks. It was, in truth, a district of gardens.

Located only a few miles from the business community,
the development had the appeal of a half-wooded country
outskirt. It was an area bounded roughly by Nayades (later
St. Charles) and Camp streets, Jackson and Louisiana avenues.
On Nayades horse-drawn cars rocked slowly by; the Anglo-
Saxon Orleanians watched the world from the seclusion of
their galleries. The houses were wide-galleried with columns,
ironwork, and dormer windows, their style that of the later
Greek Revival. At intervals in the brick walls opened wooden
garden gates, and passers-by caught glimpses of people at
their ease.

New Orleans would continue to grow, taking in suburbs

higher, ever higher up the river to old Carrollton and beyond. In all the movement, however, this Garden District was to retain an air that hardly changed with the generations. A few squares away was the "Irish Channel," and in other directions clusters of Germans' homes. A thin, varying line separated the settlements. The Irish and Germans carried on their teeming life; the Garden District held aloof. Diversity with a certain tolerance, adaptation of one element to another . . . that was always New Orleans.

CHAPTER 8

Pistols for Two

EVERYONE carries arms as in time of war." . . . "The duel is here an event of such frequent occurrence that it hardly excites an hour's notice; the only question asked is, 'Which of them got off?'—and with that inquiry the affair usually ends."

Nowhere in America was it easier to be killed. *Affaires d'honneur* had always played a large role in New Orleans; but with the lush new days there developed a predilection for such encounters unprecedented either in America or in France. Ten duels a day in a favorite meeting spot were not regarded as phenomenal; several times the number reached fifteen. During one period, each week brought its impromptu gun battle in some crowded hotel lobby. Orleanians took it good-naturedly, as they did a fog or a heavy rain.

Hearing a noise, a man looked in the direction of a stranger—and was challenged for his "insulting attitude." A recent arrival expressed an unfavorable opinion of New Orleans coffee; on the field the next day he was run through with a sword. A newcomer in a restaurant, sitting near a fencing master, by chance ordered the same three courses as the latter. The master decided he was being mocked—and a little later sent the man to his grave.

Lounging in a café, two Creoles fell into casual conversation. One mentioned Mademoiselle S. "Ah, *charmante*. The most magnificent woman in Louisiana!" the other murmured.

144

His friend turned livid. "Monsieur, that is my *cousine*. Your remark is a reflection on her!" There followed a formal clash that left one a cripple.

An Orleanian of French background once declared that he had been a principal in twenty-four duels, and enumerated them. An American, jealous of his standing, brought his own total to twenty. One Jean de Buys fought three duels with the same man.

Night after night, fencing lessons went on. Across the banquettes sounded the ring of steel as rapiers met, and sharp voices called out: "Fine! But try it again." "Monsieur, do you want to die one day in your own blood?" . . . In the eyes of many, a man had not really grown up until he counted a duel; some, it may be suspected, picked quarrels simply to prove their bravery.

All the way from colonial days comes the story of a group of military officers who one moonlit evening sauntered along the levee. They glanced about, bored, until one exclaimed: "What an evening for a passage at arms!" Without further ado a second man drew his sword, and presently they were in easy combat. "*En garde!*" The others chose partners, and the clinking of foils echoed over the field. Breaths caught as men thrust and parried, slipped and regained their balance. When it ended, one had a deep wound in his shoulder, another clutched a badly torn abdomen.

As the years passed, the dueling fashion grew ever stronger. One reason, perhaps, lay in latitude and climate: the tropical scene, the heat of the sun, the languorous nights; neither French nor Spanish were unsusceptible to such influences. Another may have been the influx of Americans, North and South, whom the Creoles disliked. The more mixed the elements, the more clashes. . . . New Orleans, too, had always been a town that offered a good time with bright cafés, gambling houses, bordellos for any purse. This reputation spread. All over the country, preachers' eyes widened as they described the manifold vices of this "wanton of the South"; their hearers, reflecting wistfully on what they were missing, resolved to sample some of it before they died. Here fortunes were made, happy hours enjoyed, restraints removed.

Manuals of dueling etiquette were published, books telling how one was to offend, or be offended; how to kill or be killed. An insult must be delivered in a certain way—a deft slap, the flick of a glove. Not a punch, nor any other ungentlemanly show of wrath—such would put the challenger beneath notice; he might be horsewhipped, but not fought. Nor could there be a duel if the challenger were lower in social rank; after all, sir . . .

The challenge must be offered courteously; no mean brawling, no crudity. A rude *défi* could and should be ignored. Normally the insult was not to be resented on the spot. No scene, no hurting of witnesses' sensibilities. Might one accept an apology? Only under certain circumstances; otherwise, no matter what either man thought, the thing had to go on.

Always, as part of the elaborate game, nonchalance. Having agreed to a duel after an encounter at a party, the two men went through the motions of friendliness for the rest of the evening. The next day the hostess would learn of the incident that had taken place at her house, along with the news that one of her guests had just killed another.

The code duello produced swaggering hot-heads, so busy thinking of ways to avenge "insults" that they gave up doing anything else—dilettantes who dashed from encounter to encounter, passing on delicate points, living for this sport of death. For the system, supposed to insure extreme care in everyday relations, promoted instead the habit of testy bickering. The high talk of "honor" was nullified by frequent outbursts of fury, and the rules were ignored more often than the romantics would believe.

In the earlier days the Creole participants chiefly sought "satisfaction"—the mere starting of a flow of blood with their favorite weapon, the rapier called *colichemarde*. The Americans, however, less skilled with the sword and perhaps preferring blunt action, took to using guns. This resulted in far more deaths than previously; and in time the Creoles themselves adopted the gun, further lengthening the death rolls.

Custom also fixed the places for dueling, usually in the outskirts. For a time the Fortin plantation, not far from Bayou St. John, was favored; then the Allard property, largely because of its towering line of oaks, their outer branches reaching to the earth. "Sous les chênes"—all New Orleans knew the spot. A trio of the biggest trees were designated The Three Sisters, and here more duels were fought than at any other spot in New Orleans. By the 1830s the location became so familiar a fencing resort that crowds gathered regularly. Word of a pending encounter spread by grapevine and many "dropped in" frequently just to see whether anything was going on!

The Lauzons, who had emigrated from the West Indies, went one night to a ball at the Salle d'Orléans. It was a large and happy family, all of its members on good terms. The favorite was Bien-Aimé, a personable and easy-going youth who was the hope of that Lauzon generation—anything but a dueling fanatic. On the evening of the ball the Salle was crowded, and Bien-Aimé crossed to the side of the room to get a chair for his sister. He happened to lift it over the head of a belle who was seated at the window. The lady leaped up, crying that she had been badly frightened. Bien-Aimé apologized, but her escort jumped forward, protesting violently. Young Lauzon asked him to discuss the matter on the gallery. There, a moment or two later, the other man slapped Bien-Aimé with his glove. Returning to the room, the youth said nothing to his family. They left the ballroom at a late hour, chatting happily. If Bien-Aimé looked a trifle abstracted, none wondered about it; the family had no reason to suspect anything untoward. Early in the morning he left the house.

Seconds were appointed and arrangements completed for the match.

That afternoon the Lauzons were on the balcony watching the sunset and still talking of last night's ball. Then, during a lull in the conversation, a voice rose from below: "Isn't it too bad about young Lauzon? Don't you know? He was killed under the Oaks an hour or two ago!" The family started up in alarm to see—approaching slowly around the corner—a carriage bearing Bien-Aimé's dead body. One of his sisters, who was spending the day with friends, went with them that night to another ball. Early in the evening, in the middle of a dance, a cousin broke the news to her. . . . And through the years there were thousands of Bien-Aimé Lauzons whose sudden deaths shattered hopes and destroyed families. Here was left an impoverished widow; there, children who had to be taken to an asylum.

And there are other stories. In the *opéra bouffe* tradition is the classic one about the "Mississippi River insult." A French scientist named Thomassi, on coming to New Orleans, stared superciliously; nothing here to equal France—but what was a civilized person to expect? The Creoles resented most keenly his belittlement of their noble stream. It should, he pontificated, be forced to flow inside its channel, or else be shut off.

The Orleanian who stood nearest him said that neither was practicable; the Mississippi was of unmanageable size and character—Europe had no river that was comparable.

Thomassi's lip curled. "We have rivers," he sneered, "that make this one seem a mere brook!"

Impayable, ça! "Monsieur, I will never allow the Mississippi's fair name to be insulted!"—and the Creole slapped the Frenchman. On the dueling grounds the Creole won, sending Thomassi to bed with (appropriately perhaps) a gash across his mouth. But the Frenchman had a final fling: "I would have killed him, except for the miserable steel in that sword I had to borrow. Now in France . . ."

Joachim Bermudez was a respected judge, who—though he had taken part in many duels—maintained an even temper in the courtroom. But on several occasions the code invaded it none the less. Once an attorney against whom Bermudez ruled flared violently, screaming denunciation. The judge told the sheriff to arrest the man for contempt. At that, the lawyer pulled a gun. The sheriff fell back in alarm, but not Judge Bermudez. He bounded forward, robe flying, took away the gun and handed the attorney over to the police!

As soon as the man won his freedom he challenged the judge, who accepted just as promptly. Immediately before the duel, however, the lawyer—having cooled off somewhat—said he regretted the whole episode and wanted to apologize. And thus entered one of the provisions of the code duello; during a certain period before the parties reached the field, an apology could be accepted, *oui;* on the way, or on the field, *non*—the murderous farce must be gone through with. In this case the prescribed period had elapsed, and the apology was ineffective. In the duel both men were injured, one in the hip, the other in the shoulder. Fortunately both recovered.

Not long afterward it was Judge Bermudez' duty to pass on a case in which a man had shot another to death in the street. Following a challenge, one of the parties had gone to court to bring accusations against the other; the consequence was the street shooting. A murder charge was filed, and the city broke into two white-hot divisions. The Washington Guards, a military group to which the dead man belonged, swore vengeance. Bermudez became involved when a writ was submitted demanding the murderer's temporary release. The Guards packed the room, muttering, threatening; if Bermudez let the fellow out, *he* would suffer. Calmly, after due consideration, the judge released him. Friends hastened to Bermudez, begging to be allowed to stay near him until the affair should blow over. The judge's eyes were stern and cold as he replied that he was not afraid.

A night or two later, as he sat at home with his wife, three friends hurried in. Toutant Beauregard, a young dentist, spoke quickly: A lynching crowd was on its way! Quietly the judge nodded, left the room, and returned with a double-barreled shotgun, which he handed to Beauregard; a sabre, which he placed against the mantel; and two cavalry pistols, which went on the table. With that he resumed smoking, and Madame Bermudez took her seat again beside him.

Suddenly the door burst open with a crash. Beauregard ran forward, gun in hand, but a cutlass blow knocked it from his grasp. The crowd pressed in—and directly before them, blocking the way to her husband, stood Madame Bermudez. She had caught up the sabre and now with furious cries struck right and left, beating back a good half of the men. Simultaneously the judge lifted his gun and a threatening youth fell dead. The judge fired at another who dodged away, badly wounded. Beauregard snatched another weapon, and his two companions picked out their targets. At this juncture the mob drew back, then decided on flight. Next morning a second dead body was found near the house. After that nobody disturbed the judge—or Madame Bermudez, either.

The judge's son, Chief Justice of the Louisiana Supreme Court, had a regrettable quarrel with a friend, a moon-eyed poet named Lapouse. An article written by Lapouse elicited an unflattering comment from the judge, whereupon the poet challenged. With reluctance, since he liked Lapouse, Bermudez accepted. It was the poet's privilege to name the distance. Near-sighted, he chose less than half the usual length, only five paces. This made it almost certain that the judge would kill the poet; but the latter would also be sure to make a hit on Bermudez.

On the field, Lapouse took out his snuffbox and offered it to each of the seconds; then—as he had done on other occasions with his friend the judge—he extended it to him. The judge hesitated.

"It's very good snuff," said the poet. "Do take some."

The judge complied. The seconds gave the signal; the men

separated. At the call both fired, and missed. The seconds hurried over. Surely this would satisfy both men? It would. Judge and poet embraced in Gallic fashion and went off the field, taking snuff from the same box.

Far different was the meeting of a Creole planter, Faustin de St. Amant, and a Kentucky slave dealer. Each had murder in his eye. As the challenged party, the Kentuckian could name the weapons; he picked pistols. St. Amant, entitled to choose the conditions, said that they would face each other beside an open grave! The American, sneering, accepted with pleasure; but it was noted that his face had paled. The next day they met by the river on the opposite (Algiers) side, while swirls of fog still rose above the river bank.

"Fire!"

A thicker smoke swept upward. When it cleared, St. Amant stood alone, staring down at the body in the wet earth. The Kentuckian had toppled over into the grave and had already stopped twitching.

Hugues Pedesclaux had a sharp dispute with a French cavalry officer. The latter named broadswords, to be wielded on horseback. A wide field was chosen, and a witness described the "handsome sight." The duelists, naked to the waist, rode high-spirited mounts; the two men, like their animals, seemed to quiver with excitement. They rode toward each other. The Frenchman was heavy but his muscles "looked like whipcord, and his broad, hairy chest gave evidence of remarkable strength and endurance." The lighter Pedesclaux had a youthful suppleness that quickened his every response. The blades cracked together, and sparks darted. Neither was cut, and the men whirled about to face each other again.

They approached warily; then, with daring gesture, each lunged out. The Frenchman aimed a head blow that would have "cleft Pedesclaux to the shoulder blade" had he not managed to ward it off. The Frenchman, sent off balance by this lunge, could not recover at once; and this gave the Creole his opportunity. Making a rapid half-circle, he regained his equilibrium; "with a well-directed *coup de pointe à droite* (having taken care to keep his adversary to the right) he plunged his blade through the body of the French officer." The Frenchman sank to the field; in an hour he was dead.

Not many Orleanians showed the wit of Mirabeau who, when sought out by the Marquis du Chatelet, replied briskly: "Monsieur le Marquis: It would be very unfair for a man of sense like me to be killed by a fool like you. I have the honor to be, with the highest consideration," etc. But after George Wilkins Kendall, editor of the *Picayune*, established himself in New Orleans, he made history by announcing he would not be drawn into such inanities. Challenged, he declared he would not duel with guns or swords, but might be willing to meet his opponent in a swift foot race! And he got away with it. Few men, however—especially officials—had the courage to take so sensible a stand. Indeed, to be a public officer was almost to guarantee oneself participation in a number of duels.

Alcée La Branche, one-time speaker of the Louisiana House, fought a duel because during a campaign an editor taunted him with never having been in one. It happened this way: In Baton Rouge lived Mr. Heuston of the *Gazette*, recently arrived from New Jersey. Heuston was well liked, a family man of cheerful disposition; friends described him as of a "generous but impulsive nature." After the campaign, Heuston said goodbye to his wife at the river landing and started on a trip to New Orleans. There, though he did not know it, the infuriated La Branche was making inquiries about him. A day later, as Heuston was playing billiards at a hotel, several men walked up. One asked his identity, then cried out: "I'm Alcée La Branche. You've slandered me, grossly!" With that La Branche lifted his hickory cane and beat Heuston about the head. The editor dropped; onlookers, intervening, at first thought him dead.

Heuston stayed in bed only a short time. Though the doctors objected, he rose, still weak, his face bearing the marks of his beating, and challenged La Branche. The Creole named weapons: double-barreled shotguns, loaded with ball, at forty yards. The meeting place was the line of oaks at Gentilly Road and Marigny's old Champs Élysées. The two men faced each other coldly. Though on the first fire both missed, it was noticed that the Creole was the quicker, the cooler. Again, on the second fire, neither was hit. A third, and the editor dropped back, hand to head. La Branche, aiming to kill, had left a deep scalp wound. In pain, blood pouring out, Heuston insisted on a fourth exchange. Now the two hundred people who were present cried out: This was enough; stop the thing! Heuston, eyes flashing, walked over to the doctors. "Feel my pulse, and see if it isn't regular!" The doctors nodded; it would go on.

La Branche stared ahead, his features "rigid and marble-like." The face of the more excitable editor was twitching spasmodically.

"Fire!"

The two guns spoke. La Branche remained upright; Heuston dropped to the ground. The bullet had gone through his lungs. For an hour he suffered agonizingly; before he died he begged a friend to shoot him through the head to end his pain. His associates now had to break the news to his penniless wife and children. Being a newspaperman, Heuston had been able to save nothing.

The sequel to this story happened during the War between North and South. General John Lewis of New Orleans, leading a column through a Red River village, noticed a sign reading MRS. HEUSTON, MILLINER. Halting, he asked: "Is that the widow of the editor?" It was. "My God . . . I loaded the gun that killed him! I've never forgotten. If we had only tried harder . . ." Dismounting, he sought out the widow and offered her any help she might need. She declined; there is no record of what she actually said. In those days the

women victims of the tragedies seldom revealed their senti-
ments, but many must have begged their God to bring down
His wrath on the men responsible for their husbands' deaths.

A congressman, Émile La Sère, counted eighteen duels, but
he never maintained his anger for long. As soon as he had
won, and if his adversary survived, he turned sympathetic.
He would help bandage up the fellow, take him home, and
sit up for nights at the bedside!

Denis Prieur, mayor for ten years, killed U. S. Senator
George Waggaman. Not long afterward Prieur's nephew,
George White, won a duel which, even for New Orleans,
had a fanciful note. At a public ball of which White was one
of the managers, a guest was a man named Pakenham Le
Blanc. The latter alleged that he had been treated discourte-
ously; he did not know which manager was to blame, but
one of them would pay. Putting all their names into a hat,
he drew out White's.

White's friends shook their heads. The man Le Blanc was
recognized as a great duelist. White, pondering, decided that
his only hope lay in shooting first. On the field the confident
Le Blanc smiled boastfully as he sauntered about. The signal
was given; White fired on the instant. Le Blanc's knees
gave way, and his gun went off wildly. By nightfall he had
died, victim of his own touchiness and overconfidence.

Then there was the odd affair of the two residents of
Richmond, Virginia. To the editor and staff of the New
Orleans *Crescent* went a wholesale challenge from a Mr.
Irving of Richmond, who had been enraged by certain
articles appearing in that newspaper. It happened that they
had been written by another Richmonder, the well-known
Virginia humorist, George William Bagby. Although, so far
as anyone could tell, they had no conceivable relevance to
Mr. Irving, he thought they had—which is perhaps explained
by the description of him given by an acquaintance: "a
maniac on the subject of duels and his honor . . . very

touchy in the matter of his 'honor.' In fact, it was impossible to work with Mr. Irving with any degree of pleasure, for he was always challenging somebody. Mr. Irving has it in his mind that death on the field of honor is the most glorious thing that can happen to a mortal, and he has been doing everything possible to accomplish such an end. . . ."

Since the offended gentleman was at that time unaware that the writer was a fellow Richmonder, his resentment was directed impartially at the entire *Crescent* staff; every man on it was declared to be a liar and a scoundrel. Understandably, this "completely demoralized" the staff. Then Irving discovered that the real culprit was Bagby, and—though Bagby insisted that he hadn't had Irving in mind at all—the two met on the field in Richmond, exchanged harmless shots, and shook hands. The New Orleans paper said it liked and respected Irving, which ended the foolishness.

Young James Morris Morgan was in New Orleans with his beloved older brother Harry, for a reunion on their way to the family residence in Baton Rouge. There was a gay dinner party at the home of another Morgan. The two brothers prepared to retire; they were to sleep in the same room. Another member of the family called Jimmy aside; he must be careful not to disturb Harry in the night, as the latter was going to fight a duel shortly after daylight. Young Jimmy was intrigued. "I instantly made up my mind that I was going to see that duel, and I never doubted for a moment that my gallant brother would come off victor."

Before daybreak Harry was up, and Jimmy raced to dress and follow him. In the dark a carriage waited before the house; one of the seconds was to be M. Hiriart of the *Bee*, "the newspaper that never apologized." Jimmy, much excited, hoisted himself up beside the driver. At the Oaks, being told that the code permitted no blood relative within two hundred yards, he retired, though remaining within eyeshot. James Sparks, Harry's opponent, was the brother of a classmate of Jimmy's; his second was a brother of Mrs. Jefferson Davis.

Jimmy watched intently. Both guns went off, and Sparks staggered. "I fairly flew to see what had happened." A glance showed that his brother Harry was still standing. Hastening to Sparks' side, Jimmy found he was only grazed; with that Jimmy turned back toward his brother, to discover that he had fallen. The bullet had struck a bone in his arm and, glancing, entered his body, passing through the lungs, emerging on the other side, and killing him.

The next day, with another of the family, Jimmy took Harry home to the upriver town. "The steamboat left New Orleans late in the afternoon, and all that night we sat by the coffin on the lower deck. Each of us was wrapped in his own sad thoughts, so the long weary hours before we arrived in Baton Rouge seemed endless. Not that either was anxious to hasten our arrival, for we knew only too well that we had a sad ordeal to go through when we met our dear father, who would be bent with sorrow, and a mother whose heart would be broken. God help me—this was to be the homecoming to which I had looked forward with such delight."

Dominating the New Orleans code duello were the fencing masters, gaudy swaggerers who could have flourished only there. Children smiled at them, women stared, and awed imitators hovered about them. To be a *maître d'armes* was to enjoy the combined glory of matinee idol, leading tenor, and military hero. The cafés constituted their realm; here they were patronized, toasted, admired. Their feats were famous, and grew in the telling. Him, why, he kill' twelve in a row! . . . They say he had to leave France because he maimed the wrong man. . . . Though the maîtres' social rank was dubious, this hardly mattered; they ruled in their own right. Usually stalwart and handsome, moving with a bold grace, they attracted women of all classes, often making conquests (so it was said) in high places. This or that husband knew, the whispers went, but dared do nothing openly. Who would match swords or guns with such a one? Other men kept out of their paths, made sure not to jostle them. Around them clustered well-dressed youths who hoped to emulate their feats, who repeated their jokes. A number became spoiled fools, earringed fops who affected drawls and exotic tastes in food; but they were safe against ridicule.

A majority of the masters opened fencing rooms in flag-stoned Exchange Alley, extending four squares from Canal to St. Louis streets. About fifty of them were ranged along both sides, spreading into adjacent streets. There they lounged, watching youths at practice and sipping wine or coffee. "Good, that one!" . . . "Pierre, you are off today." The list of maîtres glitters: Captain Thimécourt; Poulaga the Italian; Baudoin from Paris; Emile Cazère, who accepted only the cream of society; "Titi" Rosière; Reynaud; Norra. They were of all nations, all kinds. This one was as treacherous as he was suave; that one had certain qualities beneath the frou-frou and theatricality which made him a good friend to keep.

Like so many prima donnas, the masters were jealous among themselves, with a jealousy that in some cases grew to hatred. One would challenge another, with grim results. Or perhaps a meeting would be planned only as a professional exhibition, a demonstration of drama and daring. Then tempers cracked, the crowd egged on the heroes, and blood flowed red. Norra killed Dauphin. Reynaud cut Bonneval through the heart.

Each contestant tried to manoeuvre so that his favorite weapon was used, and understandably. Monthiarch the German and Thimécourt of France once met with broadswords. As the match began, Monthiarch made a great stab; had it landed properly it might have taken off his opponent's head. Thimécourt dodged, and only his scalp was cut. At the same moment his sword flashed beneath Monthiarch's arm and cut his chest. In spite of this wound, the German wanted to go on, but the seconds intervened, and he turned away bitterly.

As no doctor was present, Monthiarch—amid the onlookers' cries of astonishment—reached for a handful of tow, stuffed it carelessly into the gaping wound, and went off scowling. Why hadn't they let him continue? By this time he'd have had the Frenchman split in two!

For a while Gilbert Rosière, known as "Titi," was master of masters. A mercurial man, alternating between gaiety and anger, he had arrived from Bordeaux as a youth with a fair-sized purse, to study law. He preferred wine and late hours, the law proved stuffy, and he kept getting into arguments and duels. He did so well on the field that finally he asked himself: Why waste all this ability? Why not become a maître? When the Mexican War started, new officers rushed to "Titi" to improve their use of arms, and he became the richest fencing master in the city. But also he was steadily spending, and by the time the war ended he was deep in debt again.

"Titi" was a man of taste, of sensibilities; he enjoyed the theatre, exquisite food, and fine music, and was a devotee of the opera. Once indeed he was so deeply moved by an aria that tears ran down his cheeks. When the man next to him snickered, "Titi" turned. "C'est vrai que je pleure," he said coldly, "mais je donne aussi des callottes!"—and slapped. The next day, after a swift duel, the other man took to his bed with a wound that was weeks in healing.

Curiously, one of the best-known masters was a mulatto, the good-looking Bastile Croquère. A man of marked intelligence, he had been sent to Paris by his white father. There he fought numerous duels before he decided to return. White men practiced with him, listened ardently to his directions, hailed him as he passed on the street. The caste system being what it was, they could not invite him to their homes, but they sipped drinks with him at his academy. And no maître put on a better show: well-cut trousers, handsome coats, and (his minor vice) cameos. He wore them in rings and stick-pins, as cuff links, and on a bracelet or two.

Most lustrous of all, eventually, was the Spaniard José (or Pepe) Llulla, a lean-visaged man with a look of deceptive gentleness. Born in the Balearic Islands, he saw the world as a seaman, then appeared in New Orleans as bouncer at a sailors' hangout. In time he visited the fencing school of L'Alouette, and soon made a friend of that master. A bloodless public demonstration was arranged, the two men to show the use of wooden bowie knives. L'Alouette planned to best the youth at once, but Pepe Llulla was amazingly good, parrying, touching, parrying. The master grew infuriated; with an oath he made a deep lunge. Pepe, still cool, struck back, and L'Alouette tumbled down unconscious, with several ribs cracked. The two men were soon reconciled, however, and continued friends until L'Alouette's death years later.

Pepe, taking the other's place, proved to be his superior. He lost count of the number of his duels, but he fought at least forty. Soon hardly anyone dared appear against him. Not that he was quarrelsome; his manner was pleasant, his expression kindly. But let someone hurt his feelings, and those eyes could turn as hard as granite. He learned to be watchful; so great was his reputation that rash youths would sometimes try to run at him, gun in hand, to catch him by surprise. None managed the feat, however; Pepe could never be taken off guard.

As Lafcadio Hearn retold the story, certain persons, even bolder, suggested types of meeting at which luck might favor them: poniards in an unlighted room; or Colt revolvers, each man holding one end of the same handkerchief; or the duelists to get inside a sugar hogshead and cut away; or several pills to be placed on a table, one a poison pill, the pair to swallow them in turn. To each of these fantastic notions Pepe agreed; but either the seconds intervened or the other man dropped out. In one instance a Cuban, who did not think machetes could be found in New Orleans, proposed that weapon. Pepe gave a small smile, walked into the next room, and came out with two of them! The challenger said he wasn't feeling quite well enough to fight that day. . . .

In one fundamental respect Pepe was different from the other maîtres: he saved every dollar and became a businessman also, opening a grocery, a barroom, a contracting business, a sawmill, a slaughterhouse. He tried to introduce bullfights on a regular scale; New Orleans already had them occasionally. Then he did the thing that made New Orleans laugh most of all. He bought a graveyard, the cemetery at what is now 1322 Louisa Street.

This started a legend: Pepe wanted it to house the victims of his duels. Why, the place was full of the poor fellows! Or so New Orleans said. With Pepe it was a simple investment, though he admitted once that if he checked he supposed he might find there some of his own victims. For years visitors were taken to see this cemetery. Along with the burial rates, the proud sextons displayed mementoes of Pepe's feats, including a shirt through which he had thrust his sword. Did that one live? Monsieur, would you live with such a hole in your belly?

When Cuba rebelled against Spain in the 1870s American filibusters invaded the island, only to meet death. Most Orleanians sympathized with the Cubans; not Pepe, a burning Spaniard after all those years. Cuban partisans filled the city, and Pepe challenged them all, in splashing posters insulting them in three languages. He would take them on, one at a time! A few accepted; as they were carried from the field, interest in his offer quickly declined.

When Pepe died, friends buried him in the Louisa Street Cemetery, among the several victims he had never bothered to count. I have several times visited it, to stroll among the tombs and wonder whether Pepe's ghost and those of his adversaries ever meet and talk things over.

On at least one occasion, a June night of 1844, two women tried to have a duel. Described as "girls of the town," they rode up near Bayou St. John with their lady seconds. To demonstrate that they were in earnest, they brought not only guns but also bowie knives. Several men intervened, so the girls dropped the weapons and began to pull each other's hair. They ended unglamorously in the calaboose.

As late as 1867 a visitor found dueling common: "Men fight with the sword, with double-barreled shotguns, and sometimes with bowie knives." In a hotel lobby, a "judge" who kept a gambling house disagreed with a "colonel" who introduced him to a friend with a bad thousand-dollar bill. The judge abused the colonel, who pushed him away. The judge drew a dagger and stabbed; the colonel fired three shots and killed his opponent. The comment added: "Society at large seems to think that neither will be much lamented."

For years efforts had been made to halt the evil; laws were adopted, then repealed. The claim was once made that such measures would drive "men of honor" from the state. At one time an anti-dueling society was formed; oddly enough, Bernard de Marigny was one of the founders. But community feeling opposed such restrictions on the expression of male individuality. Charges were filed and trials were held repeatedly, but jurors never convicted. A doctor who had figured in one declined to testify, on the ground that he would be violating professional secrets! He was let off, though he had been witness to a killing.

Through the late 1870s dueling flourished. During Reconstruction, the excesses of angry men brought a new rush of encounters. But slowly the custom was dying. In a more realistic period (and one more enlightened) the thing was seen for what it was. In the end the code was laughed at, and that wrecked it. Pomposity can stand anything except a snicker.

In the 1890s one of the last publicized cases involved two newspaper writers. One shot the other through both buttocks. Thus, ingloriously, died a not-always-glorious institution.

Still to be seen are the sets of engraved dueling pistols in

Royal Street antique shops; the mossy oaks of City Park, where men died every day or so; and Exchange Alley, former haunt of the maîtres. Exchange has gone down; it now covers only three blocks, and much of it is a garish line of minor saloons, flop houses, and oyster bars. Most of the fights that occur there today are mere languid brawls that bring police with billies.

Sometimes, however, on a silent, foggy morning, the dim walls recall those of earlier days, and fencers' wraiths seem to hover close. A solitary step sounds from the corner, and a man in a dark cloak walks through the mist. It may be Pepe Llulla, coming down to open his *salle;* or a pupil on his way to meet his seconds in a carriage at the corner. . . . Pistols for two, breakfast for one.

CHAPTER 9

The Glad, Sad Band of Mummers

TO GET a stage season in New Orleans, players dreamed and made sacrifices, and afterwards boasted of it during most of their careers. "The grandest theatre in America"—so, at its height, they described the St. Charles in the uptown section. As for New Orleans itself, it was an actors' paradise, a town that appreciated the best and was willing to show that it liked what it saw.

Orleanians gave free rein to their emotions; they were not ashamed to have others see them in exultation or close to tears. When it approved, an audience went into frenzies, shouting, sobbing. On one occasion an ecstatic Frenchman leaped to his feet and almost threw himself out of his box. Even the Creole women, brought up in a conservative tradition, at times tossed handkerchiefs, corsages, jewels at a favorite entertainer. And the Americans, assimilating the Creole style, showed themselves no less demonstrative. The city loved the mad, glad, pathetic, shining crew that made up the world of the theatre.

New Orleans always enjoyed a procession, a festival. Though often a hard place for the players to reach—far off, across mountain and water—it thrived for generations as one of the great American theatre centres, not far behind New York. (Ahead of New York, even, claimed the enthusiasts.) All the stars came here, at the highest salaries. Again and again friends assembled before the actors' hotels for mass welcomes;

crowds formed at the levee to herald their coming, then followed them on the streets. Performances were analyzed, approved or criticized, and generally made the object of community excitement—not to speak of feuds and duels. New Orleans took such things seriously.

It was the drama that introduced the boon of gaslight to the city; from that first theatre building it spread over town. New Orleans much later got electric light through the agency of a certain barroom. Disapproving souls considered both incidents typical of the city.

For their part the players favored New Orleans because the town was a thrilling spot, offering dazzling sights, fine food and drink, and gay hours on Royal or Canal Street or at the lake. Some, indeed, favored it with more enthusiasm than discretion, going off on monumental benders and tumbling into unhappy scrapes. A good many sterling actors ended their careers here in this way.

During French and Spanish days, Orleanians put on amateur plays. The professional theatre arrived in 1791 with the uprisings in Santo Domingo, when French players brought new savor to the town. Louis Tabary's company entertained in tents, warehouses, and private parlors, and then in a building at what is today 732 St. Peter Street, best remembered as "Le Spectacle." The actors, however, were liberty-lovers; they startled Spanish officialdom by injecting French revolutionary songs into innocent bedroom farces, and for a time they were suppressed.

The American régime gave an impetus to theatricals, though early laws required the presence of a mayor's representative, and insisted that patrons must not insult one another, sneak in, or throw (or "pretend to throw") things. By 1808 the city had a new and splendid establishment, the St. Philip Theatre of seven hundred seats, a parquet, and a double row of boxes. After a time John Davis of Santo Domingo, staunchly French despite his name, put up his yet more elaborate Orleans Theatre. Burned down, it was replaced by a building that was a theatre and more—the central unit in a temple of assorted pleasures.

This was the same "Toto" Davis who brought gambling to Marigny's town of Mandeville. Next to his Théâtre d'Orléans the energetic "Toto" built his Salle d'Orléans, with a dance hall upstairs and gambling rooms below. No loss of repute followed; tolerant New Orleans cared little who played the games. Nearby were billiard hall, cafés, public baths, and restaurants. Largely, however, it was the theatre that drew the crowds; and they must have been durable, since the performance began at 6 o'clock in the afternoon, with vaudeville—then a comedy and an opera—followed by a long drama with a finale of singing and dancing—the end coming at about one o'clock in the morning!

All these entertainments were given in French; Americans who had no French were obliged to guess at meanings. However (as Dr. Roger P. McCutcheon has discovered), by 1806 an English-speaking pioneer was making a brave start. One Rannie gave a series of performances that ended with *The Battle of the Nile*, showing sailors sinking and swimming. "Crokadiles molesting them, and Whales, Sharks, Dolphins, Sword and Flying Fish and Mermaids Swimming." Then for years only occasional American companies appeared, until in 1818 Noah Ludlow's company floated downriver for a full season. The trick was done; an American audience had been found, though the company and subsequent ones had to use the French places on spare nights. Sometimes they were urged to appear on Sunday, always the most profitable day in New Orleans; Ludlow, not used to "anything of that sort," declined.

Gentility was not always evident; rowdy pit crowds shocked Creoles who wandered in. Ludlow himself, actor and manager, figured in several sensational incidents. A brother once sent him a poem telling of the Kaintucks' part in the Battle of New Orleans, and he set it to music. About to face

an audience largely made up of river boatmen, he borrowed
a buckskin shirt, donned a slouch hat, and threw a rifle over
his shoulder. Marching out and saluting, he was greeted by a
fury of foot-stamping. As he sang, the noise rose higher and
higher. At the final stanza—

"For Jackson, he was wide awake, and warn't scared at trifles,
  For well he knew what aim we take with our Kentucky rifles.
So he led us down to cypress swamp; the ground was low and
    mucky.
There stood John Bull in martial pomp; but here was old
    Kentucky!"

—Ludlow snatched off his hat, slammed it down, and aimed
his rifle. The effect was instantaneous, setting afire every im-
pulse of Kentucky-worship, home-love, and damn-the-
British. Men leaped up, pounded each other's backs, and
threw benches. It was such a moment as an actor lives for.

For Ludlow, however, the song became too popular—a
nightmare; he thought he would never be done with it. Moreover it nearly cost him his life once. Suddenly, from a screaming audience, an eighteen-inch pipe whizzed past his head.
The actor bowed off the stage, deciding that the tribute had
come from some Anglophile. But eighteen years later an
elderly man came up and told him that *he* had done it—in a
spasm of joy; a Kentuckian, veteran of the battle, when he
heard the glorious words he had "just let her go." Ludlow
bought him a drink.

He used to tell a moving story of his early New Orleans
days. An impoverished French actor wished to appear with
the company for the usual privilege of a benefit night. The
man proved unusually good; for his benefit he chose to stage
the pantomime *Don Juan*. Rehearsals started brilliantly. The
actor's wife, whom none had met but who was to play a
prominent feminine role, did not appear. "She is ill," he said
each time; "she'll be here soon." But not even on the night of
the performance did she turn up with him. Just before the

curtain rose, she entered—a woman of fine presence but wearing a mask that covered all of her face except the eyes. This mask she retained throughout the performance, and she proved to be an excellent actress. No explanation was forthcoming until after she had left with her husband, when the company learned that she had been a beauty until a disease ravaged the lower part of her face, eating away the nose and disfiguring the mouth.

After a year New Orleans met the man who was to make theatrical history in the Lower South. James H. Caldwell was an extraordinary combination, competent actor and better businessman. An Englishman, he had (as a contemporary put it) been drawn early to the stage "by impulses and aspirations quite common to young men of lively parts and brilliant physical endowments." An expert in "genteel comedy," less good in serious works, Caldwell rose "more through his personal than his artistic qualities." Self-educated, he had gotten along on his own merits; some found a certain hardness that annoyed them, but none ever denied that he gave the world its money's worth.

Caldwell was one of the first Britishers to sense the opportunities that awaited in the United States. A few years earlier he had gone to Charleston for his American début; within another year he was an actor-manager with several companies moving in and about Virginia. Caldwell deserved his success; he offered not the lukewarm mediocrity of most touring companies, but excellent plays, well-cast, well-produced.

Arriving in New Orleans in his middle years, James Caldwell made a quick impression; competing companies quickly disappeared. He worked hard for his crowds; for one play, he borrowed a circus elephant. Now and then he bumped his artistic toe. Once, along with a performance of *King Lear*, he presented a slack-rope troupe. A Creole journal noted tartly that after this the public "would be pleased to see more of his company on a rope." Caldwell had the true actor's ability to recover quickly from a mistake; he did not often repeat such slips.

For a time a major difficulty lay in persuading actors to reach New Orleans early in the season. They had heard about yellow fever; though anxious to appear, they would get as far as Mobile and sit out weeks there, waiting for official bulletins that the danger was over. They were not reassured when a manager in the suburb of Lafayette required players to take part of their salaries in coffins; if an actor, his wife, or any other relative died during the season, he or she would be buried "on account"!

It was Caldwell who brought here the great though eccentric Junius Brutus Booth. A few commentators have tried to blame Booth's behavior on New Orleans, saying that he fell into bad, especially liquorous, company here. Long before this, however, Booth had been fighting with rival actors and managers in England and causing theatre riots.

Booth's frenzied acting so impressed fellow-players here and elsewhere that at times they fell back from him in fright. For years he carried about with him, as Yorick's skull in *Hamlet*, the cranium of a horse-thief friend, who had ordered his head given to Booth after the hanging. During another phase, passing a spot at which another actor had jumped from his boat to kill himself, Booth also leaped, only to be fished out. Again, he summoned a minister for last rites for a "deceased friend"; under a black cloth in his room lay a miniature casket, holding a pigeon.

At times Booth disappointed New Orleans audiences; he simply did not appear. On a well-remembered occasion he offended Caldwell and the crowd by dropping into a whisky stupor in the middle of the play. The critics cried that the man was disgraced; Caldwell suspended him. A few nights later the audience was demanding more Booth, and it welcomed him back with delight. Caldwell, who usually knew how to make allowances for temperament, was just as delighted to have him.

Even Caldwell, however, had trouble coping with another of Booth's outbursts. He played Richmond to Booth's Richard the Third. In the battle scene, the tipsy Booth decided that this was a real fight. With murder in his eye, he clenched the sword and let go at Caldwell. The latter parried, skipped, dodged. Still Booth pressed him. At last, winded, Caldwell muttered: "Die, Mr. Booth, die. It's time for you to die!"

At that Booth, playing the misshapen Richard, straightened up. His weapon glittered; his voice rang out. "As long as Richard wields this blade, he'll *never* die!" By this time the audience had caught on. Caldwell signaled for the curtain, and Booth won a new, riotous acclaim.

One Fourth of July, Caldwell had unanticipated difficulties when he tried to present an elaborate musical program. The theatre was filled—river boatman below, élite above. The orchestra leader, Monsieur Desforges, was an elderly Frenchman who had been deafened by an explosion during the Battle of New Orleans (how he managed to conduct is not our concern); and for weeks he had been rehearsing his men in the overture to Boieldieu's *La Dame blanche*. To the downstairs crowd, this seemed tame stuff, and out of the dark a voice yelled: "*Yankee Doodle!*" Monsieur Desforges, not hearing, went on with *La Dame blanche*. The mob took up the cry, shouting ever louder, till the noise reached even Monsieur. For him it was transmuted into a wonderful hum of approval. His listeners were delighted! He worked harder than ever.

Backstage Caldwell bit his nails. Now the crowd began to break chairs. Out ran Caldwell to the footlights: "Play 'Yankee Doodle'!" Monsieur, hearing at last, stood dazed. "Yankee Dude? They want that?" Then he swung around to the audience and his voice crackled: "*Non*—you no have Yankee Dude!" This exhibition of fury and courage struck the audience's funnybone, and its sense of fairness as well. Applause broke out for the old man. He nodded, hitched his collar, and went back to *La Dame blanche!*

Meanwhile James Caldwell decided that New Orleans was ripe for a permanent American theatre. He would build a house of his own. "It was his peculiarity," a contemporary said, "to do whatever he did with all his might." He collected his savings and borrowed the rest from businessmen, taking three hundred dollars from each and promising tickets in return. With all that might of his, he improvised a theatre.

He chose a spot on Camp Street between Gravier and Poydras. People hooted. Up there in that empty swamp? "Streets" there were, but they were nothing more than a series of shallow ponds. It was a section of shanties, truck gardens, and wrecks of plantation homes, abandoned as industrialism encroached. While the walls rose, even Caldwell's friends clicked their tongues. It rained for days, turning the area into a vast lake. The fellow's only audiences would be the frogs!

Even how to get there was a problem. Caldwell had to put down his own sidewalks, wooden gunwales two and a half feet wide, laid end to end. River boatmen, finishing downriver trips, were glad to sell their craft for the purpose. Skeptics still grinned when the American Theatre opened on January 1, 1824. But already he was winning, as he knew he would. He offered what audiences wanted; they would take trouble to reach it. In this way Caldwell did as much as any other man to make sure that New Orleans advanced in this uptown direction. Soon other businesses were growing up about his place.

Next he provided the novelty of gas lighting. Three Northern cities had it, but Southerners considered it an expensive fad. Caldwell sent to England for a "gas machine" and installed it next to his theatre. Thousands gawked, then went in to blink at the new brightness. For additional excitement the manager rigged up a "stage garden" with gas jets for flowers. What wouldn't folks do next?

Here flourished a tragi-sweet romance, that of the impresario and the lovely Jane Placide, his leading woman. She had come only recently to New Orleans, and the town understood that the masterful Caldwell loved her as he had never loved anybody or anything else. For twelve years the city would also be devoted to Jane Placide as to few women of her day.

Though Caldwell was much older, Jane returned his affection; none who saw them together could doubt that. But with James Caldwell there was a barrier. Though he and his wife were estranged, he apparently could not get a divorce. He and Jane must wait. . . . She came of an acting family, the celebrated Placides of France and South Carolina. When Jane first arrived in New Orleans she was only nineteen. Promptly Caldwell advanced her to leading parts, and there was no question that she deserved them. Jane had a simple beauty, a charm and honesty that were enormously convincing. She played everything from duchesses to dairymaids, boys to hussies. And Caldwell cast himself as her king, her country sweetheart, her fellow-player in passion and in death. New Orleans watched and wept over the two star-crossed lovers.

Meanwhile, overnight, Manager Caldwell and the city had a new theatrical sensation—Edwin Forrest, who was to become the first great American-born actor. The impresario Caldwell's reputation had spread, and players welcomed any invitation from him. After a little hesitation he gave Forrest a chance, at eighteen dollars a week, though doing so meant bucking the judgment of his associates. For Forrest was barely twenty and had had none of the slow, basic training that the English players enjoyed; to the end of his life he would suffer from this lack. The others showed their disapproval of the boy. Such crudeness; so—so Western!

Forrest had been languishing in Lexington, Kentucky. Dissatisfied with the theatre, he had joined a circus and prepared himself as a rider and tumbler. There was also a report that he had stayed on because he had grown fond of a young actress. At this point Caldwell brought him to New Orleans, and the two hit it off at once. For the young man had magnetism, undoubtedly. Also, he was so handsome that women would be after him, or he after them, all his life.

Caldwell constituted himself the newcomer's sponsor, taking him around to parties, saloons, and the races and introducing him to patrons (and patronesses) of the drama. The young actor welcomed everything New Orleans offered, and on his own initiative sought further experiences. For instance, he made friends with the Indians at French Market and spent one summer with them outside of the city; and afterwards played redskin roles with unusual understanding.

Meanwhile Edwin Forrest was building up a box-office following. Caldwell gave him excellent roles and the youth took full advantage of every chance. Once he left New Orleans; but he came back, his fortunes higher than before. Jealousy, however, began to mar the friendship between impresario and protégé. For young Forrest was doing altogether too well, he took too little trouble to show gratitude, and he became a bit cavalier in his relations with Caldwell and the others. Worst of all, he was suddenly captured by Jane Placide's maturing beauty; he had not noticed her particularly when they first met. She did not, it appears, reciprocate, though Edwin's open devotion and his passionate whisperings were probably not unpleasant to her. She continued to smile on him, as on everybody else.

Was Caldwell amused at first? If so, not for long. Suddenly he came down hard on his would-be rival. No more glamorous roles, no more opportunities to strut in tights and half-bare breast. Forrest was assigned to old men's parts, with beard and well-covered torso. No fool, however, he seems to have decided to make the best of the situation. Working over these new parts as never before, he was soon doing roles such as Lear and Richard the Third, and proving himself more than adequate. Whatever Caldwell's motive, he had done Forrest a good turn.

Still, fireworks were on the way. Some said that Forrest grew annoyed because his parts were getting smaller as well as older; others, that Caldwell conveyed to him firmly that his attentions to Jane were unwelcome. Whatever the grievance, the result of the bad blood between the two was that Forrest challenged the older man to a duel. With a curt shake of the head Caldwell refused. He may have thought that Edwin's tantrum would pass. It did not. Forrest posted him as a scoundrel and stalked out. Whether or not Caldwell was prepared to resent the slur, he had no opportunity. For the erratic Forrest sped out of New Orleans within the hour. On the Lake Pontchartrain shore he spent weeks with his Indian friends, staunching his wounds. Eventually he returned to New Orleans, but the *affaire Placide* was over.

Jane remained Caldwell's leading player and the lady of his heart, but the divorce from his wife never materialized. Jane held her audiences, gaining in popularity with the years. She fell ill on several occasions and had to travel for her health. Now and then her retirement was announced, but each time she went back to the maestro's guidance; and the Orleanians, who understood, sighed and liked the two the more. Then at thirty-one Jane died—some said, of a broken heart. On her tomb in Girod Cemetery the words were engraved:

There's not an hour of day or dreaming night but I am with thee;
There's not a breeze but whispers of thy name.
And not a flower that sleeps beneath the moon
But its fragrance tells a tale of thee.

New Orleans declared that the inscription was ordered by Caldwell; how Mrs. Caldwell felt about it is not recorded. But we do know how Edwin Forrest, then in Paris, reacted to the news: "And so Jane Placide is dead. She imparted a grace and force and dignity to her role which few actresses have been able so admirably to combine. Her disposition was as

lovely as her person. Heaven lodge and rest her fair soul."
Both men came off well in their tributes to the woman they
had loved.

Meanwhile James Caldwell became a man of yet greater
stature. Having made his New Orleans theatre an El Dorado,
he now expanded his ventures to Cincinnati, Nashville, St.
Louis, and Mobile. "Napoleon of the Southern Stage," he
was called; less friendly sources described him as a "monop-
olist," a "crusher." He developed, alas, a love of controversy.
That quality of hardness already mentioned increased with
age. For years he battled other managers, refuting claims,
advancing his own. Did his grief over Jane contribute to all
this? In any case his enemies increased.

Now Caldwell found himself torn between the theatre and
other businesses. Having pioneered in gas lighting, he was
branching out ambitiously. After installing lights on one side
of his Camp Street, he won the right, after arguing for two
years with the city, to illuminate part of growing Canal
Street. Then he wanted authority to light up the whole city.
Turning banker, he created the New Orleans Gas Light
and Banking Company and built the first gas works west of
the Alleghenies. One hand washed the other. As bank president Caldwell favored his theatrical enterprises, granting
loans, doubling the capacity of his showhouse. He was learning rapidly!

For a time Caldwell stepped out of the theatre game, leasing
his theatres. There are indications that finance had caught his
imagination, that the easier returns appealed to him. But opponents termed this a trick. During Jane's lifetime he had
quietly bought in her name a new site on St. Charles Street
near Poydras, and now all at once he was putting up a new
theatre—his St. Charles, the grandest the South had ever
known, perhaps the biggest the nation had seen to that time.
It contained four thousand seats and four tiers of plush-lined
boxes, topped by vast galleries. From the centre hung a chan-

delier that weighed 4700 pounds and had 23,000 cut-glass drops. Outside, in front, stood ten ornate columns, and still others rose inside, in the foyers, everywhere. It was built in ninety days; on the opening night in 1835 the last touches of decoration were not yet finished. Enemies circulated stories that it was going to fall. Caldwell laughed; such tales couldn't hurt him.

Perhaps they could not, but other things did. The house never attracted the throngs he had looked for. It may have been too big for its time. Also, the 1837 financial panic hit all theatrical business, and hard. For a time Caldwell tried Italian opera, then horse shows, magicians, ventriloquists, Greek dwarfs, bird imitators, giants, midgets, women who "danced in tanks," and blackface experts. Still, there were too many lean months.

The building was jammed, however, when Caldwell brought to New Orleans the dancer Fanny Elssler, "Divine Fanny" of the 1840s. The Viennese-born celebrity was far from beautiful, but her figure and her technique were unsurpassed. She was the first important danseuse to invade the American wilds. The country was known to be indifferent to the classical dance, yet Fanny pulled the trick. The strait-laced anticipated only vulgarity from this woman with uncovered limbs, or "understandings." But even Boston turned out enthusiastically when Elssler danced there. In the audience was Emerson, with Margaret Fuller. Margaret murmured in rapture: "Waldo, this is poetry." "Margaret, it is *religion!*" replied the philosopher. A New Orleans manager commented: "Her dress, necessarily short to permit the free use of her limbs, is managed with such graceful dexterity that his imagination must be 'as foul as Vulcan's smithy' who could conceive an impure thought while gazing on her ethereal movement or her classic repose." America, pure or impure, took Fanny to its heart. Pigeons were trained to bring flowers to her; in Baltimore a group of admirers who came upon her carriage removed the horses and pulled it through the streets.

When she agreed to appear for Caldwell, it was at the breathtaking fee of a thousand dollars a night. For it was clear by now that Fanny was out for the money. Our theatrical friend Ludlow stated it bitingly: "A magnificent creature in form, but without a soul; or if she had one it was cased in iron . . . avaricious to excess, and so exacting that if she could have had her will, she would have taken the entire receipts of every night's performance; and as it was she often took the 'lion's share,' leaving the managers little more than the bones of the carcass."

When Fanny arrived in New Orleans, other managers rubbed their hands. Old Jim Caldwell had been caught; he'd go broke. Caldwell, however, knew a trick or two of his own. He raised admission prices sky-high, and auctioned off certain choice seats for incredible amounts. New Orleans came, looked on in astonishment—and burst into cheers. The wonderful thing's feet never touched ground! She "lived in the air"! The next day saw a raffle for the couch on which she had slept in the steamboat—and even, it is claimed, for the gangplank. James Caldwell could laugh.

Fanny herself, however, got into difficulties. One group of admirers decided to serenade her at her hotel. Another group, less enthusiastic, resented it when Fanny, giving a banquet that night, failed to invite them. The serenaders, gathering before her hotel, raised their voices in sweet tribute, and Fanny appeared at the window, her eyes moist. At this, the opposition burst into a furious charivari, with pots, pans, and drums. The pro-Elsslerites were completely drowned out. One man punched another, and in a moment the two sides were in a free-for-all, kicking and gouging. One fighter had his clothes torn off, drawers and all, and Fanny hid her eyes. Suddenly, in the midst of this row, a joker turned in a fire alarm; when the firemen doused the crowd with water they were turned on in fury. Windows were smashed, men sent reeling into the gutters. Fanny wept and withdrew from the window. Slowly the mob subsided and dispersed. The resent-

ful Orleanians had upheld their reputation for discernment
and staged a nice riot as well.

Within a year Caldwell's pride, the St. Charles Theatre,
burned down. It had lasted only seven years, and he blamed
the fire on a competitor. Four months later the rival house,
the New American of Ludlow & Smith, also went up in
flames. The latter firm began to rebuild, when all at once
Caldwell, by a bit of sharp practice, obtained a secret lease
on the location. The other men then took up mortgages that
he had given on *his* site, and raced to put up theirs on *that*
location.

Not long afterward Caldwell withdrew from the stage
with a mournful valedictory. The fault lay not only with his
enemies, according to him; the public also were to blame.
They had been unappreciative. The drama was "no longer
a profession for a sensitive mind." He had done for it "what
few men with capital would have thought of," and now he
was losing heavily. His appraisal may seem carping, but perhaps there was something in it; the theatre is normally a
harassing business. Caldwell may have been too ambitious at
first, and then too resentful; but while he lasted he had given
them all a good time.

After this he had a series of ups and downs, once approaching bankruptcy. Others reaped the major benefits from his
pioneering in gas lighting and street improvements. In time,
however, he regained much of his former business position.
But he could not get the smell of grease-paint out of his
nostrils and, patching up matters with his old rivals, he occasionally advised them on managerial details. At the end he
had money in the bank, a handsome funeral with the gas
company's Negro slaves to weep, and fine press notices.
Could any actor ask for more?

Under Ludlow & Smith the show went on. Their New St.
Charles saw the mid-century's sensation, those oddly mated

characters, Jenny Lind and her manager P. T. Barnum. Like Elssler, Jenny Lind was no beauty; hers was the plainness of a sparrow, the primness of an old maid. Some called her voice cold, however remarkable technically; but it made so many spines tingle that it must have had something. And Phineas T. Barnum was there to make the universe applaud that something.

In order to get Jenny to America, Barnum had signed an astounding contract; if he was to make any money at all he must put on the most stunning ballyhoo the world had ever seen. He did just this. The Elssler furor had been mild compared with the new excitement over La Lind. Boston went frantic; one New Englander paid $625 for a ticket. Jenny called the man a fool, but he turned out to be a singer himself and used the publicity to soaring advantage. Another claimed he had her glove, and he charged a quarter for the privilege of kissing the outside, fifty cents for kissing the inside!

Now Jenny was arriving in New Orleans, which was celebrating the occasion by buying "Jenny Lind shirts" and "Jenny Lind cravats" in the stores. From Jackson Square, newly built by Baroness Pontalba, thousands ran to the levee to meet the boat. When Jenny stepped forth, the critical were disappointed by her unimpressive black costume. Jenny herself was daunted by the eager throng, and Barnum—always one for a ruse—threw a veil over the head and shoulders of his daughter as he led her off the vessel. The decoy was effectual, the mob followed the Barnum carriage, and Jenny went quietly to the Pontalba Buildings. Here she found a silver door plate with her name, a gold key for her use, the chef Boudro from the lakefront to serve her. By now the square was alive with Jenny-lovers; women on balconies were waving handkerchiefs, throwing roses, craning for a look. As she prepared to open her door only one Orleanian had the daring to approach her: "Pray, Madame, are you Jenny Lind?"

The crowd waited in silence for the reply. When it came, there was nothing glamorous about it, but at least it was definite. "Yes, sir, I am"—and with this, Jenny disappeared within. But the crowd shouted so violently that she had to come out on the gallery, to smile a tired smile. Then she retired. New Orleans, however, was far from finished. Seven hours later, at about eleven o'clock at night, up marched a great torchlight procession. A pitch pipe sounded, and the thousands sang to her. Hours went by before she was finally allowed to go to bed.

A little later the annual Firemen's Day arrived. Again thousands gathered, this time with engines, horses, and bands. The usual route was changed to take in the Pontalba Buildings, and the musicians beat out the song with which Jenny was identified, "Home, Sweet Home." She emerged, to receive the grand marshal's bouquet passed to her on a long pole. This was only the start. Every fire company had to march by; the song was played again and again; each man raised his hat as the Nightingale bowed and bowed. Toward the end she was almost fainting from exhaustion.

From upriver and down, anyone who could afford her opening concert, and some who could not, came to New Orleans. At the beginning the audience was none too enthusiastic; some compared her to an alabaster statue, and New Orleans usually demanded fire, vitality. But when she sang the "Casta diva" aria from *Norma* the audience melted like snow under a Louisiana sun. Men and women clapped and cheered, shouted and wept. The town was conquered.

Toward the end of the Swedish Nightingale's visit, her manager elected to give a lecture on temperance—in New Orleans of all places! Barnum really believed in his subject; said he wouldn't touch even desserts containing liquor. The lecture (described as "sparkling") probably lent an extra fillip to Jenny's last concert. New Orleans was never a place for temperance, but Barnum *per se* was a novelty. Supposed to sail that Sunday for Natchez and St. Louis, Jenny suddenly announced that, as a Christian, she could not ride on the Sabbath. But she didn't mind singing for a Sunday night concert, and did so.

It remained for one who was neither good singer nor even moderately good dancer to eclipse the publicity record of either Fanny or Jenny. During the city's history many scarlet ladies had called there, but none with the international repute of Lola Montez, who was here in 1853. "When you met Lola Montez," commented a contemporary, "her reputation made you automatically think of bedrooms."

As for her past history, Lola had several versions, all different. Her father had been an Indian rajah, or the King of the Cannibal Islands, or Lord Byron; her mother a Scottish washwoman or a handsome upper-class Creole. This much was certain: Lola had been the mistress of King Ludwig I of Bavaria, who made her a countess. Undoubtedly, too, she was a dark and provocative beauty whose daring led her into many a sensational situation. She had, for example, had her picture taken smoking a cigarette—which automatically classified her as a *fille perdue*.

Lola had left Bavaria in man's clothes; she wore them often. She made small fortunes and threw them away, picked up a husband or a protector, then dropped him for another. It was her habit to carry a whip with which to beat her detractors. She used it once on an editor who, by a coincidence, was himself carrying one—and proceeded to use it on her. From whips the two fell to pulling hair, then to pulling guns —at which point bystanders separated them. Lola never did like editors.

After knocking around various countries the Countess Lola appeared in New Orleans for a stage engagement. Everybody had heard of her, and everybody had an opinion. Sentiment was divided. At the St. Charles Hotel a crowd of young bucks brought a band and sang to her, while a more puritanical group booed and hissed. Screams rang out, denunciations rained down, and blows. Several duels followed. All of which naturally helped the show. Presently Lola announced that she wished to "make amends for a wasted life" by becoming a nun. Later she modified this intention: she would enter, not a nunnery, but the opera. She lasted three full months in New Orleans.

Lola could always be depended on for fireworks. On one occasion she advanced belligerently to the footlights to say that she did not intend to be humiliated. She had heard that a "cabal" had been formed to hoot her—let them try that, and off she'd go! Any other actress who said that would have been hissed off, but Lola was cheered for it.

On another occasion she and the theatre manager had an altercation. She said he had made an improper advance. Some wondered what, in Lola's case, could have been called "improper." She kicked him. Being no gentleman, he kicked back. She called him a scoundrel, and he sued for damages. This delighted Lola; it was her meat. She sailed into court, "skipping like a gazelle." When the manager itemized the epithets she had fastened on him, she sang out: "Ah, my dear fellow, that's just what you are!" She talked back to everybody. To the judge she remarked that the room was so crowded it was a pity they couldn't charge admission. His Honor laughed and laughed.

For everyone, judge included, the great moment arrived when Lola had to show *where* the manager had kicked her. She was most co-operative—climbed up on a table and did a tease act, slowly lifting her skirt, higher, higher, to a point "well up on her hip." It was really more of Lola than you could see on the stage. The men went wild, shouted vociferously, fell out of their seats; one went so far as to faint. Toujours La Nouvelle Orléans. . . .

Years later Lola Montez returned, tired and aging. No manager would have her, so she hired an abandoned store and held "receptions" for a dollar admission. You could stand near her for fifteen minutes and take a good look; she would even talk to you in any one of four languages. Then she got into a fight on a steamboat, and the law was summoned. She sent out word to the sheriff: Come and get her—adding that she was naked. The sheriff, a family man, backed off the boat.

Baggage or not, there was something about Lola. New Orleans always liked a good show, and she gave it.

Modern city through a framework of the old

Wood Whitesell

Quadroon Ballroom: Now a convent

French Opera: Music, like destiny, was in the air

Garden District: The Americans built in a stately tradition

Eugene Delcroix

Garden District: A stairway designed for a lovely woman

deBrueys-Smi

Madame John's Legacy: Relic of a fabled past

Storyville: They were shocked, but they looked again

Wood Whitesell

Chimney sweep: "Lemme clean your chimley, Ma'am?"

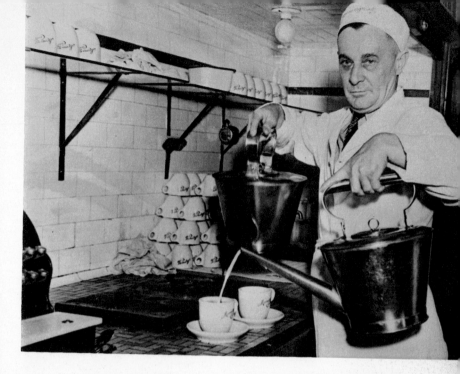

French Market: Half coffee, half hot milk—et voilà!

French Market: The waters yield their wealth

St. Roch: He looked after spinsters

Guy F. Bernard

Dan S. Leyrer

Josie Arlington's Tomb: Someone knocking . . .

Guy F. Bernard

St. Louis No. 2: Old neighbors together in a City within the City

St. Louis No. 3: "Ici Reposent"

Guy F. Bernard

Mardi Gras: Twelfth Night Queen salutes her subjects

Mardi Gras: Proteus toasts his Queen

Iron Lacework Building

Leon Tr

Sirens on the Ramparts

ON THE edge of the city, along the rue des Ramparts which had been the old boundary line, there long stood an irregular series of small, one-storied white houses. Passers-by caught glimpses of handsome wall hangings, gold candlesticks, glittering girandoles. Often a carriage would draw up before one of these houses, its elegance in sharp contrast to the humble neighborhood; and when later a man left, a handsome girl stood on the porch and waved goodbye.

The girls who lived in the cottages on the ramparts were the "*placées*" of New Orleans, the celebrated quadroons who were mistresses of well-to-do white men. The respectable women of the city, whenever the subject of the placées came within their notice, looked quickly away. Outsiders had a different attitude; for generations visitors from all over America stared at cottages and girls and went home to talk about them.

Only in New Orleans could the institution have flourished as it did. A liaison might last for a month, or for years, or for a lifetime. Certain New Orleans men were known to maintain two "families"—the white, accepted one, and the darker, unaccepted and unacceptable. Such a man divided his time between the two households, perhaps rearing two sets of children, the first acknowledged by everyone, the second ignored by all except the man himself.

The white wife? Usually she knew; her friends made sure she did. Sometimes she would break into tears and persuade her husband to end the connection. But generally she had to accept; for that was the way it was. . . . Regularly she heard things about those cottages on the border of town, and about the sumptuous "Quadroon Balls," where tawny-skinned women displayed their charms at a kind of bazaar, open only to men of financial standing. No red-necked river worker, no penny-pincher; the quadroons and mulattresses were particular.

A little house along the ramparts . . . The young man down the street is supposed to have made an arrangement last month. That one in the next square, with the four children—it is recognized that he has long maintained a place of that kind. And there is Monsieur G—— who pays his son's expenses for such a household, considering it a good way to keep him out of unknown mischief until he settles down. (A bishop of the 1790s complained that too many fathers favored this practice.)

Above everything else the traditional young man of New Orleans was proud of his masculinity. He liked his liquor, his food, his races, his girls. He wore tasteful cuff links; he owned dueling swords; by the same token, he might have his quadroon. In a number of circles, if he passed up such opportunities he might find his virility questioned. But he hardly needed to justify himself. There were the lovely ones, the evening was young, and what was he waiting for?

La vie, and a young man's nature. It may be that the climate was responsible, or perhaps the Continental attitude of tolerance; but the mood of New Orleans itself was probably the most powerful factor.

Among well-to-do Creoles, the *mariage de convenance* was common—a union made to please parents by cementing two fortunes and sets of interests. In extreme cases (like all natives, I have heard of these since childhood) the contract was signed before the couple had even met. When they did meet, the

girl often despised the bridegroom-to-be whom she was seeing for the first time; as for him, he might give her a glance—
and groan. Such a bride, tense and unhappy, became an un-
responsive or even frigid wife, so that her young husband had
an added reason for looking elsewhere.

Yes, nearly everybody knew, and accepted. But there was
often tragedy below the surface. A house by the ramparts for
two; heartbreak for one—and also, perhaps, for the third member of the triangle, the mulatto woman herself.

Hardly anywhere else in America was there a social group
analogous to that of the quadroons and mulattresses. A caste
among castes, they were not promiscuous; they might best
be termed concubines, with a status all their own in New
Orleans' world of color gradations.

These gradations could not but mystify and confuse the
stranger. He learned in time that they embraced dozens of
distinctions, that—

> a mulatto was the child of a white and a Negro;
> a quadroon, of a white and a mulatto;
> an octoroon, of a white and a quadroon;
> a tierceron, of a mulatto and a quadroon.
> a griffe, of a Negro and a mulatto;
> a marabon, of a mulatto and a griffe;
> a sacatron, of a Negro and a griffe—

and that there were still others: *métis, maemelouc, sang mélé,
os rouge* (of a Negro and an Indian), and so on. "Whether
distinguishable or not," said one observer, "it is certain that
they all exist in New Orleans." For convenience, the word
mulatto was commonly applied to all of them.

It was quite possible for some to be mistaken for whites.
One newspaper advertisement called for the return of a slave,
a "bright mulatto, Mary," described as "almost white," with
a reddish hair; "she passes for free, talks French, Italian,
Dutch, English, and Spanish." Many of the original Africans

had had skins that were not black but yellowish, or light brown, or almost red. They had delicate figures, small bodies, and aquiline noses. Then for years selective breeding went on in Louisiana, eventually producing men and women whose profiles had a hint of sharpness, whose hair was long and curling, and whose manner was soft.

Of the women in this group, an Englishwoman who came to New Orleans declared they were "probably as beautiful and accomplished a set of women as can be found." Another observer called them "gentle and pleasant," and a third considered the average mulattress notable for "*une belle taille et une gorge magnifique.*" A German nobleman was most impressed of all; to him the women were "the most beautiful in the world." "They are prohibited from intermarrying with whites and *will not* marry mulattoes," wrote Dr. John Sibley. "They prefer being kept mistresses which is assign'd as a reason for there being such a number of single women in this country."

The mulattresses' shadings were many—that of peach skin, of soft brown velvet, ivory, cream-white. The eyes were brown, or ebony, or an occasional deep blue or green; the hair, usually wavy, could be reddish or light brown. They had finely rounded figures, and they understood how to carry themselves, head high, lashes veiling the eyes. Almost always they radiated desire and allure.

They were never known as *Nègres;* they bore the title, officially in birth and similar records, of *femmes de couleur.* For New Orleans society, the letters "f.d.c." ranked them between the dark slave and the white person. In an environment that attached so much importance to skin color, they saw their hope of security through identification with the whites; and they looked down on the blacks.

"Those who are so many degrees removed from the black that the connection is no longer visible in the skin consider themselves as the 'best-blooded'; and so down to those who are only one degree superior to the blacks, whom they all treat with more contempt than even the whites do." Thus did caste extend itself. In return, the blacks hated the mulattoes for their superior pretensions. "Mules! Ain' one or other. Nothin'!" And in their "gombo" dialect the French-speaking Negroes made up bitter, satiric songs about the light girls who found, alas, that no soap would wash them white.

The free Negro group arose in several ways. Skilled male slaves managed to buy their freedom by intensive labor, or received it for bravery in war, for long service, or because of their masters' friendly feeling. Again, a white father would liberate his children, and sometimes their darker mother as well. Caroline Burson has cited a case from 1782 when a Monsieur M——, about to return to France, petitioned Louisiana authorities to approve his doing "an act of mercy by securing the freedom of Jacinta," a little mulatto girl whose mother was the slave of a neighbor; Monsieur bought Jacinta's liberty for a hundred and fifty pesos. In such cases the mother was usually freed, and by law the baby took its mother's status.

During the Spanish and early American days in Louisiana, free Negro men became mechanics, tailors, carpenters; they set up small businesses near the river, winning a degree of respect. They formed their own military corps, and various commanders, including Andrew Jackson, cited them for acts of courage. To this day, mulatto artisan groups have maintained their standing in New Orleans.

As successive generations of lighter-colored women were born, however, a certain amount of resentment against them began to appear. By 1778 these women numbered fifteen hundred, most of them "unmarried, all free, living in little houses near the ramparts." By the Spanish governor Miro's ordinance (the city has few more unconventional documents), these women were to stop dressing like whites, in plumes and jewelry; they must give up mantillas, caps, and elaborate coiffures. To persist would constitute misconduct. In place of the forbidden headgear they were to wear madras handkerchiefs—

tignons—which would make them look more humble. Although they obeyed, it was not long before they were sporting such tignons as he had never visualized—brilliant kerchiefs in red, orange, and green twisted about their heads like Turkish turbans, the ends thrusting points in the air. Let the governor do something about that! He didn't.

Early in the American era, West Indian and Cuban upheavals sent new thousands fleeing to New Orleans. With these whites and blacks arrived a large group of free women of color. Showing more white admixture than their Louisiana counterparts, they had enjoyed greater luxury. It was not for nothing that Creole males, beholding them, called them *"les Sirènes."* The white wives altered the epithet to "serpent women." In time the two terms were applied indiscriminately to most mulatto girls.

The mother of a mulatto or quadroon trained her from childhood for one thing primarily: to be the concubine of some rich white man. She would be sent to a small school or to a private tutor to learn to read and write, sew and sing. At home she was taught grace and elegance of deportment; her voice must be soft and pleasant, her manners refined. Her virginity was carefully guarded, for there lay her hope of future security; the man who came searching would reject damaged goods.

With the coming of the American régime the institution of quadroon sweethearts increased quickly. Times were easier; the town filled with young American adventurers ready to emulate the Creole bucks, who, they decided, had some interesting customs. The quadroon balls had hitherto taken place in a wooden building on Condé (later a part of Chartres) Street near St. Ann. Now these "Sirènes" had a new and radiant background. Next to the Théâtre d'Orléans of "Toto" Davis rose his Salle d'Orléans, gambling below, ballroom above. Authorities called it a dancing place without equal—airy, handsomely paneled, with a hardwood floor three layers deep and loges for onlookers. At the front an ironwork

balcony overhung broad Orleans Street; at the rear a cool
courtyard was reached by a curved stairway.

In this setting took place the dances that ranked among
the city's continuing scandals. At their height they were
directed with skill and discretion. In charge were elderly
women who understood these things. Champagne was served,
as well as absinthe and brandy, and excellent food. The orchestra was as good as any that played for the whites. And
the girls . . . only the best-mannered and most refined.
Hearts might break, but standards were upheld.

From their places the ambitious mothers watched; their
girls must be protected against obstreperous men or undesir-
ables. Usually these sponsors were ranged along the wall, but
during one period they occupied a raised platform at the end;
always they were in evening dress with fans and pearl chokers
like grandes dames at any ball. The mother of the lightest girl
in the room might herself be quite dark, but she had a right
to be there, looking on with the others.

It was not proper for a man to go directly to one of the
"Sirènes." An introduction must be arranged. There the girl
might sit in an evening costume fashioned by the most expensive modiste in New Orleans—sometimes even a Paris
gown. Up came a friend with a new arrival. The girl smiled:
Oui, she had seen Monsieur d'Aubert at the cathedral. *Oui*,
Monsieur. . . . The older women fell to comparing notes.
Ah, those Auberts. They had known his uncle, who selected
Cécile over there—how long ago, ten years? Cécile would
also be watching, with a touch of sadness. Her eyes, like those
of the others, followed the couple about the floor, and as they
went downstairs for sangaree in the courtyard.

If things went well, before the evening ended the young
man and the girl's mother would have met for a discreet conversation. By this time, if Madame were not certain of the
boy's position, inquiries had been started. Monsieur might be
willing to settle a flat sum, say several thousand dollars; or
he must make guarantees, assuring maintenance for a specified

time. He need not be rich; if he promised a moderate establishment, and the girl liked him, it could be arranged. After
that it was up to the girl to better the terms as the relationship proceeded.

The next day she began preparations for her new life. It
was much as if a marriage had been settled. Word of her
fortune spread quickly; members of her group gave parties for
her. In a way it could be termed a sale on the block. Yet the
girl herself frequently had a good deal to say in the matter.
On a first meeting she often found a white youth too abrupt,
or too casual. How would he conduct himself next week, next
month? If she had such fears she would know how to act:
"Monsieur, I must go; I am not feeling well." At a glance the
older woman would hasten to her side. The girl could wait;
a better chance would come, as it had for M. Aubert's choice.

Meanwhile the latter's partner was happy. In sight was the
goal for which she had been trained. Her children would do
some of the things she could not; they might go beyond New
Orleans into the great world. And, since this system placed
premiums on a pale skin, who knew? One day her children,
or theirs, might pass *à blanc!* To cross the line . . . every
compulsion lay in that direction.

Now, however, the details of the new house claimed her
attention. Her protector provided a cook or a maid or both,
so that she herself was free to enjoy her luxurious life. But
if she were wise (and she had been trained to wisdom) she did
not relax too much. She got up early, kept herself in trim,
watched her figure. When Monsieur called he would find
everything as he wished it: a smoothly running ménage, food
that he liked, the servant dismissed promptly after the meal,
good talk about his interests, the ever-responsive smile. Many
a white woman could have learned things from a Sirène.

Almost without exception she was faithful; it was to her
advantage to be faithful. In any case, had she not achieved
what she had been brought up for? She now took the name

of the man she called "husband," and so did her children. Her only associates were women like herself, and—just as her family did—they knew when to come to see her and when to stay away. Her mulatto brothers never appeared; Monsieur did not care for them. However, he had no objection to her going occasionally to a mulatto ball, where she sat on the sidelines and looked on.

Although the balls were seldom mentioned in local newspapers, every visitor to New Orleans made a point of attending at least one, either the unmasked kind or the masked balls customary during the Carnival season among whites and mulattoes alike; and allusions to them are found increasingly in travelers' reports from the beginning of the nineteenth century.

As early as 1806 a French traveler, C. C. Robin, spoke of the white balls as "very boring for those who do not enjoy formality," whereas the darker ones were "marked by gaiety." Christian Schultz went further: White men usually preferred the mulatto assembly to their own, "which at all times it surpasses both in elegance of decoration and in splendor of dress." Other reports tend to confirm this, the explanation perhaps being that of the two types of white dances—one for the élite, the other of a rowdier kind, frequented by sporting girls—certain visitors were not able to attend the former and thus saw only the latter.

In at least one instance, however, an observer had contact with both types of white dances as well as with the darker ones, and expressed a favorable opinion of the quadroons. This was the inquisitive Bernhard, Duke of Saxe-Weimar-Eisenach, who came to New Orleans in 1825. First he attended the refined white ball, where the ladies had a "very genteel French air" and dressed in Parisian style. Though the women danced well, "most of the gentlemen did not remain long but hastened away to the quadroon ball, where they enjoyed themselves more and were more at their ease." This was why so many at the white ball had (as he put it) to "form tapestry" along the wall!

Commonly there was an undercurrent of tension at these soirées, tension springing from sex rivalry. "I'm sorry, Monsieur, she is my partner." "No, she isn't; and you're annoying her." Quickly, as a crowd gathered, there would be a slap, an exchange of words. Many a duel had its origin in a quarrel at a quadroon ball. Nor did the rivals have to go far to settle it, for the encounter usually took place in the garden of St. Louis Cathedral. Only a half square away—where Orleans Street met Royal—this garden was illuminated by a street lamp. The men would walk across with their seconds and end the matter promptly. The girl herself might, a little earlier, have stood on the front gallery admiring the effect of the moonlight on the church towers, the way the cross shone silvery against the scudding clouds; now she watched the drama in the garden. A crisp word of command . . . the clash of rapiers . . . then silence. The quadroon girl would fall back against the wall, weeping; the music of the violins went on, and the merriment within.

These women occupied an anomalous position. They might toss their heads with pride, boast that they had in their veins the best blood of France and of Spain; but they were required to conduct themselves in a "seemly" manner, keep their eyes cast down, avoid making too great a display of their silks. A mulattress who rode openly through the streets in a carriage risked trouble; for any white woman who brought witnesses to swear that a mulattress had "flaunted herself" might have her whipped until her back was raw.

On the other hand, mulattresses were given prominent place in the theatre. During the 1820s the Orleans Theatre management was in a quandary. Few well-to-do women would consent to sit in the upper boxes since none would admit that she was not of the first social rank, and this had

created an annual loss of fifteen thousand dollars or more.
After long consideration it was decided to open that tier to
people of color. They responded at once, and thereafter it
belonged to them. The mulatto women wore jewels and low-
cut gowns in vivid hues with that touch of daring that few
whites attempted. Upstairs, near the ceiling, the blacks were
placed. The audience thus constituted a sort of racial layer-
cake. Occasionally, by ironic contrast, the "two families" of
some Orleanian could be seen within a few yards of each
other—white below, quadroon above.

As children were born to the placée on the ramparts, their
father would often make provision for their education, setting
aside funds so that, whatever happened, they would be taken
care of. And their mother never relaxed her effort to hold
her man, for she was well aware what might happen. . . .
There was Annette, who had been left overnight, to learn
that her lover was to be married next month. In Titine's case
the blow had fallen less bitterly; her partner hesitantly and
sadly told her that he was about to take a white wife, so that
their affair would have to end.

A white marriage, however, did not always end the ménage
along the ramparts. Each mulattress clung to the same hope:
her lover, even if he married, would not leave her; *they* would
be different. And some were; some of the men did remain
faithful to the death, theirs or their mistresses'. Louisiana's
laws prevented a man from leaving real estate, or more than
one tenth of his movable property, to any woman with whom
he had lived in concubinage. But these laws could be cir-
cumvented, and were; the man simply gave a male friend
access to a certain amount of his property which would later
be transferred to his dark "family."

Wealthier men arranged to send favored children to the
North or to Paris for their education. This was particularly
true in the case of sons whom the father considered gifted.
These children were taught philosophy, music, science, art;

they had good allowances; they lived in pleasant style. In the more tolerant Continental circles the degree of their shadings was not important. They were judged by their accomplishments, and a number became successful writers, poets, and men of science. Marrying well, they frequently stayed on in France and were eventually regarded as white.

When a placée's children came back home to New Orleans, however, the story was different. Abroad they had been the equal of any of their own ability and intelligence; here they were ostracized. If they wanted to do something, let them be bricklayers or housemaids! They must lower their glances before the meanest white, must wear the plainest costumes or risk a beating on the street. This situation produced endless tragedy.

The more fortunate managed to return to Europe and use their talents there. It was in this way that New Orleans lost several remarkable men—Norbert Rillieux, for example, a quadroon of Louisiana birth who returned to the state to perfect a sugar-evaporation process that revolutionized the industry, but who was so discouraged by the meagre opportunities that he found his way back to France.

A father occasionally sent a mulatto son to a Mississippi River or bayou plantation. Here, away from inquiring eyes, the boy would work out his own life. A number of them managed estates that spread with the years, and came to have slaves of their own; one had ninety bondsmen. In certain spots colonies of mulatto owners clustered together, satisfied in these places of retreat from contact with the world, yet holding their own in commercial dealings, cotton and sugar sales and the rest. They might even lend money to white neighbors.

The historian Gayarré has testified to the respect won by such darker planters. Once, riding on a steamboat, a white planter chatted with a cultured mulatto grower. When dinnertime arrived, a solitary table was set aside for the latter. Moved by the mulatto's quiet acceptance, the white man went to him with a friend: "We want you to dine with us." The darker man bowed. He would be happy to join them, but his presence at their table, even though acceptable to them, might displease their fellow-passengers. So they must permit him to remain where he was.

The year 1845 saw the publication of a book of poems by seventeen mulatto poets who at one time or another had lived in New Orleans. The poems, all in French, reveal considerable talent, a deft use of language, a sharp imagery. If only because of the general attitude here, these works betray no strong resentment, no protest against the mulattoes' status. Yet most of these men turned away from New Orleans to Europe for their careers. They became friends of such literary figures as Victor Hugo; they attended salons, gave recitals, and produced their works to wide acclaim. One had twenty plays presented in Paris. Incidentally, the book of poems bore a significant title, *Les Cenelles*—fruit of the hawthorn; that shrub, so full of thorns, nevertheless produces flowers of warm fragrance.

Less happy was the fate of many daughters of placées. If the father made no special provision, or left but a little to them, one career only was open—the quadroon balls, and the life their mothers had led before them.

As for the mother herself, after the break-up of the original relationship she might have the good fortune to attract a second "protector." Many would never attempt it, however. Too much time had passed; or they remembered too well the man they loved. Such a woman retained the cottage on the ramparts and with her savings went into business as dressmaker, hairdresser, or milliner—the traditional trades of her class. Or she might rent out furnished rooms. Her services being skilled, she usually prospered; it was said that few equaled the one-time placée in the tactful provision of good food, courtesy, and pleasant living conditions. Now and then the woman would take as husband a mulatto like herself, or somewhat lighter. A dark man? Hardly ever; the caste sentiment remained strong to the end.

To be sure, the placées constituted but one element in the mulatto population. Many others led self-respecting lives, winning positions of repute. By 1836 more than 850 free people of color were paying taxes in New Orleans on property valued at nearly $2,500,000—a figure that by the time of the Confederacy had risen to $15,000,000. In the city as in the country, they became slave owners; one woman had thirty-two bondsmen. Many owned slaves simply in order to profit by their labor; and, human nature being human nature, occasional mistreatment occurred. Probably as many, however, acquired slaves from among their own relatives and friends; it was a way of granting virtual emancipation. Repeatedly the colored owners went to the legislature with petitions to be allowed to free these relatives.

In the 1830s and 1840s Louisiana, like other Southern states, suffered a wave of hatred and hysteria against the free mixed-bloods, partly a backwash of the feeling against Negroes. Rigid restrictions were adopted to curtail the granting of freedom, and legislation was aimed at forcing many out of the state and preventing others from entering.

Such was the situation when in 1832 Marie Louise Betaud, free woman of color, sought to liberate her daughter and grandson, whom she had bought for $700. The Louisiana law now required that if any of Negro blood were to be freed they must leave the state. The elderly Madame Betaud, with no free descendants to inherit her property, had been told by her attorney that when she died all she owned would go to the state and be sold. This would include her daughter and grandson, who would thus become the slaves of whoever took over her holdings. She therefore appealed to the Louisiana legislature for permission to free her two descendants, and after some debate her appeal was allowed. She had to give bond for their support, but at least she could die knowing that they would not fall into the hands of strangers.

Madame Bernard Couvent, born in Africa, had been a slave for many years, winning her freedom as an older woman. When she died in 1837 she willed land for establishing the "Institution Catholique des Orphelins Indigents," which has been called the country's first free colored school. Though she had slaves and owned property, she had never learned to write, and she sought to assure this boon to others of her race.

Then there was the case of the soft-voiced Thomy Lafon, born in 1810, the son of two people of color. He studied in Paris, and spoke English, French, and Spanish. It is reported that at one time he sold confections to Negro waterfront laborers. Through saving his small earnings and investing them wisely, he managed to build up an estate. Husbanding it as it grew in several directions, he gradually emerged as an important property holder. He might have owned a handsome home; instead, he stayed on with his sister in a plain wooden house. He was a lean, ascetic-looking man with light skin and white hair, who could have passed as white but preferred not to do so. He lived quietly, respected alike by whites and Negroes. To people of both races he gave generously, and when he died he left his savings—some $350,000—to fifteen charitable organizations of all kinds.

It was Lafon who made it possible for the once-tinseled scene of the mulatto balls to be put to a different use. By the 1850s these balls had degenerated to a cheap rowdiness and in one more generation—by 1880—the building that had housed them stood empty.

For years a familiar New Orleans sight had been the Sisters of the Holy Family, an order of Negro nuns founded by a French girl whom a dark man had saved from drowning. To know the "little colored sisters" was to admire them. They had moved from location to location; now they heard that the old ballroom was for sale. They counted their meagre funds, sought loans, went out to beg; and the philanthropist Lafon made the gift that clinched the matter. Now much of the block, including property erected since then, is occupied by the convent and school of the "little sisters."

It is an excellent structure, that ancient gray-painted building with its windows and sharply outlined rectangle of portico above the banquette. Not far away, facing Orleans Street, is the cathedral garden where duels were once fought. In the afternoon a cross against the sky, taller than the one that lifted itself in former days, casts its shadow across the ground once trodden by the Sirènes and their "protectors."

I have several times visited the old ballroom and talked with the gentle nuns, their brown faces outlined against stiff white cowls. I have walked beside them through the courtyard where the quadroons drank absinthe with the Creole youths; later we have stood at the windows from which the girls watched the garden as the men fought over them with rapiers. Today, the room once used for the balls is the nuns' chapel; adjoining it, the smaller room where the girls often paused to powder their faces before entering, is now used for classes. All is serenity, dedication.

Yet tales are whispered. See that mark—it was there that a man killed his rival. The stain, it will never come off. . . . She went to that window the night afterward and, when no one was looking, threw herself to the flagstones below.

The Sisters of the Holy Family do not repeat these tales, of course. But now and then, in a still dusk when their young charges are not about, one can imagine oneself back in the early nineteenth century and see a slim, graceful figure hastening up the stairs, adjusting a camellia in her blue-black hair, wondering eagerly whether tonight she will find favor with some rich and handsome "protector." Sirènes, serpent women . . . I hope that when you visit their old building you will recall some of the kindlier stories about the golden-skinned placées, and not only the harsher ones.

CHAPTER 11

Bronze John Pays a Call

IN THE spring of 1853 New Orleans looked back delightedly on a crowded winter. No, sir, never had a season like that one—more ships, cotton, parties, masked dances, everything. And now that April had arrived, here was spring at its gentlest, when one could enjoy balmy afternoons and cool evenings. The hot weather would come soon, of course, and already some people were preparing to get out of the city: the wives and families of the well-to-do, certain merchants and traders, agents who were here only for the commercial months.

There had been years—New Orleans still recalled them—when this exodus had been motivated not only by the heat but also by the terror born of an epidemic. There had been, for instance, that dreadful summer of '37 when the city had been struck by cholera and yellow fever together. The Orleanians had not forgotten that! But a good many years had passed since either scourge had paid a really serious visit. Conditions were changing, weren't they?

May sped by. The thermometer jumped, and the rainy season was slow in coming. As usual, a few doctors were complaining about sanitary conditions in the city, but—also as usual—their complaints commanded little attention and no action. The doctors were probably exaggerating, and anyhow that sort of talk could be bad for business. It was what gave New Orleans a bad name. Don't believe half of what you hear. What you don't know won't hurt you.

New Orleans was used to its sanitary conditions; they were what it had always lived in. Any observant stranger, however, would have had reason for suspicion as he walked about the streets. The city, lying lower than its levees, was a saucerlike expanse in which the rainwater collected in gutters, in shallow ponds under the houses, and along the outer swamplike stretches. There was no system of underground drainage. During rainy weather the water stayed where it fell, grew stagnant, developed a green scum that looked like velvet and stank. And into this water were thrown the city's slops, garbage, and dead animals.

During dry spells, it was choking dust that gathered everywhere. Even the streets that were cobblestoned were not free of dust, since wagons and carriages dug ruts between the stones—ruts and holes filled with dust or, as soon as it rained, with mud and water.

Once in a while city "scavengers" would rake the refuse out of gutters and ditches, and push it aside in piles; but it all washed back as soon as rain fell. A newspaperman once said that he could identify any city street by its special odor. Occasionally citizens signed petitions calling for improvement, but nothing happened. The town stayed dirty and continued to reek.

From the earliest days, Orleanians had been cursing the mosquitoes. The tiny things weren't dangerous, of course; everybody understood that. But they could make an evening an experience close to martyrdom. It has been claimed that it was to escape their bites that New Orleans men turned from the short trousers of the 1700s to the long ones of the next century more quickly than men of other cities. An indispensable adjunct to living was the baire or mosquito net. As Benjamin H. Latrobe declared: "It is easy to slip under the bar at night without admitting any [mosquitoes], and there is an indescribably pleasant sense of security in hearing their clamor on the outside without the possibility of being annoyed by them." And I can testify, from childhood memories, to the fine superiority one felt in hearing that impotent buzzing on the other side of the net! Embroidering on necessity, the Creoles ornamented the baires with figured gauze, even with lace. Lawyers erected frames in their offices, big enough to cover table and chairs, and worked under the nets. Mosquito-proof coverings capped birdcages, and the housewife put a sack of muslin over her head and arms and did her work under its protection. Now, in May of 1853, Orleanians were slapping again at the little annoyances. Another summer of fighting these things; ah, well.

On May 10 the bark *Siri* slipped into her berth; though few in New Orleans could have known of it, her captain and two or three crew members had died in Rio de Janeiro before she sailed for the Mississippi. The same May day saw the *Northampton* arriving with four hundred Irish laborers and their families; there had been sickness on board, and burials. A week later the *Camboden Castle* was in from Kingston, where at least seven had died of the fever—the dreaded yellow fever that Orleanians called "Bronze John."

Unloading the *Northampton*, waterfront laborers passed the ship's hospital and thus learned that Bronze John was upon the city. The dockmen quit in a body, and hungrier replacements took over. By now more vessels had tied up. Seamen were moving about, meeting girls, drinking with friends, sleeping in crowded rooms. One or two sickened, but the doctors who attended them falsified the records in order not to offend the city's business interests. But this could not go on indefinitely. When friends brought a stricken sailor to the Charity Hospital and he died, the health officers turned in a truthful report. The newspapers ignored the matter, and the rumors that began to circulate were firmly contradicted. All careless gossip! Needless alarm! There *have* been a few cases of illness, but only ship's fever—that's all. You know how such men live. . . .

Then came the delayed rains, heavier than usual: hours of

savage downpour that washed over the receptive ground, lifting heaps of gutter stuff to the banquettes. Intermittently the sun shone, and the town steamed in the heat. Daily the hospital received more fever patients; each night a few were carried out dead. On the wharves the files of laborers thinned. Twinges of alarm started again, only to be quieted: Just working people, not yet acclimated. For it was the sincere belief of many (doctors included) that Bronze John did not attack native Orleanians—Creoles, or Negroes, or older American residents. To the fanatical old-timer this seemed all right; let the outlanders die. . . . When some skeptic raised the question of the new cases, it was explained that the fever would attack certain spots: the close-packed Lynch's Row in the Irish Channel, sailors' boardinghouses along the river, the marshy land occupied by newly arrived Germans.

But the number of dead increased with the weeks—seven this week, nine the next, then twenty-five, and now—on July 9—fifty-nine. The Howard Association (a group formed earlier to deal with epidemics) made a brief announcement of certain plans for coping with the disease—which infuriated the optimists; it could frighten people into an epidemic. The city council rebuked "alarmists"; the fever was "sporadic," confined to "overcongested spots." Then on July 23 the papers issued the figure for the past week: 204!

Good God, it was on them! Terrified men ran to their boarding places, snatched up whatever belongings came to hand, left the rest behind, and raced out to the street, where they halted cab drivers and thrust bills into their hands: The river landing, fast. But so many were headed for the landing that the vehicles crashed into each other. At the wharves men and women formed agitated lines, begging to be taken aboard; the privileged bribed their way into cabins. The congestion was due to the fact that there were few steamboats along the levee. During the warm season the wharves usually stood nearly empty. To make it worse, towns upriver and along the Atlantic coast had already started to declare embargoes: Nothing to be accepted from New Orleans, nothing to be sent there; armed guards were posted to make sure that the loathsome disease was kept at a distance.

Now, Orleanians by the hundred were rushing—by carriage, wagon, cart, any vehicle they could find—to reach the homes of friends and relatives along the Mississippi, or indeed anywhere outside the city. The poor trudged miles to escape; women caught up children with one hand and their skirts with the other and scurried after their men. Don't fight with the manager about the rent; leave the stuff here. We've *got* to go. Some of them already carried the seeds of death; within a day or so, no matter where they found themselves, they would be in agony.

No more street cries were heard in New Orleans; the marchandes, cake-sellers, knife-sharpeners, fish peddlers stayed at home, frightened or sick. The wheels of business ground to a stop, and managers watched the declining ranks of their clerks. There was scant need for them; who was there left to buy things? Except for the vehicles hurtling out of town, or those of the overworked doctors, the streets were bare. Even the bars, New Orleans' long-favorite gathering places, were deserted.

For weeks not a day passed without heavy showers. Skies blackened, and summer lightning darted, flaring over gray houses and grayer faces. When the rain stopped, the water trickled on all sides; weeds sprang up thicker than ever, and from the dirty liquid the mosquitoes swarmed by the millions.

The disease was insidious. First the victim felt a little indisposed. "Nothing—just a headache, a touch of chill." Then his temperature rose, though not enough to worry about. He would go out, eat a meal; then his knees gave way, and he took to his bed. By this time, the fever had made inroads. The temperature went far up, and the patient thrashed about in acute discomfort. His eyes grew bloodshot, his mouth went dry, and he demanded water. Delirium broke, and the sick man struck at those who tried to restrain him. There might be a "false recovery"; but soon the situation grew worse.

The victim's face darkened as he struggled, the veins distending as if about to break. Blood oozed from lips, gums, and nose, and there was retching, the dark substance in the basin being the bitterly feared "black vomit." Even then he might get better, though not many would believe it.

Few agreed on the cause of Bronze John's visit. It originated in rotting wood. No—from tiny specks in the air. Not at all—it was "pestilential effluvia" from river bank and swamp; digging those canals around the city had disturbed the ground and brought it on. As for remedies, Orleanians drank lime-water, swallowed sulphur or violent cathartics, or put onions in their shoes. Quinine was popular, though another school preferred opium. Cruel "cups" were applied—instruments with tiny, razorlike blades that cut into the skin and drew out the blood until the patient turned white. And hungry leeches were applied, to suck and swell until they threatened to burst.

The next report listed a total of 555 officially dead of the fever. (How many more not officially listed?) The next week, worse: at least 947! Every square in the city was counting its victims.

At this juncture there returned to New Orleans the Rev. Mr. Theodore Clapp of the Unitarian Church. He had been north to seek relief from what was called a "general debility." Now he felt that his people needed him. By train and water he had traveled for a week without pause and had now reached the levee. "Whilst waiting to get my baggage," he wrote, "I could smell the offensive effluvium that filled the atmosphere for miles around, resembling that which arises from putrefying animal or vegetable matter." He was far from well, and his condition made him more than normally susceptible to contagion.

Arriving at home, he lay down; but the news of his return had spread, and calls for his help began to pour in. During all that day and the days that followed he moved among the dead and dying. He found people falling sick one by one in their homes, trying to care for each other until the last had dropped to the floor. There the bodies lay, bottle-green flies swarming upon them, fattening, until the stench of the bodies forced the authorities to drag them forth. At a boardinghouse for draymen and laborers, the minister learned that in less than two weeks forty-five corpses had been carried out. Nearby, a poverty-pinched woman had the burden of a family of eight; inside of a month all had died, to be followed shortly by the woman herself.

From other witnesses, other episodes. A husband and wife were together, both gravely ill. The doctor ordered him taken to the hospital; she was too sick to be moved. The pair clung desperately to one another. "Let us alone, we want to die together." The doctor summoned two men to help him wrench them apart, and the wife fell back in convulsions. By the time the husband was admitted to the hospital, the death rattle was sounding in his throat; a day or two later his wife was also gone.

Callers discovered another couple in bed, their bodies cold. A baby was sucking at the yellowed breast of the woman, crying against the chilled arm that held him even more firmly than in life. On the floor lay another child, and the maid had dropped near the doorway, her hand stretched toward the knob as she clawed for escape from this room of death.

Officials died, and plumed hearses drove in stately procession. But one man remembered longest a scene before a humble house. Passing, he spied two workers carrying a coffin of unplaned wood smeared with lamp-black, as was the custom. Behind it stumbled a twelve-year-old boy and his sister. Funeral employes tossed the coffin into a wagon and, applying the whip, started for a cemetery two miles off. It was midday, the sun's heat overpowering, but the boy and the girl, hands clasped, started the long walk together. As they went they murmured, "Pauvre père . . . pauvre père." When an onlooker tried to make them give up the idea, they shook their heads. Investigating, he learned they were the last members of a large family of French immigrants. He could never locate them again, and he decided that they, too, had died.

Through the city swept the tide of fear. Who would be next? Who could escape? Wagons and carts were still clattering along every road to the country. Some, in ignorance or terror, refused to let doctors or members of the Howard Association enter their houses, and desperate men seized guns to defend themselves.

Doctors were ordering cold treatment, hot treatment; open windows, closed windows. One decided that there was some mystic efficacy in the juice of fresh oysters. Coatings of lime were spread along the banquettes; "its exhalations were supposed to be antiseptic," according to the Rev. Mr. Clapp. If a remedy seemed to work, all hailed it; then, after a dozen who used it died, it was abandoned.

The city tried dramatic devices. Cannons boomed at street corners to clear the air of "effluvia." Barrels of tar were dragged out and fired; the gas works gave citizens any amount of tar they would take away, and in yard after yard blazes flared. At the successive shocks of the big guns, fever victims fell into convulsions and covered their eyes against the frightening glare. From the levee New Orleans looked like a city under military onslaught. On breezeless evenings curling smoke columns spread over the town, and the light of the tar fires illuminated bodies that lay blackening where they had collapsed.

A couple, planning marriage, decided to wait no longer. The first minister they applied to refused; with death so close around them, marriage would be blasphemy! A second was too busy. Reluctantly a third agreed; but before the wedding party had left the house the girl had dropped gasping into a chair; a few hours later, her bridegroom helped to bury her in her wedding dress and veil.

In the hospitals dying women begged to have their babies brought closer for a last look, and then prayed that the babies would follow them to the grave. Other mothers, losing all their young, begged God to take them too. A pregnant woman, close to delivery, was brought in with her husband. The baby was born as the mother lay in late stages of the fever. The husband died, and then the desperate wife; the baby lingered for a few days, and then followed them.

Men hurried about with frightened stares, avoiding friends, standing back as they talked with tradesmen and taking their packages with gingerly care. Others swaggered; it wouldn't strike *them*—and even if it did, what was the use of worrying ahead of time? Still others—and this is characteristic in any plague—showed hysterical gaiety. Men would meet at bars and drink heavily; would order meals of the finest game, stuffed turkeys, and highly sauced fish. They prowled cafés and dance halls, where they sometimes found a girl or two.

A lovely blonde matron determined to forget for a night the scenes of agony around her. When her husband left the city on a brief trip, she accepted an invitation to join a lake-front party. There the merry-makers drank toasts, danced in the moonlight, crowded about the gambling wheels. The young woman sang as she waltzed at the water's edge. Disease and death seemed far away. Late at night the party rode back to the city in a carriage, and the joyous spirit still bubbled. "Faster!" cried the girl as they rolled over the Shell Road; whips cracked and women's voices rose gaily. From shacks along the route where men sat with dying relatives, eyes followed the vehicle in wonder and bitterness.

When next day the husband returned to New Orleans, it was to find the boarding place nearly empty. "All dead!" a servant whispered. "All but your lady, and the fever catch her jus' today." When he reached her side her face was drawn, her delicate complexion a heavy yellow. The doctor shook his head. "She did everything that would help to bring on an attack." That night, in the rain, the husband and a friend placed her body in a box. As he left the cemetery, they were halted by an attendant. "Wasn't that Mrs. ——?" The husband nodded, and the man made the sign of the cross. "Great God! I seen her last night when she passed along here, laughing."

Daily the toll grew. Bulletins from the Board of Health, put up on poles and boards, drew crowds with white faces. The men who posted the notices today were seldom the ones who had done it yesterday, for the fever reached everywhere. Mistakes in preparations for burial grew common. A family, carrying a box to a cemetery, opened it there for a final sad look, only to discover that they had been given another corpse in error. Mix-ups became the expected thing: nothing was normal, nothing as it should be. Over all the city was confusion and terror.

Several young men, keeping an appointment made much earlier, met at a daguerreotypist's. Only one, a doctor, was solemn; while the others joked, he dropped on a couch and fell asleep. One of the friends slapped his side. Why not stage a tableau, with the doctor representing the dying patient? Filling a basin beside the sleeper with ink to represent the black vomit, they struck lugubrious poses while the daguerreotypist photographed the group. A few days later, all save one lay dead. It would be appropriate if the earnest doctor had been the survivor, but he was not. Close to exhaustion, he took a boat to Mobile for a short rest. Arriving, he sent back a note to a friend telling how peaceful it seemed, away from hideous New Orleans. As the friend put down the note he glanced at the newspaper; it told him that the doctor had just died in Mobile.

Still longer became the lists of the dead. Skies darkened and black clouds pressed low like leaden hands over the city; the devout cried that the Lord had forsaken New Orleans. Bronze John's method grew ever more grotesque. A policeman would be stricken as he walked his beat, and robbers cleaned out his pockets. A nurse caring for the sick collapsed before them, and they managed to get well in time to bury her. Makeshift hospitals were found abandoned, reeking. Doctors, nurses, orderlies—all had died. On the floors, in beds, at windows, stretched the swollen forms of the last patients; or perhaps one living man moved feebly in delirium. In such cases officials gave firm orders: Go in, pour disinfectant, drag out the dead. Take 'em anywhere—out into the yard, or to the cemetery—and set 'em afire; anything to prevent further infection.

Funeral pyres burned in the night; over the whole area spread the smell of charred flesh. In the morning a half-consumed hand would be discovered, a grinning head that had escaped the flames. They were minor horrors in the great horror that was New Orleans of 1853.

With the ever-increasing dread, even simplest loyalties disappeared. A sixteen-year-old girl falling ill, the family sent for a carriage to take her to Charity Hospital. The house was dark; men, women, and children sweltered in the heat; every opening was clamped against the "effluvia." When the driver knocked, two men brought out the girl in heavy wrappings, placed her in the back seat and, handing him the fare, ran inside again. If the driver wondered at their heartlessness, it was not for long. He had other worries.

Needing a drink, he stopped for one or two. When he arrived at the hospital, a weary clerk stood on duty. Opening the back door of the cab, the latter put the usual questions: "What's your name? Where you from?" There was no reply. The driver jumped down. As he touched the girl, she fell over heavily, a corpse. Shrugging, the clerk turned back: "Get her away."

The driver sped back, beat at the door of the house, the locked shutters, the gates. At last a thin voice sounded, and the cabman shouted: "I got your daughter. Dead!" He heard a groan, and the shutter slammed. No one would come down. Now alarmed, the driver went to a cemetery. The sexton demanded a certificate, told him to leave or he would call an officer. The cabman returned to the house, lifted the body to the front steps and left it, the head hanging out of the blankets. The next day passers-by called a public cart to remove the body. A week later the house was emptied; every member had succumbed.

One week brought a total of 1500 deaths, some 1300 of them due to the fever. By now the city knew the error of the old claim that natives were immune. Everybody seemed to be dying; who could escape?

Bury the dead, bury the rotting bodies! That was the universal cry, the main task. However full the hearses were packed, they could never accommodate them all. Carriages were put to service, wagons, carts, anything. Men grabbed wheelbarrows and pushed along a casket or a stiffened figure.

All roads led to the graveyard, and the old slow pace was gone. Get there fast, get it done with, then come back for more! Over wet streets the vehicles raced, drivers and corpses bouncing when they hit holes. Wagons crashed into one another and overturned in the mud, to spill out the shrouded figures. As they approached the cemeteries, the congestion grew. For square after square, endless files stood for hours. "Nothin' to do but wait, mister. Nothin' to do."

Cemetery attendants worked day and night, and still could not catch up with their work. Bodies lay in boxes, piled up like crates of dry-goods. They remained there for a day, or two or three. When so many were brought in daily, it was impossible to get to them.

At the mortuary chapel on Rampart Street, drays and

wagons lined up with their boxes. With so many arriving, a full death service could not be expected, so a tired priest waited at the entrance, to drop a little holy water on one, then on the next. It was better than nothing; it might help to bring peace to the poor souls. . . .

Workmen were paid twenty cents a body; but the labor grew ever more backbreaking, and they struck. Then they were granted a few cents more per corpse, plus the promise of a good supper to fortify them, and they returned. They found boxes piled higher than ever; in the heat and rain, the coffins were bursting open. Relatives begged: "Please bury my mother!" "Take care of my baby, won't you?" Desperate men picked up shovels and buried the bodies themselves. The stench in and around the cemeteries grew so overpowering that passers-by had to hold handkerchiefs to their noses. So hogsheads of lime were poured over the festering piles, and barrels of tar burned in the cemeteries, adding new odors and new sights.

Still more drastic measures were required. Men dug trenches and pushed the bodies in, one atop the other like bad fish. A quick covering with mud, and attendants struggled on to further chores. When the next rain washed away part of the thin coating, additional stenches rose, and occasionally the sight of an arm or a bloated face. Another wheelbarrow of mud here, Pete. Cover that one over, fast as you can!

Frenzy bred nightmare scenes. Families fell into quarrels, fist-fights, challenges to duels, all arising from disputes over whose wife's body would go first into the earth. The unending dirges had to be stopped; they were too disturbing. Of necessity officials no longer demanded certificates and boxes, and many people were merely wrapping the bodies in thin cloth and dropping them at the entranceway.

People were being buried alive, when a comalike state was mistaken for death. One worried man begged friends to make sure this never happened to him. Missing him, they went to his house, to be told he had just been taken off in a cart.

The cemetery they were directed to proved to be the wrong one, and it took them some time to reach the right place. There they located a sexton. Yes, he'd buried that fellow a while back, in a trench—yes, right there. Seizing shovels, they uncovered the man near the surface, his mud-filled fingers reaching upward as he had struggled to free himself. By now he was dead; as he had feared, he had suffocated.

Through the streets rode high-piled wagons. The Negroes chanted: "Bring out yo' dead! Any dead today aroun' here?" . . . Hundreds were being disposed of without record. Unwilling to see their relatives treated so carelessly, many resorted to burying them in the family courtyard, where—to the flickering of candles—they frantically dug the last resting-place of father or wife or sister. Carts were driven furtively to the levee, where men lifted out bundles with weights attached. Travelers saw them floating—a twisted child, a woman with long hair streaming in the water. Corpses were caught by logs along the bank and there they stayed, bobbing slowly in poses of unconscious appeal.

In the presence of so much death, callousness increased. Men in bordellos, spying a cortège, drank a toast to it. Gambling assumed fantastic proportions; idlers bet on the number of deaths in their blocks, the relatives they would lose in a week. Vandals would break into a house while the family were taking a child's body to the cemetery. Weakened persons were knocked down in alleys, stripped of jewels and purses, and left to die. In a hospital a wily barber-nurse watched the patients with unusual care; when any of them became delirious or too weak to resist, he stole the small possessions they had concealed about them. But he himself caught the fever and died in one of the beds he had looted.

Yet another side of humanity showed itself. Women who had gone to more healthful places insisted on returning to do what they could. Wealthy matrons visited the shacks of the

poor, and poor people came to help at the bedsides of the
well-to-do. Shy persons, who had had scant contact with
their neighbors, now proved their courage and helpfulness.
Girls from bawdy houses became nurses, and circumstantial
accounts are given of madames who made remarkable records
in caring for victims.

The elderly quadroons won particular admiration, moving
about unflinchingly, contributing their skills to the ailing, and
achieving a new prestige. Doctors never ceased to praise them
for their work. Many of the quadroons died, but others survived to attain positions as professional nurses. Through the
whole grim period nuns, ministers, and priests offered glowing examples of self-sacrifice.

Presently yet another scourge had arrived, that of simple
want. With business halted, disaster faced those who had always lived close to the bare subsistence line. Neighbors became one another's protectors; one well-to-do couple, for
instance, took on the care of thirty families, "as if they had
been of their own kith and kin." Hundreds of tales of human
generosity survived those black months.

The climax of fear arrived when for the week ending
August 27 more than 1600 died—of these at least 1370 being
yellow-fever victims. A frenzy ran through the city, then a
new determination. They would work harder, they would do
what they could, though everything seemed lost.

From all over the United States gifts of money and food
were arriving. Many thought the city would never recover,
that it might be abandoned as a stinking plague spot. But
slowly conditions improved. Each week brought a slight de-
crease, fewer deaths, fewer again. For the first time Orleanians
could face one another with hope. Though the fever continued to strike, it was with decreasing force.

By mid-September only eighty new deaths were reported
for the week; and now the weather changed. The rains ended,
breezes swept from the lake, and the sun beat down with less

ferocity. The mosquitoes disappeared—a minor blessing at least. Families were returning, stores reopening, one at a time, then by the dozens. New Orleans was becoming itself again, with its theatres, operas, restaurants, and crowded levee. All aboard for the Mississippi again!

Though exact figures are difficult to arrive at, it is probable that during this period 15,000 persons died of all causes; estimates range from 27,000 to less than 9000. Many deaths were never entered in the records; or they had occurred in the suburbs or outlying settlements; or the people had died in flight some distance away.

Thousands of orphans filled the existing institutions, so that new ones had to be established—which helped to make New Orleans what some have called "a city of orphanages." Despite devoted care many of the youngest children died. For months others would look up whenever a new face presented itself; in the youthful eyes was a hope that this might be the missing mother or father. An adult friend told how he came upon one of the orphans, writing on a torn paper:

My Father's Grave

My dear father, I love you of all my hearth. And you did
Died so quick. And I think that I see you always
And I which that you would life. You was so good.
Our hole famely were . . .

The boy listed four names. The stranger asked a question. "They all died, too," said the child, and began to cry.

Eventually one large group of the homeless were assigned to new institutions. They were to be separated—boys to this institution, girls to that one. A girl ran to her brother, a few years younger than herself. "No! No!" she wept. "I told Mama when she died that I'd look after Sam. If you take him, I'll kill myself!" They were allowed to stay together, and later a family adopted them.

The city went on, but for years when America thought of New Orleans it thought also of plague. In former times the town had suffered through fear of its epidemics, losing men and women who would otherwise have come here to live. Now thousands, among them some of the most able in the country, swore they would not try to live there again. Worse, perhaps, this and other infestations bred a spirit of resigned acceptance. There would always be these things; man could do nothing about them. An observer wrote: "I like the people of New Orleans; they are not afraid of epidemics, and when they die they do not whine about it."

Yet those Orleanians also failed to do much about their problem, to make an effort, within the range of available information, to forestall future risks. Intermittently, for years, they endured other plagues, but they let their streets and surroundings remain wet and foul. Sanitary officials demanded, urged, demonstrated that—though the causes of yellow fever and other scourges were not yet clear—their incidence could at least be reduced through certain basic precautions. Not very much resulted. In a Sanitary Commission report of 1853, the year of this greatest of epidemics, it was declared: "New Orleans is one of the dirtiest, and, with other conjoint causes, is consequently the sickliest city in the union, and scarcely anything has been done to remedy it. In no part of the world is a thoroughgoing reform so much needed as in New Orleans." Undiscriminating admirers described the town as the "Acropolis of the South"; the more realistic changed the word to "Necropolis."

Yet slowly, out of its testings by torment, New Orleans learned how to cope with its problems of sanitation and semitropical disease. When Bronze John's secret was discovered, when science established the role of the mosquito in its transference, the town became the heart of a vast experiment to show how medicine could wipe out one of the "eternal" scourges. It went to its task with vigor, with crusading spirit; and it won. Breeding places were ended, stagnant pools dried, old cisterns cleaned and screened. In showing how the fever could be defeated, the city offered a lesson to the world.

New Orleans then began to rank as a healthy metropolis. And, too, out of the sufferings of the earlier days came by-products of good. The city emerged as one of the great hemispheric centres of medical research and training. Through the years it has given the world a series of great men of medicine, men who fought the fight against sickness by the river, and ended as conquerors.

CHAPTER 12

Years of the Locust

FOR a long time Orleanians have told the story of an impressed visitor of the last century who stood on a gallery and sighed over the cool beauty of the moon. Watching it whiten the roofs, he told his hosts: "I've never seen a moon like that." To this the old Negro who was setting a table in the next room made prompt reply: "Mister, you shoulda seen that moon befo' the War!" It is a later variant of the story about the Creole gentleman who grew annoyed during the early American days when a mild earthquake interrupted a dance. Things never happened like that, he complained, in the days of the French and Spanish.

The inner significance of such tales re-emerges again and again in the chronicles of New Orleans. What *was* always seems better than what *is*. As for the influence of the War of the '6os, Orleanians tend to believe that it was responsible for all their city's ills. The city did suffer, and heavily, both in the war and during Reconstruction. But these may not be exclusively blamed. What they did was to accentuate and strengthen certain trends that had been in the making for many decades.

For a full century New Orleans has rarely had a municipal administration that did not shame it. Bad government has been normal government, and the rancid odor began to rise at least twenty years before the War. Not the Creoles but the

Americans were to be blamed; taking over control, it was the latter who were responsible for the corruption and careless thievery that made the city resemble a latter-day banana republic, as well as for the adoption of murder as a political weapon. Two eminent respectables who introduced the new mode in the 1840s went on to triumph in national affairs. They represented the two leading parties of the time. The Democrats provided "King John" Slidell, whose name was ultimately to be linked with James Murray Mason's in the *Trent* affair. And the Whigs contributed Judah Benjamin, eventually Secretary of War and Secretary of State for the Confederacy. Each of them, during his Louisiana period, won the scandalized attention of the country in an episode described delicately as sharp practice.

In order to capture an election, John Slidell mechanized politics and put the steamboat to a new use. At the time of the presidential election of 1844 he managed the notorious "Plaquemines Frauds." In those days voters could cast ballots anywhere in their parish (county); and Orleans Parish extended to the Gulf through the marshy Plaquemines region. On election day "King John" proceeded to the levee with two steamboat-loads of worthy Democrats. Churning down-river, they stopped and voted at one isolated precinct after another. It was alleged that the boys voted three times, just to be sure; but the truth is that Slidell's plan was less crude than this. Since the state would go to the party that won the largest number of precincts, he steered his votes with care, floating them in at this point, then at that, so as to bring the local totals up to suit his plan. Though the device angered the Whigs throughout the country, the national Democrats were delighted by it. Here was demonstrated a new talent—a fine individualism and enterprise. "King John" was made.

As for Judah Benjamin . . . two years before, the Whigs had managed a neat coup of their own. By law a man could prove himself a property owner, qualified to vote, by showing a license for his carriage or cab. Just before election Judah

Benjamin, high in the party that professed to look down on
vulgar Democrats, stood by placidly while his aides handed
out to several hundred followers the cash to buy licenses
for nonexistent vehicles. The fact that most of the new li-
censees could not afford even the doorknob of a cab made it
only more hilarious.

Within a few seasons, things grew so much worse that
such tricks seemed like enlightened conduct. The Democrats,
seeking lessons in better methods of election rigging, brought
in a guest instructor, Chris Lillie of Tammany Hall. Chris
taught them how to run in triple voters, how to vote by names
taken from tombstones, how to gouge the eyes of opponents
who insisted unreasonably on going to the polls. And as time
went on, each side took to saying that it had to do such
things because the other was doing them; and each was right.

Presently the Whig party declined and then disappeared,
its place being taken by that piebald phenomenon, the
"Know-Nothing" or "Native American" movement, anti-
Catholic and anti-"foreign." Strangely the Know-Nothings
won recruits in Gallic New Orleans, even among the Catholics; and, as elsewhere, well-to-do citizens turned to the new
party as an agency for striking at the unwelcome power of
naturalized Americans. Blood flowed even oftener than before; mobs hunted down Irish, German, and Italian scape-
goats, beat them unconscious, and dragged them over the
cobblestones by the feet. The Know-Nothings soared to
power in New Orleans, winning repeatedly. Election day
meant that a man sharpened his bowie knives, inspected his
pistols, and stood ready, if necessary, to kill his opponents to
keep them from the ballot boxes.

By this time the city's police department seemed to be
controlled by men who could fairly be called criminals; while
citizens slaughtered one another on the streets these officials
looked in the other direction, intervening only when their
side was losing. There was constant turmoil—inflammatory

attacks, partisan appeals, ambushes on the banquettes. The chief justice, brother of "King John" Slidell, was felled with brass knuckles as he tried to vote, and the head injuries he received put an end to his career.

In 1857 Governor Wickliffe, in a message marked by considerable heat, told how organized bands had taken control of streets "to commit acts of violence upon multitudes of our naturalized fellow-citizens." He estimated that a full third of the voters had been frightened away on election day; and he cried out against "outrages which tarnish our national character and sink us to the level of the anarchical governments of Spanish America." As a consequence the legislature established a new office—superintendent of New Orleans elections—hoping thus to keep them at least moderately honest. It was a hopeless task. A "Native American" mob congregated to tear down the new superintendent's house and kill him. His reaction was first to send his family away, then to summon friends with whose help he turned his house into a fort. The mob changed its mind.

As the city election of 1858 approached, there crystallized an exotic phenomenon: a reform movement, with Major P. G. T. Beauregard (later of Confederate fame) as candidate for mayor. The politicians answered it by sending a mob into the registrar's headquarters, to snatch lists and remove all names opposed to the Know-Nothings. The process took days; and the police did nothing.

A vigilance committee of a thousand members sprang up, issuing a call to "free our city from the murderers who infest it." It proclaimed itself the temporary government, as members shouldered guns and took over the Cabildo at Jackson Square and the adjoining state arsenal. Using an element trained in hard filibustering among Latin Americans, the vigilantes ripped up granite street blocks and dragged cannon into place.

Meanwhile hundreds of Know-Nothings milled before the white columns of City Hall; they demanded guns and got them. The weak mayor, frightened at the prospect of gory battles, vacillated. The Know-Nothings drilled; at one point a colonel rapped out an appeal for followers to storm Jackson Square and blast it out. Two rival armies formed, fingers on triggers.

Government all but collapsed. When police were summoned, none appeared. The militia, also summoned, mostly stayed at home. Back and forth between the two armies spies reported hourly. Business was paralyzed, while mobs began to loot stores. Several times bands of hundreds moved into fighting position; once the vigilantes mistook their own side for the enemy, killing four and injuring nine. Each time, luckily, an open break was averted, though by a narrow margin.

Election day arrived; despite all the alarms the vote was light. Sadly, the reformers had won no strong following; the people simply remained away. That night the vigilance committee abandoned its buildings, leaving behind piles of guns. Leaders ran to steamboats, hid in the swamps. For days victorious Know-Nothings beat opponents on the streets. Though eleven men had died, no investigations were ever made. Too many had been involved on both sides, and New Orleans was content to go back to rule by corruption.

Is it any wonder that crime flourished? The city had long had an underworld, clusters of waterfront dives of shifting prosperity. By this time, however, Gallatin Street had become the centre of criminal activity. It lay at the border of the French quarter, a short thoroughfare near the old market, but its make-up and appeal went beyond the French. It was also American, Spanish, German, Oriental, anything and everything—a reeking collection of saloons, barrel-houses, gambling joints, nickel and dime hotels, bagnios, headquarters of thieves and stranglers, "offices" of prizefight impresarios with shady connections, fences' shops.

An American Casbah on a small scale, Gallatin Street witnessed nightly killings, stabbings, riots, and the murderous clashes of rival bands; and above all these sounded the click of gambling wheels, the tinny crash of pianos, the whine of quarrelsome women. Here went criminal operators who needed quick help; men with dangerous goods found here a temporary retreat and expert assistance in disposing of them. To Gallatin Street gravitated saloon keepers who got into trouble elsewhere, harlots who became too violent, wranglers that no other neighborhood would stand. Sailor's joy, poor man's paradise, it was the centre of a hundred unsolved mysteries. When harassed visitors arrived in New Orleans, hunting missing relatives, the advice given them as a last resort was: "Have you tried Gallatin? But don't go there alone!"

The street woke with the dark and went to sleep with the dawn. Only the most daring, or foolish, policeman ventured there at night without a partner; generally the police preferred to go in squads. A peeler was fair game for anyone from a dope addict with a knife to a drunken strumpet with a chamber-pot to heave from a gallery.

Among nonhabitués, only those who knew the leaders and their connections ventured into Gallatin without protection. At best they might wind up without their watches or gold toothpicks. A Gallatin resident couldn't resist temptation; it wasn't fair for swells to walk around that way, just asking for trouble. Inside the garishly ornamented buildings waited gamblers who hated a fair game with the passion of a religious zealot; bouncers whose fingers itched until they had broken a few heads; brawny blonde harpies who, when business was bad, walked out to grab their men and drag them in.

The women danced in casual aprons or chemises, or nude. If the liquor wasn't doctored, something was amiss. A number of girls carried their own knives, shaped to their special wishes, decorated with hearts and cupids, and notched. Versatile ones alternated as dancers, tarts, and street thieves. At one extreme were brilliantly bedecked newcomers, ready for anything that came up; at the other, hags fallen into drooling want. No man of sense called on the Gallatin girls with more than a dollar or two; whatever he carried, he would be relieved of it before he left, even if several had to sit on him to rob him.

Walking casually through the place, experts could tick off the reliables and their records. Mike Haden—cut his brother's throat because the brother got mad when Mike, then thirteen, stole bananas; Mary Schwartz—ripped out a man's eyes when he gave her a quarter instead of her usual four-bit fee; Butter Joe, who in his day, before his brain softened, had lowered his head and cracked scores of skulls. That one over there, with brass knuckles, slingshot, and a bat? He was celebrated because, with a single aim of the bat, he could crush an arm at the elbow.

The street had one unbreakable rule: A man could do anything he could get away with, but he had to take care of his own dead. Call a friend, drop the body into an empty yard, drag it to the river; just get it away. Gallatin had more side alleys than any other part of New Orleans, and those wet, dark stretches had their uses. A bouncer at a prosperous place, after knocking a visitor unconscious, made a casual check of the man's pockets and tossed him there. At once a pair of petty scavengers started for the prone figure, to fight for the prize. Anything they found was theirs—tarnished cuff links, belt, tie, shoes. A few minutes later, still another prowler would creep in, to take shirt, trousers, and underwear. If the weakened victim tried to struggle, a brick would take care of him. The story is told of one such final thief who came by after his predecessors had removed even the victim's socks. Damn it, nothing left! Or was there? He struck a match; in the light he caught a reflection from the open mouth. A gold tooth! In a moment he had it and was on his way to a pawnshop.

And the boys had their friends to "look after them" up at City Hall.

Meanwhile what had happened to that dream of New Orleans as the world's greatest port? There seemed to be more trade than ever in the 1840s and the following decade; despite such interruptions as epidemics, the town continued to fatten. But those who looked closer observed that the city's share of the total business was decreasing.

Years before—about 1830—a canal had been dug from the Ohio River to Lake Erie, and another from the lake to the Hudson, the two giving New York City direct connection with territory that had long depended on New Orleans as its port. Then Pennsylvania and Maryland went to work to dig *their* canals. The old West was being tapped for its flour, wheat, and rawstuffs, and growers need no longer take the winding downriver trip. The consequences of this change were a long time in reaching New Orleans; there was so much traffic, so much business. Actually, the city was receiving a larger amount from the upper valley than ever before—but it should have been getting even more.

There was, further, the matter of railroads. Though Louisianians talked a lot about building railroads, they did only a little. Two or three lines were under way; by 1860 a single line left the state, to nearby Jackson, Mississippi. But other Southern cities were getting ahead of New Orleans in this respect: Savannah, Chattanooga, Charleston. . . . As early as 1845 a few informed Orleanians had grown dismayed. That small New York town, Buffalo, had taken more flour and wheat from the West than had New Orleans itself! And half the other "Western" stuff was now going to the Eastern seaboard by rail and canal rather than the river.

Certain gains in other directions helped for a while to conceal the real picture. More and more the city was concentrating on the lower valley and on cotton. More slaves were filling the fields of the Deep South and Southwest, and King Cotton was rolling more bales aboard the steamboats. New Orleans was realizing her destiny as capital city of the Deep South. But what if cotton should ever fail? Few raised that question; most Orleanians were dazzled by the silver flood. Let the rest of the country go, cried the cotton enthusiasts; our city's fortune lies right around here! There was undoubtedly, in this attitude, a factor of angry resentment against the North—a feeling that was growing all over the South.

More markedly than in most Southern cities, however, New Orleans had a contrasting element: Unionists who wondered whether the wasteful system of slavery was not beginning to strain the economy, and whether the enthusiasts were not going too far. One group of practical citizens urged further that—if the break came and the extremists won—the place of New Orleans and of Louisiana was (as they put it) "with the border states," not with Mississippi and Alabama and Georgia. Nature herself had connected Louisiana with the upper states; the whole river valley constituted a unit. Here centred the city's future; to align itself otherwise would be "unnatural and antagonistic to its obvious interests and destiny." Furthermore, as a city committed to commerce, with scant industry, it depended on its trade with the world. Throw this away, and where would New Orleans be?

New Orleans was to find out. Though strong interests opposed joining a seceding confederacy, when the break did come Louisiana made the plunge, the Creoles and the Americans leaping in with equal fervor. New Orleans' French accents and the flashing reds and yellows of her Zouaves were notable in the battles of the next four years. For a time Orleanians visualized their city as Queen of the Confederacy. She was the cotton capital; wait until the North found herself dependent on cotton, and Europe wanted it and came for it!

For a brief span the city boomed. But the Confederacy's cotton policy was doomed. The Federal blockade slowly throttled the port; then, with little warning, a Union fleet was steaming toward it. The Federals numbered almost exactly the same as the British forces had in 1814-15. Below the city stood two forts, ready to rake down anything that tried to slip past, and a line of hulls was chained across the river

as an additional protection. Of course they would never get
by. But Flag Officer Farragut (whose father had come from
this vicinity) gave the order to attack. For five days the Con-
federates resisted bitterly, boldly; almost won—and then lost.
New Orleans lay helpless, with hardly more than a token
force to defend her; the South had concentrated its men elsewhere.

Church bells rang out the grim signal; thousands fell on their
knees. The less pious ran to the riverfront, set fire to warehouses, looted supplies, lapped up whisky that gurgled in the
gutters. In the violent light of her blazing port, New Orleans
dropped out of the war.

Ben Butler of Massachusetts, who became the military ruler
of New Orleans, is the most hated man in the city's tradition.
It is not difficult to see why. Though, as a New England
Democrat, Butler had voted fifty-seven times in convention
for Jefferson Davis as a presidential possibility, he despised
slavery; he had been a labor attorney, favoring a ten-hour
day and other radical reforms. Also, hadn't his father fought
under Jackson to save New Orleans from the British? He said
he had come to help return it to the United States. A man
of fervid opinions, Butler was probably as tactless a human
being as the town ever knew.

Yet even an Orleanian may admit that his city gave "Beast
Butler" a degree of provocation. Mobs spat on soldiers and
reviled the American flag; women poured filthy water on his
men, feigned vomiting spells at the sight of them, and went
into guffaws at Federal funeral processions. (Some of the
lighter ladies pasted Butler's picture in the bottoms of their
chamber-pots.) Much of this, of course, is understandable as
the rage of a demonstrative people confronted with an un-
dreamed-of situation. General Butler responded with high-
handed tactics of his own: confiscations, forced sales, the
brusque removal of families from houses that he and his staff
wanted to occupy.

In a burst of anger, the general promulgated his notorious "Woman Order." It declared that, since American soldiers had been subjected to indignities from females "calling themselves ladies of New Orleans," thereafter any woman who "by word, gesture or movement, insulted or showed contempt" would be "regarded and held liable to be treated as a woman of the town, plying her vocation." Though the order was never actually carried out, for Butler there was the devil to pay. He was denounced in England, and Jefferson Davis, whom he had once praised highly, declared him an outlaw.

With his brother, Ben Butler engaged in certain business activities which seem to have been dubious operations on a large scale. Throughout the war, as is well known, men on both sides engaged in clandestine trade and profited hugely by it. Though there is no proof of any particular Butler taste for silver, Orleanians to this day identify Ben as "Spoons Butler." Their fathers and grandfathers applied another term to express their rage against him; having one eye crossed, he became "Old Cock Eye." Creoles, using the French pronunciation, made it "Old Coke Eye"!

On one point both North and South might agree: Butler gave New Orleans a scouring such as it needed but rarely got. During the war, bitter men hoped for a yellow-fever epidemic that would wipe out the Yankees. If only to save his men, Butler saw that verminous gutters were swept clean, and the city's surface shone with a new cleanliness. And the man performed one final, sardonic act. He ordered carved on the base of Jackson's statue in the square the words General Jackson had used against the Nullifiers: THE UNION MUST AND SHALL BE PRESERVED. It was a hard thrust.

Butler left New Orleans after only six months, and the city settled down to years of changing values. As docks lay empty, hunger drew close. Nearly all business depended on the river—dry-goods stores, restaurants, hotels. Moreover, the basis of the city's economic being, black bondage, was now disrupted. Under Federal control during most of the war, New Orleans had watched the opening attempts at a new labor system and at a local government in which for the first time slavery and cotton did not dominate. Working people took office; and old natives were astounded by hour-and-wage legislation that struck them as fantastic.

Reconstruction arrived here earlier than in most other places in the South. Adjustments started under Lincoln; the President proposed gradual enfranchisement for the new freedmen, efforts at mutual adjustment. When death ended his plans, racial hatred blazed higher. On one raging day whites and blacks clashed over a projected assembly, and into the hall where the Negroes were trapped the whites poured repeated volleys. Then, as the Negroes ran out, they were clubbed and shot in the streets. Score: forty-four blacks killed, and four whites.

National Reconstruction grew more rigid. As governor, Louisiana had a handsome young white adventurer, Henry Clay Warmoth; as lieutenant governor, a Negro named Oscar Dunn, far more honest than many a white around him. It was, of course, a day of irregularities, of mounting extravagance. Item: One hundred thousand dollars' worth of chandeliers for the state capitol; item, a gold spittoon for every person in office.

Yet this is not the full story. It was a time of revolution, and new social classes, whites as well as blacks, were beginning to win a voice in government. It is not often noted that the blacks got only the crumbs from the feast; the rich food went to the whites. From neither old master nor new associate did the Negro have a chance to learn the thing called responsibility.

Meanwhile New Orleans suffered. No one, I think, made a more pointed comment than that of swashbuckling young Governor Warmoth. To a man who talked of corruption, he cried: "Why, damn it, *everything* is demoralizing down here. Corruption is the fashion!" Hadn't it been that way for a long time? When a delegation protested against the stealing in a bond issue, the governor agreed with its members; but, he said, he had found every leading New Orleans broker lobbying for the issue. A native Democrat of the day, investigating carpet-bag schemes, discovered that practically every one of them involved respectables of his own party.

Stealings, killings, gougings . . . a pattern not entirely new in New Orleans. To complicate it further, crops went bad and neglected levees broke. Meanwhile, although railroad mileage had vastly increased in the United States, spreading into great new regions, the channels of the Mississippi had been neglected, with consequences that might have been anticipated for the port of New Orleans. People who had always been poor were poorer than ever; for other portions of the population poverty became the normal way of life. I remember one of my grandmother's stories. A neighbor of hers had a kitchen whose interior was visible to the families on each side. Daily, during these lean years, the neighbor woman moved about the kitchen, stirring with big spoons the contents first of one pot, then of another. Not until much later did my grandmother learn (by accident) that those pots had always been empty. Our neighbor's pride had led her to stir their imaginary contents so that none who caught sight of her would suspect her want.

In the French quarter and below it, along the Creoles' Esplanade Avenue, and up in the Americans' Garden District as well, big houses stood dark and dingy, ironwork rusting, paint peeling in strips. Families sold their jewels, their furniture, their homes, to live a diminished existence in the background. Antique dealers made hauls of art work, family portraits, silver tableware, that would eventually find their way to all parts of the country. One man would learn for the first time to labor with his hands, managing through the years to pull back his clan by wrenching effort. The next man, unable to make the effort, would sink beneath the surface.

For some there was true tragedy in this process of decline. A proud Creole woman had a son who took the only job available to him, as a shoe salesman. After a while, taking to drink, he disappeared with fifteen hundred dollars. The mother went to the employer: "M'sieu, we will make it good. Please take this." It was the deed to the family tomb, worth several thousand dollars, their last resource.

The 1870s came, and factionalism broke out among the Reconstructionists. On September 14, 1874, armed men rose against the metropolitan police. Score: thirty-two dead, seventy-nine wounded. Then, two years later, Reconstruction was ended in New Orleans through a brisk bipartisan deal. And so, were things now made pure in New Orleans? After a detailed study one Southerner, Garnie McGinty, concluded: "The political change was not very pronounced, either for better or for worse. . . . The Democrats hungered for the spoils of office and were about as extravagant. . . . The change of political control did not bring any outstanding modification of political principles nor any great improvement in public morals."

These years of restoration, too, gripped Louisiana firmly in the greatest lottery ever seen in this country. By and large, officialdom basked happily; for the lottery's bribes were generous. It could afford them; annually it siphoned $500,000,000 from the American people.

New Orleans had seldom lost its taste for taking chances. Churches of several faiths had sometimes raised funds by lottery. In 1868, under the carpet-bag government, a group of men obtained from the state a twenty-five-year lottery charter, paying the legislature $300,000 cash for it. Later, as part of the presidential election "understanding" described above, the lottery people put up another $250,000, by which they managed to get the lottery authorized by the state constitution. The Louisiana Lottery pledged donations to charity hospitals, asylums, yellow fever funds, the French

Opera—any worthy cause indeed, and a few not so worthy. Its critics cursed it as the "Golden Octopus." In most places such an organization had to pay back three-quarters or more of its take; under the indulgent Louisiana law the lottery paid back only half. Operational details were honest; the company could afford that luxury. Two Confederate heroes, Beauregard and Early, were each paid $30,000 a year to sit on stage and preside over special public drawings.

New Orleans went lottery-mad. Small drawings occurred daily, grander ones twice a month, yet grander twice a year. People talked lottery, dreamed it, bought tickets by their dreams. Voodoo books became the town's best sellers. Wha's a black cat wid no tail mean, Papa? . . . Seen two nun' in a row; what number I should take, you think? The credulous went to church to try to get their tickets blessed. Women boasted that not once in years had they failed to buy a daily ticket. They pointed to the barber who had won $300,000. At one time an inquiry revealed that thousands of smaller bank depositors had withdrawn their funds to play lottery.

The company expanded, acquiring banking connections. No loans for reformers; if you want a crop financed, Mister, keep your mouth shut. For a time the major problem lay in the legislators' greed. They wouldn't stay bought. The firm had to maintain a permanent pay-off fund; to its large pay-rolls it added nephews, cousins-in-law, and uncles of public officials. Yet even in New Orleans opposition developed. Ministers, women, and uncowed businessmen organized in protest. By the early 1890s the term of the twenty-five-year charter was drawing to a close, and the lottery men put forth their most strenuous efforts, offered their biggest bribes. The state rang with the oratory of men who "yielded to none" in the worship of Southern womanhood, the support of the sanctity of the home, the love of children; and would therefore vote for the lottery.

Lawmakers signed pledges against the Octopus; then, as the bribes mounted higher, broke their pledges. When a deadlock developed, a sick member was warned that he would die if he went to the capital to vote. He went anyway, and died; but his side, the lottery, had carried the day. When the governor, Francis T. Nicholls, refused to sign the bill, the lottery officials hastened to court and odd decisions blossomed, belying the previous state law. In the end, however, the people won. The Federal Government took firm action; and the Louisianians, carrying banners and singing hymns, cut the Octopus apart.

New Orleans could hold its head a little higher.

Meantime, in another fashion, the city had once more stirred the nation. Before the war hundreds of Italians had arrived here; after it they came in increasing numbers, settling about the poorer parts of the French section. Encouraged by steamship companies and employers seeking cheap labor, they crowded into humble houses and former mansions now partitioned off into dozens of rooms. Their bright garments swung on lines; rows of garlic and spaghetti hung in courtyards from which the glory had departed.

Ever since then the French quarter has had a marked Italian subflavor, unmistakable for blocks in a row. The Italians became fruit handlers, market men, operators of oyster luggers; in time the Gascons at the market gave way to them. A large element were Sicilians, their ways "different" from those of older Orleanians, who frowned on their "Little Italy" and ignored them.

As years passed, an occasional Sicilian was found dead of violence, and a secret organization was rumored—the "Mafia." Well-to-do Italian merchants were threatened. In Italy itself government officials were moving against the Mafia, and many of its members fled to New Orleans, where they used their favorite weapon—the sawed-off shotgun hung inside the coat by a hook. The quiet of former Creole neighborhoods was shattered as shots rang through the courtyards. Killings increased, always among the Sicilians. New Orleans shrugged. As long as they don't hurt us. . . .

Overnight the Mafia was involved in a dispute over low-paid banana loaders. Two elements, the Provenzanos and the Matrangas, fought to monopolize the labor supply, and the Matrangas, connected with the Mafia organization, drove off the Provenzanos, who had political connections. Chief of Police David Hennessey, friendly with the Provenzanos, intervened on their side. After communicating with Italian police officials, he announced he had strong evidence against the Mafia.

On an October night of 1890, as Hennessey neared his home, shotguns roared out, and a band of men scattered to adjacent streets. When the friend who came to the dying officer's help asked who had attacked him, he gasped: "The Dagoes!" The city was more startled than it should have been; here was the fruit of its policy of looking in the other direction. The mayor named a committee to work with the police; they accumulated identifications, remarks overheard on the day of the killing, and other telling evidence. Charges followed against nearly twenty men.

The Italians hired leading local attorneys, and one or two of less savory reputation. The heated city followed the long trial of the first nine men; feeling had become so violent that several of the prisoners were beaten in jail, one seriously wounded with a gun. Though the state's case looked strong, a rumor circulated that expert jury tamperers were functioning. And it seemed to be confirmed when the verdict came in —not guilty for some, mistrials for the rest.

The day was Friday, March 13, 1891. Unfortunately for the Sicilians, two ships had just arrived in port with 1800 new immigrants. Italians were rejoicing at the verdict, holding supper celebrations; wild stories spread that they were going to "take over the town." In the next morning's paper "all good citizens" were summoned to a mass meeting on Canal Street "to take steps to remedy the failure of justice." The invitation was signed by a committee of sixty, including highly prominent Orleanians.

What was about to happen appeared obvious. The Italian consul tried desperately to locate the mayor, who was not to be found. The governor was in New Orleans but did nothing toward calling out troops. The crowd assembled; a march started to the prison at old Congo (now Beauregard) Square, where the Negroes still danced on Sunday. The sheriff had left, saying he was trying to find help; his subordinates, locking in all the other prisoners, opened the Sicilians' cells and told them to hide where they chose.

The mob battered down a side gate, and the prison was theirs. For nearly an hour the committee's leaders conducted a man hunt, while the larger crowd outside shouted at each blast. The committee had set down eleven names, including those of several who had not been tried. It found them, one by one—youths or mature men, crouching in corners, beneath stairs, on exposed galleries. The victims begged; with hands crossed as if in prayer, they swore their innocence: "Give-a me chance." . . . "Don'-a kill me." . . . "Don' . . ."

And the leaders shot them, one by one. Eager helpers crowded forward to pour additional bullets into the bloodsplashed bodies. Two were dragged out and hanged to trees. At the end the chairman ordered the mob home; and the non-Italians believed to have tampered with the jury went unmolested.

For some hours it appeared that Italians would be murdered indiscriminately. Hundreds fled from their homes, either hiding or appealing to friends to take them in. I recall my grandmother's story of the way many tried to conceal themselves in toolhouses, garrets, backyard privies. "Save-a me, please! Save-a my chil'ren!" It is a happy family memory that she took several of them in. Hours passed; the blood heat cooled, and no more were killed.

The affair became an international episode. Americans'

opinions were divided, largely by section, North or South. One side defended the killings, saying that but for this drastic action the Mafia might have swept New Orleans. Speaking for the opposite view, one magazine said sternly: "The New Orleans massacre is a horrible illustration of the working of a municipal government among us at its worst. None of our cities is as badly governed as New Orleans."

A grand jury, investigating, reported that it lacked enough evidence to act. Italy withdrew her minister at Washington, and there was a little talk of war. President Benjamin Harrison termed the killings "deplorable and discreditable . . . an offense against law and humanity," but added that they had not originated in "general animosity to the Italian people." Orleanians fumed at the President's words, but when an indemnity of $25,000 was paid the matter ended.

Years of the locust, years of scant hope. Yet better times were on their way. New Orleans would rise again; in doing so it would demonstrate that quality of durability which is one of its dominant traits. It had never been a soft, malleable place. Apparently doomed to decay and squalor and obscurity, it came back.

In the 1870s the mouth of the Mississippi, the port's outlet to the world, gradually silted up. Vessels were growing bigger than ever, and they could not slide through; here was as harsh a threat as New Orleans ever faced. The answer was a towering feat of engineering, the Eads Jetties, to force the river to clear out its own passage. The port recovered; today it is again second in the United States, ever more important in its relation to Latin America.

Yellow fever—Bronze John—was beaten in 1905. Much later came the conquest of the flood danger. Almost every year the city watched with dread its levee gauges, and as recently as 1927 it was menaced by the worst flood in its history; it saved itself by breaking through a levee nearer the river mouth. Today a spillway above New Orleans can take off the water before it reaches the city, and Orleanians believe that the hazard of the Mississippi is now a thing of the past.

Throughout its history the bad drainage system has presented a recurring problem—not only a source of discomfort, but a grave risk to health. During the present century New Orleans installed what is perhaps the greatest system of pumps in the world, disposing of that problem. Then, in 1915, the town awakened to the risk of bubonic plague from thousands of rats brought in by ships and from their escaping into the older sections. A tremendous project was launched—house-to-house inspection, checking of individual premises, general cementing of floors, and other measures. It was a rat-hunt unprecedented in this country.

Freer, cleaner, healthier . . . but in the process New Orleans succeeded in retaining much of its native flavor, the inherent character that makes it *sui generis*. All this, however, belongs to the story of the later days that were often hardly less prodigal than those before them.

PART III

Lustrous Town

CHAPTER 13

Music in the Air

O NCE there was a middle-aged little woman in the French quarter, long since reconciled to spinsterhood. She had clerked, assisted a milliner, helped make Mardi Gras masks. Then in the 1870s a *cousine* gave up a confectioner's concession at the French Opera House, and allowed her to take it. Within a month the colorless spinster had become a bride, having chosen among several eager claimants. And the explanation was that the man who married her got free admission to the opera—a boon worth any sacrifice of his liberty!

To walk about the French section, then or earlier, was to find oneself in a city of music in the grand style. Melody showered the streets. From the window of this galleried house rose the notes of an aria; Madame was repeating a second-act number from last night's opera. Over there, carrying a basket of crabs on her head, a marchande sang still another solo. At that corner a light mulatto was shaking his finger: "Not a great voice, but so *charmante!*" He should know; in twenty years he had never missed a Sunday performance. And the grocer across the way nodded confirmation of the remark; he was from Palermo, and he too knew. . . .

Two stout businessmen argued: "Ah, good—yes, but not so good as La Dauterive. When I was a boy . . . that divine trill, the way she held it, two minutes—no, three! And who could ever die of consumption so well?" As he paused, up

rolled a carriage to let out the new *ténor leger.* The two men
bowed as the young singer sauntered past, head thrown back
in Byronic style. Women leaning over galleries recognized
him and thrilled with delicious excitement. To be a leading
singer, that was a thing for you, yes! Nothing he did was
private. Where did he eat? With which member of the
company was he . . . ?

All New Orleans watched the amours of the singers. What
did he see in that sow, big enough to make two of him? . . .
Guérard, she could do better than that *basse;* he looked like
a longshoreman! And the population usually understood why
a certain baritone had not appeared for a performance—
whether it was a too-hilarious evening at the lake, or a too-
pronounced scratch from a diva's nails.

Just ahead rose the gray walls of the French Opera House
itself, at Bourbon and St. Louis streets. By three-thirty in the
afternoon a few were already lined up for the *troisièmes* and
the *quatrièmes*—third and fourth levels. The opera here was
no luxury, but one of life's necessities. The housekeeper,
planning her week, might omit meat from a meal or two;
tomorrow, soup and nothing else. But seldom would she fail
to set aside the twenty-five-cent pieces for the family's visits
to the temple of music. If that were not possible . . . ah,
what would life be worth?

It did not surprise Orleanians to hear that So-and-So, awaiting a check from Paris, had gone without dinner to buy his
usual seat. A man could always eat! Then there was the old
paterfamilias who seldom went out. He dozed in the sun in
his patio; friends visited with news of those "dead on the
post." Yet when his opera evening arrived, he took out his
neat suit, unchanged through the years, and hobbled forth.
Without *l'opéra,* how much less life would mean.

Not even deep mourning, requiring a family to wear black
for a year, could keep the Creoles away. For those in mourning there were discreet *loges grillées*—secluded boxes fronted
with lattice work. Here they would enjoy the good music

and not be gaped at. Enceinte ladies sat in such boxes until
the crucial day itself. From this custom arose the familiar
story of the wife who watched a first act with delight that
gave way to apprehension: "Jean—I'm so sorry, but I cannot
stay for the ballet!" And the baby arrived in the carriage on
the way home.

In a locality in which every man considered himself a
critic, there were many potential performers. About the Opera
House lived amateurs who had complete roles at their command, who practiced the year round, hopeful of a call;
meanwhile they amused themselves by singing and talking of
opera in their friends' parlors. Even the urchins were ready
to serve; almost anyone could perform without rehearsal the
role of a street boy in *Carmen.*

Young men hung about for a chance to go on as members
of soldiers' ensembles. It meant, if nothing else, opportunity
to meet the more interesting backstage ladies. "Those ballet
girls," an elderly Creole chuckled to me, "they were so bright,
so—so sympathetic. Only when I got to know them well did
I understand why Papa had been anxious that I shouldn't!"

Old Bourbon was the opera street of New Orleans. Here
clustered dozens of shops connected directly or indirectly
with the institution; here boarded players, musicians, dancers,
and technicians. About the courtyards and restaurants sat
assistant managers, costumers, wives and sweethearts of the
singers, chattering, shouting in a half-dozen tongues. These
sparkling personages gave new relish, new variety to the
town. Regularly members of the companies liked New Orleans so well that they elected to live here, marrying and
becoming part of the community. A place that put such value
on good music, good food, good living—they found it wonderful.

A grande dame remembers a night when a pair of leading
singers entered a restaurant. They had enjoyed a triumphant
evening, she as Carmen, he as Don José. As the door opened

a young businessman spied them. He rose to his feet and bowed in their direction. An electric excitement caught the roomful of guests. The young man reached for his wine glass, lifted it; without a word, by unspoken consent, every man and woman in the room got up and joined in drinking to the two glorious ones at the door. Then the place broke into cheers and applause, and the couple took bows, kissed hands, and wiped away their tears. Could their other ovation on stage have matched this?

The music was the thing, and New Orleans had a right to be proud of its music. It could claim rank as the first American city in which opera was established on a permanent basis with a resident company.

While such performances were making a feeble struggle in New York, the opera flourished here, with performances of a completeness and splendor to match many on the Continent. The river city for a time supported two French companies, while the uptown American theatres presented visiting troupes, notably the famous Havana company; and from New Orleans went companies that toured America to rousing success, bringing grand opera to audiences that had never before heard it.

Over the years a surprising number of operas received original American presentations here, a few seasons after their Paris premières. Noel Straus has noted that when the Metropolitan Opera revived Spontini's *La Vestale* in 1925, statements were made that America was seeing it for the first time; but *La Vestale* had been introduced in New Orleans on February 17, 1828, as contemporary newspapers show. Repeatedly the musical reference books give première dates for productions in New York and other places, whereas the New Orleans performances preceded them by years. And many a European singer of highest repute came to New Orleans for one season or several and went back to the Continent without showing himself or herself in any other part of the United States.

Back in 1791 that early troupe of French refugees, bringing the professional theatre to the city, included bills of short operas as well as nonmusical productions. The early playhouses of the 1800s—the Spectacle de la Rue St. Pierre and the Théâtre St. Philippe—interspersed operas with dramatic works. After a time the gambler-impresario John Davis gave the city his commodious Théâtre d'Orléans; he is said to be the first Orleanian to go to Europe in search of singing troupes.

The Creoles took their opera straight, no cutting, no tampering. Once James Caldwell offered a production of Rossini's *Semiramide* and omitted the last act. The audience burst into rebellion, shouting, shaking fists, and throwing canes at the magnificent gas chandelier. On another night, one of mixed music and drama, an old gentleman from below Canal left the American theatre indignantly because, instead of *la belle musique*, a girl walked out and sang (as he put it) "one petite baby catch some sleep"! Yet Caldwell and his competitors did bring many opera companies that pleased the most discriminating.

By the 1820s opera was in its stride, with large companies and large orchestras. Critics were growing more appreciative; but they could also be sharp. One reproved the French management because the quality of the chorus' singing transported the audience "into a warehouse of wet-nurses accompanied by several hundred babies." Another was happy that a new singer did not, like his predecessor, "beat his flanks to get a note from his chest."

Romantic Orleanians, ever ready for a glamorous heroine, had their reward when the twenty-two-year-old Julia Calvé (no relation to the great Carmen, Emma Calvé, who sang much later) arrived in 1837 to give a new upsurge to the lyric drama. "La précieuse cantatrice," "la belle Calvé"—the journalists devised many epithets for her. Rossini had encouraged her as a child, and New Orleans went beyond Rossini. Several accounts tell of her petite figure, her magnificent head of black hair, and her eyes, described as "the most beautiful in the world."

It was Julia Calvé who took a leading role when, two years later, Meyerbeer's *Les Huguenots* was offered here for the first time, in its American première. Taxing, difficult in a dozen ways, the massive drama stirred the city as had few others; it became the opera New Orleans loved above all for nearly eighty years. Regularly the season had to open with *Les Huguenots;* the Creoles could not get enough of its pageantry and passion in the grand style.

La Calvé traveled about America; a poetic admirer implored her in print not to be "a bird of passage" but to stay always in the French city. She accepted his suggestion, establishing residence here. Soon she met Charles Boudousquie, a socially inclined businessman who took an ever-greater interest in the opera house—as well as in La Calvé. He proposed to her, and she accepted; after a time the popular Boudousquie, yielding to the lure of the opera in another way, became the manager of the institution. New Orleans applauded its beloved little star and its favorite impresario. Serene and smiling, Calvé went on to further glories, and the productions under her husband's direction reached ever higher levels.

It was during this period that the Swedish novelist Fredrika Bremer attended the Théâtre d'Orléans. She thought the stage offering "very well given," the prima donna deservedly a favorite, but the audience more interesting yet. Seated in their rows of boxes, the women presented "the appearance of a parterre of white roses." No colors were worn; the costumes were gauze-like, and the ladies had bare necks and shoulders, "some very bare indeed . . . some with flowers in their hair." The ladies were pale but not unhealthy-looking; Creoles seldom had ruddy complexions. She found that the white pearl powder commonly used by the Creoles produced a complexion of great softness; yet the art was "too frequently apparent . . . an unpleasing effect." But the Creoles can hardly have minded their Swedish critic, who herself had a long red nose and dressed in costumes like purple tents.

By and large it was an audience that liked music for itself. Its members had been trained from their youth to know and appreciate opera. They would never have tolerated those two nuisances that were later to be so characteristic of fashionable audiences—belated arrival in the middle of an act, and the chattering of box-holders that forces the true devotee to strain his ears in order to follow the music.

The opera-goers could be cruel. Repeatedly we read of some youthful singer who, making his first appearance, nervously hit a bad note. On the instant there was hissing, and the artist was ruined for New Orleans; it would be years before he dared return. True, this seems hard; but New Orleans retorted that it had been taught to appreciate the best and it wanted no apprentices.

Annually the city awaited the announcement that was a major event—the lists of operas and singers. On that morning men stopped one another, and women paid calls to discuss Boudousquie's plans. "How does the list sound?" "Will it be as good as last year's?" "My cousin in Paris likes Mademoiselle Evon. But that tenor—*mon Dieu*, a moose!" As the time approached for the arrival of the company from Europe, the press published all the details it could get. The troupe had left France; it was due next week; a reception was being planned. Hundreds went to the docks to meet the boat. And on the first few nights everyone picked favorites, ready to defend them for the season.

Feelings could flame between partisans. In 1857 a feud developed between Mesdames Colson and Bourgeois. Professor Albert L. Voss has called my attention to the spectacular situation. In April the *Daily Picayune*, in a story headed "Verdi versus Verdure, or the Battle of the Bouquets," told of "a performance the like of which we have never before witnessed on any boards." The opera was *Il Trovatore*, with Colson as Leonora and Bourgeois as the gypsy Azucena, and most of the French town seems to have turned up in order to applaud the rival stars. Before Azucena had even finished her first aria, her supporters had started "a horticultural exposition that lasted at spasmodic intervals throughout the evening." With Leonora the effect was the same, if not more flowery, and also louder. Verdi, it was then remarked, composed "some of the loudest music that the modern school of Italian opera can boast," but from that moment onward the orchestra and the singers could barely be heard above the demonstrations.

Bravos and bravas broke from galleries, pits, and boxes. Hands clapped, canes pounded, and men called "Hi-hi" for unbroken minutes at a time. No matter what either of the singers did, she was applauded. Action was interrupted, practically forgotten, as bouquet after bouquet fell on stage. "Like Proserpine, gathering flowers, herself a fairer flower," the two rivals swept back and forth, delightedly picking up their gifts. Other members of the cast became supernumerary stage cleaners, everyone from noble to page boy helping carry off bushels of tributes.

When the curtain fell on the third act, all of the fragrant ammunition had been used up; but partisans ran out to raid flower-sellers, shops, and the homes of friends living nearby, with the result that by the opening of the final act the theatre resembled a garden. There came a brief silence, during which a bit of Verdi could be heard; then with Leonora's aria, a bouquet dropped like a shot, to be followed by another and another in unending fire through all the scene. At the climax it was "a fusillade, a battery, a bombardment."

The last scene was the gypsy's. Azucena had hardly reached the final phrase of her aria before the floral storm fell upon her. She was supposed next to take her rest on a bench in her cell. Catching up some of her flowers, she placed them there, then "lay down to sleep, literally, on her laurels"! When her rival, Leonora, entered, *her* admirers had no more tributes left, but they made up for this in pounding, shouting, bawling. The gallant Troubadour sang unheard through his role; the other players went through theirs—appealed, defied, and died, all in dumb show. "Verdure had won, and Verdi was nowhere."

Ten days later, even this spectacle was outdone. This time, no mere flowers could express the audience's love for La Bourgeois; the hearers arrived equipped with more potent weapons. As the gypsy hit a high note, a heavy *crack* echoed through the audience—a torpedo! Another, and then throughout the rest of the evening burst detonation on detonation. The theatre filled with smoke. The action on the stage was obscured, but the crowd was expressing its feeling for the evening's Azucena. At the end there followed another indication of regard—"a casket containing a thousand-dollar diamond bracelet and a splendid diamond ring." Again, toujours la Nouvelle Orléans!

This same rivalry brought death to at least one man, narrow escapes to others more fortunate. La Bourgeois was due a benefit, and she picked Victor Massé's *Galatée*. It was expected that—as was customary—the role of the statue-come-to-life would be assigned to the other star, La Colson. Mme. Bourgeois, however, picked Mme. Préti-Baille, a former member of the company who had recently been replaced by La Colson. The situation held several kinds of dynamite; anger spread, half the city apparently feeling that Mme. Préti-Baille ought not to appear, the other half insisting that she must. Indignant partisans announced that on the night of the performance they would hiss the Galatea.

Several young Creoles met informally to discuss the situation. One of them turned to Emile Bozonnier: Where did he stand in the matter?

"Anybody," replied Bozonnier promptly, "who goes to a theatre to hiss a woman is a blackguard and ought to be slapped."

Another of the group, one Gaston de Coppens, glared at

the speaker. "Are you aware," he demanded, "that *I'm* one of those who will go and hiss that woman?"

"I wasn't—but the fact won't make me change what I said." With which the two let the issue rest for the time being.

The night of the benefit brought out a large and nervous audience. There was furious applause for Préti-Baille, and there were furious hisses. The performance ended in a riot. Outside, after it was over, Bozonnier and Coppens met. Coppens asked, "And what about that slap?" He got it—and the inevitable consequence was that the two faced each other on the field. Though badly injured, Bozonnier survived. A short time later the *Daily Delta*'s critic, Emile Hiriart, depreciated La Bourgeois' admirers, was challenged by several of them, and agreed to meet them in turn. The first two matches were not fatal; in the third the critic killed his opponent.

In 1859, a dispute over a few hundred dollars resulted in the most notable single event in the history of New Orleans opera. A new owner, on acquiring the Théâtre d'Orléans, increased its rent. Manager Boudousquie protested, but in vain. Then he asked himself: Why not a new house, the finest in the country? Proceeding to prompt action, he formed a company and called on the architect, Pouilly, builder of the St. Louis Hotel. This was in March, and Boudousquie wanted the great building ready for the winter season. Pouilly called the deadline ridiculous, and refused to undertake the task.

The manager then went to James Gallier, Jr., thirty-two-year-old son of the man who had built the St. Charles Hotel, the Pontalba Buildings, and City Hall; and Gallier promised to finish the project in time. Within a month the contracts were signed. Men worked day and night in shifts; the city permitted great bonfires to be built at the corner as a help to evening operations. On time, by November 28, the architect delivered "the lyric temple of the South."

The French Opera House was a plastered brick structure

of Italian design, four stories high. On gala occasions 2500 persons could be fitted in, though normally there was space for only some 2000. Many termed it America's best-designed opera house, especially because it was so planned as to afford a clear view of the stage from any seat. The ground floor (*parquet*) had upholstered armchairs, and this same principle of comfort ruled through most of the house. Above the first floor rose four gracefully curved tiers of boxes and seats.

The four stage boxes (*loges d'avant-scène*) were prize possessions. And the lower floor had other boxes, partitioned, called *baignoires* (bathtubs) because they were shaped much like the upright tub of the time. Above spread the *corbeille*, the lustrous horseshoe with its fifty-two stalls, twenty *loges grillées* (covered for those who wanted privacy), and *loges découvertes* (uncovered ones). The *secondes* or second balcony had loges, with seats behind them; the *troisièmes* or third balcony had only seats. Last of all were the *quatrièmes*, the steep fourth balcony, which had only benches. Though someone christened it *Paradis*—for obvious reasons—the waggish applied the term *poulailler*, chicken coop!

The coloring was soft white, red, and gold. The main entrance outside projected over the banquette, with pillars to the curbstone. Two broad flights of stairs led to the foyer, hung with chandeliers and great mirrors that were the ultimate in opulence. On December 1, 1859, the doors were flung apart for Rossini's *William Tell* and the next day's newspapers described the women in *grande toilette*, the visits between boxes, the drinking of champagne in private parlors behind the boxes. One of the great opera houses of the world had begun its career.

It was a highly successful year. The second season had barely started, however, when M. Boudousquie was groaning over a procession of mishaps. By this time his wife, La Calvé, had retired, and he was in desperate need of a star. Some accounts say that his prima donna had jumped blithely on a chair and broken her leg; others, that the lady proved to have a bad voice. Disaster impended—until Boudousquie bethought himself of a slim, dark Italian girl, not yet eighteen, of whom he had heard and whom he had been considering.

At the moment, Adelina Patti looked like a questionable asset—a former child prodigy who might wear badly. (Most child prodigies do.) Both her parents had been opera singers, and the black-eyed girl had heard music from birth. The large family—all of them either sang or played some instrument—had encountered difficulties during the first years after they had come to America, and their possessions had often gone to the pawnshop. When Adelina was only six she was one day sitting and listening to an older sister's struggles with a taxing exercise. "But why don't you do it *this* way?" the child suggested—and proceeded to demonstrate, astounding the others with her rich voice. By the next year she was being helped up onto a table in a public hall to sing for the assemblage. Then she was taken on tours, alternating concerts and sessions with her dolls.

The Pattis prospered on their prodigy's earnings. For about five years they retired her for rest and growth; then in 1859, making her debut as Lucia at the New York Academy of Music, Adelina scored handsomely. A year later the family aimed for Europe, and sent her to New Orleans as a way point. And now, in desperation, Boudousquie turned to the girl. Word had spread that she had a good voice, but when Adelina went on stage that first night the applause was merely polite; New Orleans had to be shown.

Then, as the first rare notes poured out, men and women looked at one another in amazement, and the bravas resounded. In the foyer the excitement exploded: Such tones, such smoothness, such liquid quality—and plenty of volume, too! New Orleans had its star, the glorious flowering bud of a Patti; and the season was made.

Quickly Adelina went on to her next role, and the next. She was signed for more performances; Havana allowed her to cancel scheduled appearances, and again her engagement was extended. Then, finally, she sailed away to win the world's applause. But New Orleans would never forget the part it had played in her making. It could exult when it heard Verdi's answer to the request to name his three favorite *prime donne:* "First, Adelina; second, Adelina; third, Adelina!"

Back to New Orleans, several times, came the Patti whom the world now considered its greatest singer. She was no longer the lean, intent child of 1861; now there was wisdom and calm satisfaction in those shining black eyes. Also, she was a great lady, an international figure. Most important of all, the voice had become only more golden, only more velvety.

She did something that few other singers have managed: for decades she preserved her opulent powers. Though she could sing Wagner, she wisely did not; and never did she use her voice more than two or three times a week. As for rehearsals, she never attended them. Once, touching her throat, she told another singer: "What comes out here never goes in again."

Adelina showed herself shrewd in other directions, too. She knew her value and was prepared to get it. For a time she received $5000 a performance, "payable in advance,"—a fee that few singers could command today. A single tour netted her a half-million dollars; the manager said he had lost money, but that was hardly Adelina's concern. And Adelina, who had once worked to redeem the family's pawned possessions, in time became the richest singer in the world.

On her first return to New Orleans her career was approaching its zenith. The city, applauding vociferously, recalled the ardent girl of those earlier days; and many begged permission to call and kiss her hand. Then she went on to other successes in London, Paris, St. Petersburg. She was married three times—to the Marquis de Caux, equerry to Napoleon III, to the handsome tenor Nicolini who had been

Radames to her Aïda, and finally to the Baron Cederström of Sweden. As the century moved into its last decades she was becoming hardly more than a name to younger opera-goers. From her castle in Wales, where she had her own theatre, she often emerged to sing in opera or concert; for she refused to "retire."

In 1904 New Orleans heard Adelina again. By this time she had been before the public longer than any other vocalist in history; eventually she was to count a full fifty-seven years in her professional career. But not even the careful Adelina could hold back time forever. She was now sixty-one and she was making herself ridiculous with one "farewell concert" after another—so many that managers took to advertising her appearances as "positively farewell," none of them quite believing the adverb. (Indeed, it was ten years after this, in 1914, that she made what was actually her last appearance, at a Red Cross benefit in London's Albert Hall.)

Now, as she advanced to the footlights and faced her New Orleans audience, it was not the same Adelina, or the same voice. A handsome woman, yes, skilfully made up; a voice handled adroitly, with the art of a great technician. But only a thinning trickle of sound issued; the pearllike tones were gone. Though her arias and ensemble numbers were cautiously transposed to "favor" her limitations, she still missed occasionally. New Orleans reflected that it had been a long time—from 1861 to 1904. Some few could recall that first appearance, and they sighed. A New Orleans legend had passed. . . .

For the opera itself, there were good seasons and bad. The early 1860s, when war gripped the city, were no years for music. As soon as hostilities ended, however, an Italian troupe arrived in 1866 to grateful applause. A new director, Alhaiza, prepared for a gala season. With considerable effort he arranged for a company of fifty-seven members. Newspapers carried the happy news that the singers had arrived in New

York, then that they had left for New Orleans on the steamer *Evening Star*.

Within a week the editors were staring appalled at stop-press dispatches. In a hurricane off the Georgia coast, the *Evening Star* had sprung a leak. Of the nearly 275 aboard, only a few were saved. Every one of the artists had drowned, and with them James Gallier, Sr., father of the Opera House architect. Few other tragedies have so deeply affected the city. The opera people had always been close to its heart; and now this sudden and terrible thing! There was public mourning, and the rival house—the old Théâtre d'Orléans—closed in tribute.

A month later a second blow struck the city. The Théâtre d'Orléans itself burned down. Hastily the French Opera picked up artists from several sources, and managed to put on a successful season. The following years were rewarding; opera had come again into its own, a core of latter-day Creole life. Though the French Orleanians had suffered badly in the war, any who could scrape together the means to buy a seat seldom failed to attend.

The French Opera House had manifold uses, being the gathering place for a hundred causes, benefit performances, mass meetings, and receptions for honored visitors. In 1888 a visitor decided: "It is a theatre built by Frenchmen for Frenchmen, after the old, old French style. There is not a modern suggestion in any of its appointments. Foyer and greenroom, parlor and restaurant, staircase and stalls and boxes conspire in their curious arrangement and relations to convince the visitor that he has suddenly been transported to a theatre of the last century."

Here the Carnival organizations staged their balls. Here society grasped its sceptre firmly. Here the débutante made her bow to society; though there were to be parties and suppers given for her, this appearance was the heart of her first season. If the family could afford it, she wore a Paris gown;

if not, a gown from a New Orleans modiste. Add long white
gloves, a fan, and, invariably, a bouquet with hanging rib-
bons—and she was ready. As the family drew up in its carriage before the Opera House, and a Negro attendant helped
her out, many eyes watched in the light of the gas jets. Her
more intimate friends pushed forward. "Ah, chérie, so soon!
It seems like only yesterday that you went to sleep in our
box!" "Marie, if only m'mère were here to see!"

The family moved slowly up the stairway. A commotion
arose behind them as a large group alighted from one of the
horse-drawn cars—a special "opera car" with its excited and
voluble Creoles. Here, too, was Mrs. Samuel Delgado, a
grande dame who would soon preside in her great box. White-
haired, bright-humored, she dressed usually in pastel satins,
pinks and blues, and wore plumed hats; for the opera she
donned flowers, jewels, and her whitest white. Since she
found it impossible to walk up the long staircase, two men
carried her in the chair that had been brought in her carriage.

The débutante reached her family's box. From several
directions they acknowledged the waving of hands, the nodding of ornamented heads. On all sides the scene showed little
change from that of earlier years—the women's dark hair, roses
and camellias against the combs, satiny shoulders, quick gestures. From below, a bell sounded, lights were lowered, and
the first notes of the overture rang out.

One observer decided that nothing showed the power of
music so eloquently as the face of a Creole girl at the opera;
he described "the nervous twitch of the hand that grasps the
railing in front of her box, the glow in her eye, the heightened
color of her cheeks, the rapid change of expression, responsive
to the change from joy to sorrow in the hero, gladness to
lamentation in the music."

When the lights went up, however, the débutante had more
than music to think of. She must not miss the signs of recogni-
tion from any dowager; she must look gay and entertaining

and also entertained; she must try discreetly to attract every young man she had ever met. The last purpose was, momentarily, the most important in life. Would she be a belle, or merely "tapestry along the wall" like the ladies observed years ago by the Duke of Saxe-Weimar? The older generation had its eyes on her. "Her grand'mère would never have had a half-empty box like that!" "Pretty, but she does not seem so popular, *hein?*". . .

To the débutante's relief there soon approached two male cousins, and Oncle Théo, who kissed her hands. There, *Dieu merci*, her brother had found three unattached youths. . . . This went on for three intermissions, with sips of wine, bonbons, many bows. In the background, a little tearful, sat Maman, who remembered her own début. Toward the end, tension lifted; the daughter was really enjoying herself. It hadn't been so bad, had it? She had come through with a crowd of admirers; she was launched.

Shining years alternated with duller ones, reorganizations, new starts; for the most part, the standards seem to have been maintained. Through the years New Orleans could point to these American premières, a few from a long list:

At the Théâtre d'Orléans

Donizetti—*Lucrezia Borgia*, February 27, 1834
  Lucia di Lammermoor, May 28, 1841
  L'Élisir d'amore, March 30, 1842
  La Favorita, February 9, 1843 (New York première, June 25, 1845, was by a New Orleans troupe.)
  Don Pasquale, January 7, 1845
  Les Martyrs, March 24, 1846
Halévy—*La Juive*, February 3, 1844
Meyerbeer—*Le Prophète*, April 1, 1850
Spontini—*La Vestale*, February 17, 1828 (Philadelphia, so-called American première, October 10, 1828, was by this New Orleans troupe.)

At the French Opera House

Meyerbeer—*Dinorah, or The Pardon of Ploërmel,* with Patti,
    March 4, 1861
Thomas—*Mignon,* May 9, 1871
Lalo—*Le Roi d'Ys,* January 23, 1890
Massenet—*Hérodiade,* February 13, 1892
Saint-Saëns—*Samson et Dalila,* January 4, 1893
Gounod—*La Reine de Saba,* January 12, 1899
Giordano—*Siberia,* January 13, 1906

Some of these dates show New Orleans premières in cases
in which New York has claimed precedence, usually at later
dates; they differ with a number of dates given in musical
encyclopedias. Comparatively little research, however, has
been done in the story of the New Orleans opera, and the
facts given above are from actual records of performances
and from reviews which appeared in the newspapers the day
after the performance.

And in New Orleans took place the débuts of singers who
later won fame in Europe or New York: Riccardo Martin;
Constantino, who came to New Orleans almost unknown and
went on to New York, where the Met and the Manhattan
sought him, the latter winning; Clotilde Bressler-Gianoli; and
Emmy Fursch-Madi. This list, too, is long, and old Creoles
still grow ecstatic over the memories of this one and that.
The community itself produced a number of distinguished
conductors and composers, and from the 1820s until almost
the end of the century New Orleans troupes toured the country, giving performances in New York as in other places.

Until well into the present century the city retained its
electric enthusiasm for opera. There was, for instance, that
dazzling hour in 1909, which still brings tears to the eyes of
old men who recall it. In *Trovatore* the tenor Escalais, who
had long been a leading tenor at the Paris Opera, came to the
great aria, "Supplice infame," with its three possible high C's.

In rare voice, Escalais went through the number magnificently; the audience shouted and stamped. He took his bows, then resumed his position for an encore. Again he went through the aria, and again he hit every one of the high C's—better, perhaps more richly, than the previous time. Again the audience broke out; the ovation seemed unparalleled. Then he stepped forward a little and people held their breaths. He was going to try it a third time! Yet again rose the taxing notes, each as full as before. Another storm of applause; and for a fourth time the man began the solo! A deep silence fell, and spines tingled. New Orleans history was being made; here was something that they could tell their children. When Escalais finished, men and women jumped to their feet. The reception must have been intoxicating, the greatest, perhaps, of Escalais' life. And then, as the experts gasped at the tenor's daring, he lifted his hand—and sang the aria a fifth time! Not once did he dodge or slur; in all he had hit fifteen high C's, in a glorious demonstration of power and control.

This was news; the next day the *Times-Democrat* and the *Daily Picayune* carried the story in stirring terms. "Wonders of the tenor voice have never before been so marvelously demonstrated . . . an ovation in every sense of the word, and one justly deserved." A Creole descendant of today recalls that evening: "We were children then, and in bed, when Papa burst in. From the hall downstairs, he shouted to us, and he kept on shouting as he climbed the steps. We thought something tragic had happened, and we ran to him. There he was, his face red, his voice breaking; 'Fifteen high C's, I tell you—fifteen!' " All over the French section, men and women were telling of that immortal episode.

Slowly the Opera House fell on bad times. The French quarter declined; certain Creoles attended religiously, but their playhouse was like some of them—dimmed, worn, old-fashioned. The younger people preferred a different kind of en-

tertainment. Each season cost a greater effort, and now and
then a year went by without any opera at all. The chief handicap was increasing expenses. Roused by the threat of bubonic
plague, the city authorities ordered an extensive overhauling
of all floors in the old section—which included the Opera
House. Then Carnival organizations, on which the Opera's
managers were depending more and more for revenue, demanded reductions in the management's charges. Finally, the
September of 1915 brought a devastating storm that left the
structure in worse condition than ever.

Overnight a savior appeared; William Ratcliffe Irby purchased the building and presented it to Tulane University,
with funds for its restoration. With the ending of World War
I a new season was announced, and it began bravely. Old
faces returned, and many younger ones turned up. An effort
was initiated to make the city see what was being brought
back—the grace and zest, the tragedy and high comedy of
the grand style in opera. On December 3, 1919, *Les Huguenots* was offered again—that beloved favorite, played so many
times, applauded by so many Orleanians through the years.

Early the next morning someone smelled smoke. The Opera
House was ablaze. There was little chance of saving it. The
fire ate at the stage and the dressing-rooms, the brilliant
horseshoe, the second and third and fourth levels. Cornices
crashed, sixty-foot sections toppled. Half of New Orleans
must have gone there during the morning and through the
day of December 4. As a boy of nine, I was taken to the
scene; I remember the steaming wreckage, and my surprise
that the ladies with the odd foreign accents were crying so
hard. This one had been the company's Delilah, that one the
Gilda. This singer had lost jewels in her dressing-room, that
one a complete wardrobe.

But New Orleans had lost more than that—a glory that
might never return.

In recent years the city has seen a renaissance of music,

concerts, and symphony programs, with a New Orleans civic orchestra; more music is heard, perhaps, than ever before. The New Orleans Opera House Association has succeeded admirably; and again there is talk of rebuilding the grand old place. More than one Orleanian will die happier if this comes about.

CHAPTER 14

The Bright Lights of Storyville

THEY were coming to New Orleans—more of them than in the old days—to point, to be shocked, and to ogle. The dozens of worth-while sights naturally included Basin Street. Or you could call it the Tenderloin, the Tango Belt, Storyville—it had several names; in the 1890s you knew that all of them denoted America's greatest "restricted district." Nowhere else was there anything quite like it; a broad rectangle, legally created, legally maintained, which had (as they told you) "everything."

"Everything" ranged from mansionlike establishments with mirrored ceilings, oil paintings, and a charge of $50 a night, to the individual girl who roamed the streets with a carpet on her back and charged a quarter. It was estimated that from one to two thousand women practiced in the district, and that many times that number of persons lived off the business—collecting rent, serving food and drink, playing music. In all parts of the city, including those eminently respectable uptown residential areas, reputable citizens grew richer on the proceeds of district property. Year in, year out, the rent was probably the most assured in the city. Once when a delegation of informers called on the mayor with a protest, he summed up New Orleans' attitude toward the problem of the restricted district: "You can make it illegal, maybe. But you can't make it unpopular!"

New Orleans had seldom tried very hard even to make it illegal. From the early days it insured a supply of informal
companions for visiting sailors—barmaids, dancers, friends of
the evening. In any case, the town had inherited the traditional French attitude: Human beings were human beings—
why not let them indulge their natural propensities with a
minimum of fuss? Planters, it was said, rented out particularly
interesting mulatto girls at $20 or so a month. The poor man
had his waterfront dives. And soon more opulent bordellos
were being established for the wealthy; why penalize a man
just because he is rich, Monsieur?

As the American régime opened, stricter local regulations
were adopted, aimed not at suppressing the prostitutes but
rather at preventing them from creating breaches of the peace.
They must not, for instance, go out to drinking places, but
must stay at home and let business come to them. In the 1840s
and '50s alert businessmen arranged with city officials to
create bagnios near the big hotels, the St. Louis and St.
Charles, and several were set up on Poydras Street near a
church.

It was before the war, in 1857, that licensing was first attempted. If a madame paid $250 a year for a license, and a
girl paid $100, they could operate anywhere above the first
floor of their house; in prescribed areas they could work on
the first floor as well. But the professionals called any licensing, any special areas, unfair and discriminatory; and the
courts held it unconstitutional. Even then certain politicos
were considering establishing a restricted area, and had their
eyes on Basin Street, a small thoroughfare that paralleled
Rampart Street, along the French section, and above it across
Canal Street.

Suddenly several three-storied mansions were built on Basin
Street. Good residents, wondering, soon learned their purpose. Wagons brought heavy furniture, statuary, and mirrors,
this equipment being followed by thoroughly painted women,
each accompanied by her stable of girls. When neighbors

protested to City Hall, they got nowhere. The biggest of the places had been put up by a ranking police official, a recorder, and certain members of the council; additional authorities were probably connected with the other houses. Canny investors, recognizing a trend, bought Basin Street property for themselves, and the quieter residents moved out. The licensing attempt had failed, but Basin had begun to thrive.

The city as a whole heard increasingly about the street, through gaudy madames such as Hattie Hamilton with her bawdy house called Twenty-One. Her "friend" was Senator James Beares. Hattie had been a respectable housewife in Havana until her businessman-husband discovered her affiliation with a widely known call house. A change was indicated for Hattie; after varied adventures, she wound up in New Orleans with her senator. The senator recommended her place to his friends and constituents. Hattie kept it well, and her clientele (and the senator's) were well pleased.

On a May evening of 1870, the senator and Hattie drank together for hours at Twenty-One. The Negro butler heard a shot. Going in, he found the senator dead with a bullet in his stomach, and Hattie with a gun in her hand. The efficient butler summoned the senator's brother—and when the police arrived there was no gun. Hattie went to the station house, but thanks to the brother's efforts she was released without questioning. The police charged the butler as an accessory; but presently he, too, went free. Both he and Hattie knew a great deal too much.

Hattie's Twenty-One declined, and the leadership in the profession passed to Kate Townsend, with her Basin Street establishment a half square above Canal, on the site where years later the Elks' Club was to be built. Giving Kate her due, a newspaper said she "reigned as queen of the frail sisterhood for many years, and was probably known in every quarter of the land." Contemporaries estimated that it had cost $100,000 to build and furnish her place, with its red velvet hangings and hand-painted tables. In Kate's own room the bed hangings were of lace, "an exquisite basket of flowers hung from the tester," and the chamber-pot was inlaid with gold.

Early and late, Kate insisted on refinement. Her girls must act and talk like the *haut monde;* Kate claimed that they were as cultivated as anybody in town. Whether cultivated or not, they and Kate thrived. She grew enormously fat; even when carefully "placed" in her corsets, she bulked inordinately. Nevertheless she remained handsome. "Her face always wore a smile, and as she was known to be very wealthy, she was much sought after."

Kate had her sweet man, Troisville Sykes, known as "Bill." As often happened, the big woman liked a little man. "Bill," member of a well-established family, was short, narrow, anemic, a mild fellow but no fool. Kate "mistreated him cruelly," slapping him to the floor, throwing him out, then taking him back. In the early '80s Kate's place declined as competition grew more pronounced. Kate turned moody and developed an obsession; repeatedly she told listeners that one of these days she would cut Bill open.

And "one of these days" eventually arrived. Returning from a drinking party, Kate shouted for her man. But he had locked himself in his room and Kate staggered off. A day or so later, when she had sobered, Bill went to her. Apparently, however, she had not quite recovered her temper. A banging noise and a series of screams brought the girls out of their rooms. They heard Kate's black-and-tan dog barking angrily inside. As they stood there, Bill emerged, his clothing ripped and bloodied. "Well, she's gone," he said, almost casually. "I had to do it." The little man showed them a nine-inch bowie knife and a heavy pruning shears, both heavily coated with blood. "She drew the knife and I took it away. She pulled the scissors and I used them on her." He was as mild as ever; even his regret lacked emphasis.

The news spread fast, and hundreds gathered to stare at the enormous Kate, stretched out on her big bed with the lace bar and the basket of flowers hanging from the tester. The dog was now whining in the corner. At the funeral—a grand affair—the girls passed champagne, because Kate had said she would want it that way. A jury, trying "Bill" Sykes for murder, set him free. Then, no less mildly than before, he produced Kate's will, signed ten years earlier and leaving everything to him—an estate worth $82,000. But officials remembered the law (aimed partly at mulatto mistresses) that allowed only a fraction of an estate to go to a person who had lived in "open concubinage" with the deceased. When the lawyers finished, Bill got less than $50; the little man's sweetness to big Kate had netted him almost nothing.

Matters were getting out of hand; questionable houses were springing up all over the city. In 1897 Alderman Sidney Story, a respected businessman, on completing a study of restricted districts in Europe, proposed for New Orleans the formation of a single red-light area. Despite sharp criticism, such an area was staked out covering thirty-eight squares around Basin Street. The girls themselves objected; so did owners of houses in other vicinities, who would be losing their rents. Nevertheless the Louisiana Supreme Court upheld the city. This was the genesis of "Storyville"—for, no matter how vigorously Mr. Story protested, the area got his name and kept it.

From everywhere, by boat and train, the women flocked to Storyville. Most of the nonprofessionals moved out of the district. For blocks there stretched unbroken lines of cafés, saloons, flop-houses, gambling places—and the houses themselves. Thousands of people were presently sharing in the business, one way or another. Among all of them grew up a certain feeling of kinship; they were the Tenderloin, and the world outside led a separate life unrelated to theirs. "Anything you like, Mister, any way you like it."

Basin Street itself had the richest spread of houses. Here carriages drew up before hitching posts; doormen in livery had the establishment's name embroidered on their sleeves.

Maids took the caller's name, and a diamond-hung madame emerged: "Ike, have you been sick? We've all been wondering." Or: "I'm afraid we haven't met. Oh, the judge sent you?" In several places, a caller felt out of place if he did not wear evening attire, for in the damask-draped drawing-room sat girls in ballroom dress, and before making a choice he was expected to buy drinks for all. Prices were four or five dollars a bottle for champagne; beer, a dollar.

Next morning he rose to find his shirt freshly starched, suit pressed, breakfast ready. All the conveniences of home, said the irreverent, and a lot more fun. If he were particularly well off, or a high politician, the client could take over a house for the night, invite his friends. Everything on me, boys. . . . A number of these houses extended credit, and a customer properly vouched for could run up a large bill. The madames knew New Orleans; well-placed female impresarios could call up banker friends and "get a credit line on anybody."

Gaudier places installed the new electric lights, stained-glass windows, awnings over the banquettes. Inside was splendor in the manner of the '90s—heavy velvets, ottomans, love seats, draped alcoves, embroidered pillows, and pictures of shepherds, the President, and Shakespeare. All the elegance you could ask, with the Bard thrown in.

Appealing to local pride, a few madames noted that by giving preference to home-town girls they were providing employment for countless deserving natives. One of them boasted that none would "hear any foul language in my house—not a word he wouldn't want used before his wife and blessed tots." In flush times the really high-class establishments could afford women entertainers who did "nothing else" but sing or dance, though normally the staff had to double in skills. In some instances houses issued cut-rate serial books; pay a lump sum, then for weeks simply tear off a ticket for each visit.

With a flourish houses announced that they had just gotten new girls who had "royal blood," or were at least members of the nobility—traveling incognito, of course. Competitors hooted, and frequently proved that the so-called countess was only a can-can girl from Philadelphia, or that the princess had been a "living statue" who had played New Orleans a season ago. A "Lady Estelle" was once presented wearing a tiny mask; because of her high birth, she was "shy," it was explained. This worked until a customer, recognizing a mole, exposed her as Maggie Johanssen, who a few years back had been charging two dollars down the street.

One mulatto girl, calling herself an Indian, Minnie Haha, direct descendant of Longfellow's heroine, displayed as proof of her claim an oil painting labeled "Mr. and Mrs. Hiawatha, Minnie Haha's Ancestors." An especially ingenious madame advertised that at her place could be found a few women of good social position who, wanting pin-money, were ready to meet strange gentlemen. She picked her customers with care and for years afterward blackmailed them successfully. But the height of something was reached by the madame who offered, as a truly unique experience, a mother and her daughter for the same visit.

To stay in business some women operators adopted novel business techniques, flooding the town with engraved cards and merchandise lists, or distributing to the offices of selected "friends" eloquent notices of specials they "couldn't afford to miss." An elderly Orleanian told me how, as a young man, he used to wonder why his employer, on receiving a certain kind of message, would look around quickly and then dart out. Presently the younger man found the explanation; by error he opened one himself. It offered an opportunity: If the employer wished, he would be the first to know a girl who was half-Greek, half-Chinese. The Orleanian chuckled: "I didn't show that letter to the boss. I went around myself."

There were less tinseled places: middle-range ones, lower ones, and two or three varieties of the lowest. Along side streets, especially Franklin and St. Louis, thrived the cheapest—

one-storied wooden cribs, rows of single rooms in each of which waited a bureau, a bed, and a woman. The law forbade her to sit on her steps "in indecent posture," and she was not supposed to accost. Still, when trade was bad she and others moved to doors and windows and called out: "Hey, Mister, I wanna ask you somethin'." Or: "Wanna good time, Papa?"

One low roof might cover a row of fifteen or twenty cribs. A surviving record shows that an owner's agent collected $3.50 a night from each girl, in advance. If he had put a crib to any other use it might have brought in perhaps $8.oo a month.

Not far off, on various rows and alleys, any man who strolled by risked not only his possessions but also his life. A half-dozen women would come out to snatch his hand, each trying to pull him into her room. One might grab his hat, and he would have to follow her to get it back. If he did not follow, three or four others caught him, and in he would go. He might have his mouth pulled open and the liquor poured in. In any case he wound up with pockets picked and the memory of a curious experience.

Law or no law, dozens of prostitutes walked the street. These were older women, flabby, brawling, offering themselves for a half-dollar or less; having no place to take their customers to, they used sidewalk or alley for appointments. It was along such a street that an Orleanian, passing one evening, was accosted by a Mexican girl. He asked how old she was. "Fo'teen, Mister." He shook his head and started off. She called out: "Too old? I got a friend inside—she's thirteen!"

After dark something was happening every minute in the district. Pianos banged and women yelled, gambling wheels rolled and bartenders pacified drunks. Above it all hovered the smells of beer, cheap whisky, and perfume. Up and down the streets moved boldly dressed men, looking for customers for their girls or keeping check on those who went in and out. In the saloons sat fancy men, waiting until the hour came

for the girls to close the shutters, when they could join them
again.

To their "representatives," the girls and the madames had
to make the right payments. A place could be raided for dis-
turbances, and failure to pay off was certainly "disturbance"
of a kind. Ward leaders, precinct officers, higher-ups—each
took his cut. At the bottom was the flatfoot on his weekly
rounds; regardless of whether business was bad or good,
every girl must pay him anywhere from two bits to a dollar.
Orleanians remember how, as they passed, they spied incon-
spicuous piles of silver, at the edge of the outer stairs, which
nobody touched except the peeler. Want to get thrown in
the can?

New Orleans now had a "second mayor," Tom Anderson,
King of Storyville. Tom had started at the bottom. A bright-
faced, well-built lad, he knew his way about at an early age.
People liked him; when he said a thing, he meant it and
carried it out. An enterprising boy, he did favors for friends,
worked his way in with the politicians. Getting on, he
opened two café-saloons, "The Real Thing" on North Rampart Street, and "The Stag" on Gravier.

Attending to these businesses and watching his chances,
Tom Anderson gained in political repute. City Hall turned
over to him various matters to be handled in and around the
district; he handled them well, and was given further duties.
He became an important figure in his ward, and eventually
he had a glittering new place, his "Arlington Annex"—saloon,
restaurant, and general headquarters of the district. "The
Mayor's Office," it was christened, and Tom was pleased.
By now City Hall was giving him carte blanche; jokesters
called the district "Anderson's County."

Tom saw that things ran smoothly, without waste, and
above all quietly. The district was organized as never before;
Tom passed on everything from obstreperous bawds to the
employing of Negro musicians. Visitors to the section,

whether sightseers or not, paid their first call at Tom's place, to watch the tight-lipped men who scurried in and out with messages for the boss; the pimps and their girls; youths with slicked-down hair on their first trip down the line; older hands known to every madame.

Tom called them all by their first names, from hustler to trombonist, from beer runner to specialist in provocative dances on mirror-hung platforms, given for aging men's delight. He knew who was arriving in the district next week, and who was on the way out and why. The moustachioed "mayor" was gaining in girth and assurance. Never talkative, he grew only more silent with the years. When he spoke, however, the district hopped to it.

One day Tom met a police reporter, Billy Struve, a non-writing journalist who got facts that no one else could get; mere writers did the rest. Billy knew things about everyone in town, they said, and told a lot of them. Tom Anderson offered him three times what his paper could pay him, and now Billy was working for Tom, as majordomo—his eyes and ears.

It was Billy Struve who handled one of Tom's sidelines, a heavy-paying one, the *Blue Book* of the district, a Who's Who of girls and madames, with addresses, phone numbers, and comment. The madames advertised in it, and so did bars, restaurants, breweries, bath-houses, laundries, pawnshops, and a lawyer or two. A new edition was issued every year, with photographs of interiors, parlors, and bedrooms. According to the *Blue Book* itself, it was aimed at "the man who wants to be a thoroughbred rounder." "To know a thing or two, and know it direct, go through this little book, and when you go on a 'lark' you will know the best places to spend time and money." Every man should own it, "because it puts the stranger on a proper grade or path, as to where to go and be secure from hold-ups, brace games or other illegal practices usually worked on the unwise in Red Light districts." Here are a few entries:

May Evans. One woman among the fair sex who is regarded as a jolly good fellow, who is always laughing and making all those around her likewise. While nothing is too good for May, she is clever to all who come in contact with her. The signal of May's mansion is *All the way.*

Dorothy Denning. Known as the "idol" of society and club boys, and needs but little introduction, as she is known by the elite from New York to California for her wit and loveliness.

Grace Lloyd. Comes of that good old English stock from across the waters; she regards life as life, and not as a money-making space of time. Miss Lloyd is also known for the grand and rare collection of Art Tapestry.

Tessie Gordon. Petite Marietta or Tessie, as she is better known by the boys, is a fascinating little brunette who hails from Havana. There is "class" to Tessie. She greets all her visitors with a quaint, Oriental dignity, gives them the "glad hand" and a pleasant "How do you do."

Floro Randella, better known as "Snooks," the Italian beauty. A visit will teach more than pen can describe.

Vivian Stone. Where swell men can be socially entertained by an array of swell ladies. Miss Stone is above all things a favorite with the boys—what one might say, those of the clubs. Vivian is contemplating having an annex added to her present home, as her popularity has gained so that she cannot accommodate her friends.

Jean Carlton. Located so that the most particular person in the world can reach it without being seen by anyone.

The Firm. Noted for its selectness. Everybody must be of some importance, otherwise he cannot gain admittance.

Diana and Norma. Their names have become known on both continents, because everything goes as it will, and those who cannot be satisfied there must surely be of a queer nature.

Margaret Bradford. While still young in years, has nevertheless proved herself a grand woman. One of the few who can say she has friends who are friends indeed, and who are with her in all her adventures.

Gipsy Schaeffer. To operate an establishment where everyone is to be treated alike is not an easy task. There are few who stand better with the commercial people than Gipsy.

Miss Antonia P. Gonzales. Always a headliner. Has the distinction of being the only Singer of Opera and Female Cornetist in the Tenderloin. She has had offer after offer to leave her present vocation and take to the stage, but her vast business has kept her among her friends.

For years Tom Anderson's particular friend was the one from whom his place took its name, Josie Arlington. Tom's role in the *Blue Book* is indicated by his full-page advertisements; Josie's, by the graphic photographs of her establishment's interiors—Vienna Parlor, American Parlor, Turkish Parlor, Music Room, and bedrooms. She dominated the volume, as Tom dominated the district.

Josie was home talent, formerly Mary Deubler of a good German family. Her beauty had a tantalizing quality; she had gone "on the turf" (as the district called it) when she was sixteen. A certain Lobrano took her to dinner and did not bring her home until nearly eleven o'clock. This, of course, could mean only one thing. Her father slammed the door, and, though Josie knocked and knocked, he kept it barred against her. Meanwhile Lobrano was waiting outside. He was afraid he couldn't support her; but he had another suggestion: She would support him. He knew one or two madames; with his backing, she could do well for herself. Lobrano proved to be a prophet.

However, after a few years, as Josie opened her own place and Lobrano moved in, so did some of her relatives. He quarreled with them, accusing them of sponging on her. In 1890 her brother bickered with Lobrano; Josie mixed in it, as did her girls. It ended with the brother dead. When Lobrano faced the gallows, Josie remained loyal through two trials. Then, when he went free, she bade him goodbye.

She was going to lead a new life, a refined life. She fired her girls because they were crude, and hired new ones. She announced, too, that she would have only society leaders as clients. She carried out a good part of her intentions. Her new house, "Château Lobrano d'Arlington," was three stories high, with stained-glass windows and a cupola; rates were $5, or much higher for special favors. The *Blue Book* described it as "A palace fit for a king. . . . Absolutely and unquestionably the most decorative and costly-fitted-out sporting palace ever placed before the American public, the most attractive ever seen in this or the old country. Within the walls will be found the work of great artists from Europe and America. Many articles from various expositions will also be seen, and curios galore."

Josie had a cardinal rule—no virgins. "I'll never have a girl ruined under my roof." For her it was a matter of principle. She had a niece to whom she gave a convent education, and the girl was said to have had no suspicion of Auntie's real interests. By this time Josie had acquired a handsome house on Esplanade Avenue, where she stayed for years with her niece. The young girl occasionally met Josie's lawyers and business advisors, and it was her belief that Josie was simply "in business."

After a flush decade, Josie's way of life, even with the additional refinement, began to tell on her. There seems to have been a fire, or an accident, after which she took to thinking. Out in fashionable Métairie Cemetery she built a pink marble tomb for $15,000, with stone urns sending up stylized flames and smoke. Before the metal doors she installed a large bronze figure of a maiden leaning forward as if to knock. What did that symbolize? One school of thought interpreted it as Josie herself on the night she stayed out and Papa wouldn't admit her. Others maintained it symbolized Josie's regulation—no virgins admitted.

Now in her mid-forties, Josie began to talk to her girls and her customers about salvation. For some reason this did not help trade, and Tom Anderson and his associates, worried,

persuaded her to give up the life entirely. She did so; but—
always canny—she leased her place to another woman. In
1914 Josie died and was taken to the big pink tomb. Afterward the niece married one of Josie's business helpers.

Years later a railroad signal pole went up on the road outside the cemetery. Someone cried, "But what's happened to
Josie Arlington's tomb?" The pink marble now looked almost
red in the signal light; those flames seemed truly to be burning. Even after death, red lights for Josie. . . . Thousands
gathered every night. As a youth I watched with them, and I
can recall the eerie effect, the frightened exclamations. Then
city officials got busy and the signal light was moved. Next,
one morning the bronze virgin was missing! The superstitious
nodded. That maiden hadn't been able to stand it. People
were saying she had walked all the way to Baton Rouge.
Finally she was found on a nearby trash heap, and restored
to her rightful position.

Tom Anderson became ever more prepossessing. His hair
and moustaches whitened, and he assumed the mien of a judge.
To the district came all the eminent sight-seeing visitors:
John L. Sullivan, "Gentleman Jim" Corbett, William Farnum,
Wilton Lackaye. Tom entertained them at supper parties and
had experts take them down the line, as guides now escort
visitors for the Spring Fiesta and the Natchez Pilgrimage.
Also, as he had always done, Tom helped anybody in difficulties: broken-down prizefighters, stranded actresses, or girls
of the district who had gotten in trouble and been sent to the
"ice house"—the Isolation Hospital. More and more people
were anxious to shake his hand and chat with him. His callers
were professional tourists (including women) there for a peek
at the saloons, the richer palaces, the girls in dimly lighted
cribs. Frequently the district's working people grew annoyed
at these thrill-seekers and let go with their opinions—which
only enhanced the thrills of the jaunt.

By 1908 the Terminal Station, biggest in New Orleans, was

opened along Basin Street. Incoming strangers stared in fascination, as if from a front seat at a theatre. No Orleanian who used the station could deny he knew what the district looked like.

By now Tom's close associate was Gertrude Dix, one of the most popular managers, a calm, efficient woman who ran one place for him and had general supervision of a second. The 1911 *Blue Book* had this to say of her: "Miss Dix, while very young, is of the type that pleases most men of today—the witty, pretty and natty—a lady of fashion. Her managerial possibilities are phenomenal to say the least. Miss Dix has been with us but a short time but has won all hearts. It is good for one who loves the beautiful to visit Miss Dix' handsome ladies. There are no words for her grandeur of feminine beauty and artistic settings. Phone Main 299." And Gertrude, as we shall see in the next chapter, was a lady who could fight for her rights.

She could not, however, match the bizarre appeal of a pair of glamorous star madames, whose names were famous over America. Both were octoroons, successors in a fashion to the Sirènes of an earlier day. Lulu White's clientele said she was not exaggerating when, describing her stable of mulatto girls, she called them "the most beautiful women in New Orleans." She in turn complimented her customers by identifying them as "the very best people in the city."

Lulu's "Mahogany Hall" had been there before the district itself, and lasted through its history. She had her name spelled out in a stained-glass transom. The house was of brick, sturdily built, with iron balconies. In an early tilt with her critics she was described as owning $2000 worth of furniture, a chandelier of cut glass, a red carriage with horses, a pair of earrings worth $7500, and diamonds valued at $10,000. She also had the only white piano in New Orleans, as fine a thing as stood in any uptown drawing-room. She wore a red wig and a red evening gown, and she sparkled from head to light-brown toe.

Not one to entrust her praises to the uninformed, Lulu issued her own booklet, with introductory notes: "In presenting this souvenir to my multitude of friends, it is my earnest desire to, in the first place, avoid any and all egotism, and secondly to impress them with the fact that the cause of my success must certainly be attributed to their hearty and generous support of my exertions in making their visits to my establishment a moment of pleasure. While deeming it unnecessary to give the history of my boarders from their birth, which would no doubt prove reading of the highest grade, I trust that what I have written will not be misconstrued, and will be read in the same light as it was written; and in mentioning that all are born and bred Louisiana girls, I trust that my exertions in that direction will be appreciated as yours has been to me."

At this point she switched—tonily—to the third person: "This famous West Indian octoroon first saw the light of day thirty-one years ago. Arriving in this country at a tender age, and having been fortunately gifted with a good education, it did not take her long to find out what the other sex were in search of.

"As an entertainer Miss Lulu stands foremost, having made a lifelong study of music and literature. She is well-read and can interest anybody, and make a visit to her place a continued round of pleasure. And when adding that she would be pleased to see her old friends and make new ones, what more can be added?"

Lulu's rival was the Countess Willie V. Piazza. "If you have the blues the Countess and her girls can cure you," the *Blue Book* promised. "The Countess has made it a study to make everyone jovial who visits her house. If there is anything new in the singing and dancing line that you would like to see, telephone the Countess, and her girls will oblige." And the Countess had a sense of humor: a music box was installed in her mattress.

As age crept upon her, the Countess Willie took a trip to

Europe. On her return, it was noticed that she had a peculiar look. Some said that she had had her face delicately enameled. Whatever the new finish was, it hid the wrinkles; but she dared not smile lest she crack it. Mischievous guests would try to make her laugh, until she shrieked: "Stop, damn it. I paid high for this face, and I want to keep it!"

And meanwhile, around the corner, up the street, from half-open doors music was pouring out—a new kind of music. The Orleanians called it "jazz."

CHAPTER 15

"*Elgin Movements in My Hips*"

OUT of the stillness of the evening a horn uttered its impassioned plaint. A drummer began an endless, insistent beat, pounding, pounding. Other players took up the music's wail, each in his own style, sometimes jarring, but for the most part blending with the rest. Feet shuffled, and a hoarse voice sang in a mood that was half sad memory, half tragic appeal. Then the tempo quickened, the mood brightened; and always, under it, through it, came the pounding beat, drumming through the night.

It wasn't the music of the upper-class Creoles in their Royal Street courtyards. It sounded nothing like the polite European works heard in Garden District drawing-rooms. There was little suggestion of such French and Italian arias as one heard at the French Opera. Nor did it obviously resemble the laments and the work tunes that the Negroes sang in the fields, or even the kind of black man's music that New Orleans was used to hearing at Congo Square. Yet, actually, it derived from each of these in greater or less degree; here and there it had something of all of them, plus a quite new and different element unmistakably New Orleans in character. For, in the "new" dark part of town, jazz was being born.

Few whites were more than vaguely aware that this section existed—a huddle of dingy shacks sprawling over an irregular area on the uptown side of Canal Street. Through the middle ran Perdido from the direction of the river toward the lake, and South Rampart cut across it at a right angle. The name Perdido, meaning "lost," had come down from Spanish days; the original road was supposed to have lost its way in a swampy tract. With its poor drainage, most of the area was still mud, and—since nobody else wanted it—the blacks had taken it for their own. Unpainted hovels, rickety shops, the beginnings of tenements and dance halls—these were what filled it now. In the days of freedom after the war thousands of Negroes had congregated here, the population growing ever denser with the passing years. The people around Perdido were accustomed to poverty and sickness, to the violence bred of hot, undisciplined tempers, and to the knife and the gun for settling quarrels. There was misery, yes; but there were also hours of laughter in the sun, rest on a lazy Sunday afternoon, and at night the happy release of the music that welled up from the black musicians' hearts.

The ancient dances at Congo Square (by this time called Beauregard) had continued until the 1880s. Year after year the dancers had worn away the grass and made deep grooves with the stamping and scraping of bare feet in the mud. White observers noticed that Negroes used sticks and bones to beat drums that were sometimes mere boxes, while white-haired elders chanted strange, quivering words and younger ones danced. In the women's dances, their bodies twisted but their feet barely left the ground, whereas the men leaped and jumped into the air. Here were heard chants dimly recalled from the Negroes' homeland, and the pound of primitive African rhythms. On the sidelines children were dancing in imitation of their elders, and vendors cried their rice cakes, beer, pralines, and *estomacs mulâtres* or gingerbread. Among the onlookers wandered salesmen carrying curious packages—good-luck charms and bad, the Voodoo for which many of the blacks came to Congo Square. The white people who watched would never forget the scene, and the Negroes of postwar years grew up with its sounds in their ears, its tempos in their blood.

The white man's music was far from unfamiliar to the black people. In their servants' quarters, or as they walked the streets, they caught its strains—the music for quadrilles and schottisches, waltzes, and polkas. Some of them, too, had regular seats in the Paradis high up against the roof of the French Opera, and on the way home they hummed or whistled arias and choruses. But they made their own music as well.

Ever an imaginative improviser, the Negro was absorbing New Orleans' multilingual music, changing, transmuting, fusing it into a thing of his own. He composed as he went, as all simple people do—joyous stuff, wildly enraptured, or sad and bitter, or a mixture of the two, songs that were gay one moment and despondent the next. He had no teachers to tell him how to sing and play, so that he remained free to develop his own style as his moods dictated. The moaning phases of this music may have sprung indirectly from Congo Square chants, its deep, prolonged tones lamenting the sadder hours; but there were also rich and ringing passages eloquent of warm exultation. To the New Orleans blacks "freedom" signified the right to express the music that was in them.

Throughout enslavement the Negroes had been fashioning rude horns, flutes, and drums—anything that could produce sounds; actually, these were pebble-filled gourds, long whistles, pipes punched with holes, violins made from cigar boxes. And now that emancipation had come, and with it the chance to earn money, scores were saving their nickels and dimes toward the purchase of the shining, "real" instruments they saw in the pawnbrokers' windows. That these were now available was due to the return of the white musicians from the war, either poor for the first time in their lives or else growing poorer during Reconstruction. The pawnbrokers on Rampart and Canal, anxious to get rid of the bulky instruments, kept prices low, and the Negroes walked in, bargained, and sometimes went out the happy possessors of dilapidated cornets, trombones, or clarinets.

Now there were wider opportunities for them because they had real instruments—things built to be played! Few were acquainted with printed music, but what did that matter? They could still make music come out, couldn't they? Indeed, it was a tradition for years that a popular musician should not be expected to play by note. One New Orleans player, when told that he ought to learn to "read music," asked, "But whadda we do when the lights go out?"

Soon the boys were gaining command of their new instruments, making them sing and growl, striking sudden high notes that tore at the ears, executing twists and turns and furious runs, then single notes repeated and modified and repeated again. The beat was subtly altered—sometimes anticipated, sometimes delayed, as though a lazy man were playing along without giving much attention to it. The horns were made to emit a hoarse sound like the speech of a man with a sore throat; or a player would produce a "dirty" or "raddy" tone that made hearts beat and pulses hammer. This was barrel-house stuff, lowdown, elemental. Altogether, the effect made certain hearers dislike the music intensely, finding it ragged and unmelodious. Its admirers—and it had many—called it syncopation, or ragtime, or jazz.

The dominant principle was improvisation, accommodation. The head man plays the theme, the basic melody; from then on, Papa, you're on your own. Each man had, so to speak, a certain amount of elbow room; he could run up and down the scale, play variations at will in a process of spontaneous adjustment; one complementing another, now ahead of him, now behind, slurring, slipping. At certain points most of the men would rest, leaving the field to one player, who knew what to do with it. But, for the most part, this early jazz was the product of joint effort, every man working along with his neighbor. When a supercilious competitor dubbed the men "fakers," he got his answer: Mister, we can fake better than some of your people can play!

Two sets of players, chiefly, were developing the new type

of music. The first, the "Americans," dominated Perdido, and the others lived about the French quarter. The French Negroes, like their former masters, looked down on everything American as "crude," favoring sweeter, gentler music; but they could not long keep themselves aloof from the influences steadily growing stronger around them, and they soon joined in creating jazz.

Though most of the earliest songs are lost, a few can be identified. "Tiger Rag" has been traced to a French quadrille; authorities have charted part of its evolution. The once-popular "Goodbye, Bag" was originally a work song of Negro mill men who chanted it as they handled bags of rice. Then there were songs of satire in gombo Negro dialect that poked fun at pompous figures about town, troublemakers, arrogant persons of all shades of color. Even an operatic aria or two has been found in early jazz songs.

New Orleans, never a place without music, now rang with it as never before. Dark bands played at picnics, at contests, at neighborhood dance halls and saloons, on river packets, at the lake front, and in parades—especially the Mardi Gras parades, in which everybody sang, danced, and marched. Their finest opportunity, however, came with the grand funerals that marked the high point of Negro activity for years. In freedom, many benevolent societies, fraternal organizations, and burial clubs were being formed, and nearly every person in the Negro community managed to scrape together the necessary pennies for a membership. A man or a woman who couldn't make sure of a fine burial—God, what a shame! And basic in every burial contract was the provision for an impressive parade.

On the way to the cemetery the musicians walked slowly: a few steps—halt; a few more steps—long pause. Behind moved the hearse and then the weeping family surrounded by friends. To the music ("When the Saints Go Marching In"), the more susceptible performed a trancelike dance, feet scraping, shoulders drooping. The prolonged, dirgelike moaning was overpowering in its emotional compulsion. A fine man, that one! Lord, why'd you take 'im? Gonna miss 'im bad—yeah, bad! . . . Along the banquettes, apart from the official procession, was ranged a New Orleans institution, "the second line," made up of Negroes with only a spectator interest in the occasion. Generally young and jobless, they were boy and girl amateurs of jazz—a kind of bobby-sock crowd; and when word went forth that a favorite band was going to take a corpse to the grave, they turned out by the score.

The throng accompanying the hearse increased as the funeral procession moved on. Heads popped from attics, gardens, and alleys, and men, women, and children ran out. Ironing was left unfinished; the pots of red beans and rice dried up on the stove. A fun'ral, a big one, yes! Though the burial societies did not particularly favor this increment of marchers, the crowd was generally silent and restrained on the route to the cemetery; and in any case little could be done about it. This is a free country, ain' it?

At the cemetery the body was interred and the chief mourner had his or her hand shaken. Then the musicians bowed formally to everyone, hitched their suspenders and started homeward. From now on they were on their own, to perform as the mood hit them—and the mood was invariably festive. Trumpets were raised and jazz tumbled forth, jazz hot, jazz frenzied. The "second line" strutted, high-stepped, shook it and shook it hard. Shouts rose; amateurs took out home-made implements and ragged it. The favorite song began, "Oh, didn't he ramble?" It had a glorious climax:

> "He rambled all around
> Till de butcher cut 'im down!"

Now and then trouble developed. Funeral officials would grow annoyed at the overagile, overloud antics of the "second line," and words would lead to brickbats, to threats of gun play. Git along, you trash!—You go to hell! In extreme cases police might be called to restore order. One of my early recollections is of such a funeral band; returning to its head-quarters it created so much violence that I was summoned home.

Happily the custom of ostentatious and noisy funerals still survives in milder form. When a former Zulu, the Negro Mardi Gras monarch, died in 1948, it took the procession hours to traverse a few blocks. On the way back, though the king had been widely respected, the band couldn't help play-ing "I'll be glad when you're dead, you rascal, you!"

Those were the days when Milneburg (that lakefront place named for red-headed Alexander Milne) came into its own. There were picnics at the lake edge, pavilion dancing, con-tests, club parties, and private entertainments—all of them prompting calls for the jazz musicians. Whites as well as blacks were hearing the new music and, though some did not admit it willingly, wanting it played at parties and shows. Every Sunday old "Smoky Mary," the train on that pioneer short-line railroad, took cars out to Lake Pontchartrain along Bernard de Marigny's former Champs Élysées. One of the cars was always filled with musicians; having the place to themselves, they could put their instruments on the seats and in the aisles and enjoy themselves. They talked over their plans for the day and for next week, and from time to time practiced runs and choruses. It was grand to be a player.

Behind their car there was always an extra one, empty, into which troublemakers would later be tossed—the rowdies and drunks who during the day at the lakefront would create dis-turbances. Kept in that car as in a rolling jail, they were turned over to the police when the train arrived back in the city late at night. Meanwhile the blues and jazz and moan songs had been sounding over the lake. It was these easy-time occasions on Pontchartrain that gave rise to the classic, "Milneburg Joys."

Naturally, keen rivalry soon developed among the bands in a series of almost amicable battles with no bloodshed. Various firms—beer companies, small lottery lines, manufacturers of cure-all medicines—would hire one band or another to ride about on an advertising wagon; or a dance hall wanted the boys to offer a foretaste of the night's entertainment. The band would start a slow trip about the streets, stopping at intervals to blare out. Inevitably, it would soon meet another organization doing the same thing, or perhaps returning from a funeral. On the spot, by tacit agreement, an impromptu contest would be staged. The wagons halted, the men limbered up—and then out it came: the high notes forced higher and higher, the sliding tones pouring forth in an irregular flood. Nobody shirked; everybody tried to outdo his "opposite man." An excited crowd would surround the wagons instantly. Let the best man, let the best band, win! Players mopped their brows, trembled, the veins in their temples distended. This was "bucking." One set tried to "cut" the other, and music was heard such as has never been heard since—luminous passages, golden outbursts, ever stranger things happening to the beat. It dragged, it spurted, it pounded triumphantly.

"Make it hot!" cried a young dancer.

"That gimme the crawls!" screamed his girl partner.

The crowd swarmed from one band to the other, deserting whichever flagged, racing back when it broke into a new paroxysm of sound. When the decision between them was at last arrived at, one band rode off triumphantly while the other sat back, spent and dispirited. That night the winner got the crowd, the loser faced an empty hall.

Meanwhile the word "jazz" had sprung up, somewhere and somehow. There are those who say it originated in Chicago and was accidentally applied, in derision, to an early New Orleans band; this school believes, too, that at first the word had a sexual implication. There is, however, a weakness in this allegation of a Chicago origin: the French have a verb *jaser*, to chatter or prattle, and the word was reportedly heard now and then in New Orleans with the general sense of "excite, pep up." "Jass it up, boys—things gettin' dull." (In those days the word was spelled *jass*.) In any case, the music was originally referred to less often as "jazz" than as "ragtime."

First of the great New Orleans jazz figures was Buddy Bolden, a barber who blew his horn to glory. He had two loves, music and women; in both he was a virtuoso, and through both he won money, local fame, and jewels. Friends remember how, as he marched along, one grinning girl held his coat, another his hat, and during his moments of rest a third took his horn. Let Buddy smile too long at any one of them, and the other two tried to tear her eyes out.

Buddy made up one song after another; when he wasn't playing his horn, his rich voice was stirring the girls, "giving 'em the crawls." His playing had one feature that later jazz authorities recognized as indispensable—"the trance," an ability to sink himself in the music until nothing mattered but himself and the cornet, in fervent communion. As Buddy played, the girls brought him jiggers of whisky; they tied nickels, dimes, and quarters in handkerchiefs and tossed them to him. He would take the money and throw the handkerchiefs aside, but still the girls threw the money, and themselves, at him.

As the 1900s approached, New Orleans had dozens of fair-sized Negro dance places, in and around Perdido, up along South Rampart, and below Canal as well. Big Easy, Come Clean, Funky Butt—the list is a long one. It was at Funky Butt that a small, bulkily built boy listened nightly to the silver magic of Buddy's notes. Nobody paid any attention to him then. He was young Louis Armstrong.

Deeper, deeper, Buddy Bolden plunged into his music. Ever more deliriously rose the notes. He dominated the dancers of black New Orleans, playing at saloons, lakefront parties, and certain white parties. As they walked through the night men and women heard the wild notes climbing the scales, and knew it was The King. The King worked hard, too hard, at his music and at his girls. He began to startle the dancers with almost demoniac musical passages; then he sloughed off and went sad. In 1907, in the midst of a parade, with his women all around him, he halted, screamed, and frothed at the mouth. A little later the family took him to the state mental hospital at Jackson, and for nearly twenty-five years he remained there, a broken man.

In the meantime the red light district had done its part, and more, to get jazz music going. Ragtime didn't originate there, but Storyville gave it valuable encouragement and impetus. The madames found that customers liked the music, especially the slow, muted kind, and were more liberal when it provided an interesting background. Saloons, barrel-houses, honky-tonks—all these wanted it, too.

The earliest jazz masters played in marching style; there was no place for the piano in funeral parades and open-air entertainments. With the demand from the bawdy houses and other "inside" affairs, jazz underwent an alteration. The piano and the violin crept in; some of the important figures of ragtime won a start as professors in the houses. The girls and their guests liked musicians who "played it cute," grimacing, jumping, clowning. These specialists, willing to oblige, became jokesters, too.

"A drink all around, and ask the professor what he wants." When the professor led the boys in an especially provocative number, everybody chipped in and filled the hat with coins for him. One of the most exuberant of the piano men was Ferdinand ("Jelly Roll") Morton. Apprenticed to a barber, he found the white and black keys in his heart, and embarked on a fervent career; it was "Jelly Roll" who composed "Milneburg Joys." For a long stretch he entertained at Tom Anderson's Arlington Annex.

Another early musical figure was a pianist named John the Baptist, who played with a gut-bucket touch. He starred with the octoroon Countess Willie V. Piazza, the madame with the music box in her mattress. The Countess' rival, Lulu

White, had adopted her nephew Spencer Williams after his mother died. For some years Spencer lived around Lulu's "Mahogany Hall," and from his fingers came the provocative "I Ain't Gonna Give Nobody None of My Jelly Roll." He also made Lulu yet more celebrated with his "Mahogany Hall Stomp." Even Spencer, however, could not match the contagious theme of Tony Jackson's composition, reminiscent of Countess Willie's establishment—"Elgin Movements in My Hips, with Twenty Years' Guarantee"!

The success of the Negro jazz players had both a conscious and an unconscious influence on the white musicians of New Orleans. Though a number of the latter dispute the Negro origins of ragtime, it seems probable that the whites followed the way opened by the blacks. They had to "rag it" or they would lose their chances at popular jobs. In the 1890s Jack Laine ("Papa Laine") emerged as the first important white jazz player, and his music and that of his contemporaries made their own style, generally called "Dixieland."

Of French descent, "Papa" was the son of a member of an orthodox military band. He became an entrepreneur, organizing small aggregations of his own and developing a "New Orleans" manner, usually with drums, clarinet, cornet, trombone, guitar, and violin. Other white-jazz pioneers were Leon Rappolo, "Kid" Orey, and "Pops" Foster; aficionados of the era can name a dozen others.

Meanwhile scores of white boys were forming rough aggregations with improvised instruments, to walk through the streets and follow their luck. By 1895 part of New Orleans was laughing at the antics of a "Spasm Band," later called the "Razzy Dazzy Spasm Band," whose organizer was the singer Harry Gregson (later captain of New Orleans' detective force); he crooned through a gas pipe. Its shifting membership included Emile Lacombe or "Stalebread Charley," who had a box fiddle; "Chinee," with a bull fiddle made out of a barrel; "Cajun" (Willie Bussey), who blew a harmonica; and "Warm Gravy," "Whisky," and "Monk." Some jabbered and scratched themselves like apes; others crawled on their knees and stood on their heads. They played in front of the Opera, before vaudeville houses, and in the district.

The Spasm Band especially liked the district for its sights, as well as for its sentimental *femmes galantes,* who shed large tears and large tips over them. One night while Sarah Bernhardt was playing New Orleans she made a Storyville tour. The Spasm Band members raced to entertain her, skinning elbows and using up their last ounce of breath. The Divine Sarah was enchanted; her voice pealed in appreciation. Reaching into her purse, she handed out two or three small coins. The boys snorted; they preferred the bawds, any day!

Among the experts, others were coming along to take Buddy Bolden's place; Bunk Johnson, "Bad Eye Joe" Oliver, Freddie Keppard, and, above all, Louis Armstrong, today's major jazz figure. Negro New Orleans regards old "Satchmo" as its hero, its golden black boy extraordinary. Louis, born here in 1900, grew up with jazz. His mother was a cook; his father, separated from her, took small jobs. The big-lipped, big-nosed boy was good-humored, forever skylarking. Many liked him, and they called him Dipper, Satchelmouth, and eventually Satchmo. From the first he crooned in a throaty, gravelly voice.

Louis joined the "second line" at the funerals, frequented the dance halls (standing outside), lapped up the sounds that floated into the heat-drenched summer nights. Leaving school early, he sold papers, and presently a Jewish coal seller gave him a job as helper on a wagon. It wasn't long before eleven-year-old Louis and some friends formed a small singing aggregation that hit boxes with sticks, scraped tins, blew harmonicas—anything to make a noise. One boy stood on his head on a bean can and spun round while the rest cried encouragement.

Louis' jobs took him to the district. There he heard "Jelly Roll" Morton play, and he was lucky enough to get a chance to sing for the girls. As he got older he watched the fancy men, especially Clark Wade, a dark gallant whose women kept him in silk shirts and brilliant suits and who wore diamond on his garters. Casually Clark would lift his trousers to show the shining things on his legs. To get a job as a pimp—it must be a wonderful thing. . . . When Clark died his friends gave him a funeral that lasted for hours. In long, broken files the women sobbed and beat their breasts. Never be 'nother man like Clark—no, *sir!*

But such was not to be Louis Armstrong's life. On New Year's Eve, when he was twelve, another boy taunted him; he ran home, got his stepfather's gun and fired into the air. Though no one was hurt, a detective took him in charge, and the boy got an indeterminate sentence in the Waifs' Home. When a kind official there gave him a chance to join the reformatory band, Armstrong lips met their first true horn; what issued made listeners jump. After a bit Louis was leading the institution's band, and presently—within a year—he was free again.

Things did not go well at first; Louis tried one job, then another. Then a fancy man hailed him and they had a few drinks. Opportunity was tapping: a vacancy had opened in a band that played outside the district, and Satchmo took it. Soon he was moving about among the organizations, his high notes blaring out in a startling flow, his husky voice making listeners straighten up and grin.

Louis Armstrong was inching closer to the district. When he was seventeen it looked as if he might get a place there. Tom Anderson had turned over the matter to a helper, and Satchmo was ready to be called. But then, during the fall of 1917, the thing happened that was to change the history of Storyville and of jazz as well. The United States was at war with Germany, and the military were kicking about the way soldiers and sailors picked up diseases in the district. Army and Navy alike demanded that it be shut down, or the whole city would be declared out of bounds. Mayor Martin Behrman objected: The situation was all right; everybody expected such things in New Orleans. City officials went to Washington for conferences. In vain. Washington clamped down, and New Orleans had to pass an ordinance: In less than a month, at midnight of November 12, prostitution would be illegal everywhere in the city.

Few believed it would really end the district. Tom Anderson—with all his influence, he wouldn't let it happen. Tom, calm and judicial as ever, went around, making calls, talking reasonably, practically. As the deadline approached, fire insurance companies canceled Storyville policies, and it was feared that the whole area might be burned down in the night. About twenty-four hours before the deadline, Tom's friend Gertrude Dix went to court to make certain points: The district was being operated under law "for the protection of public morals and public health, good order and the peace of the community"; she had a contract for her house that would cost $6000 during the next two years; "having confidence in the good faith of the city" she had invested $15,000 in equipment and furnishings; and what was threatening the district was confiscatory and therefore unconstitutional. But the judge shook his head, and the bells began to toll.

Furniture dealers swarmed around, buying beds, tables, and bric-a-brac. "Twenty dollars? I paid $400 for it in July!" The girls were being cheated and there was nothing they could do about it. Wagons rolled up and down. The few who did not have to sell ordered this and that carried out; then, with their Boston terriers and their birdcages, they trudged after the vehicles. The lower-priced residents heaved mattresses onto their backs and walked away.

Where to go? A large proportion were leaving town, talking of double crosses and dirty reformers. The less excitable hunted rooms, in the hope that "it would all blow over"; yet few wanted to take them in, even as roomers. One of the women, Edna Wallace, who was twenty-two, had decided to leave a little in advance and had taken a job in a shrimp-packing factory. But the job lasted only a week; the women, learning what Edna had been, refused to work with "one of *them*." Returning to the district, she snatched a revolver and fired it into her stomach. They took her to the hospital; she, at least, would have a roof over her head for a time.

As midnight approached, Tom Anderson sat glumly at his table. Lulu White, Countess Willie V. Piazza, and the rest stared disconsolately into their glasses. In the saloons, in the last few houses, the jazz bands tried to lighten the gloom, sending strident music through the smoky air while the pianos played it soft. Blues in the evening, Basin Street Blues. Oh, he rambled over town, till the butcher cut him down. . . . The men tried to comfort the women, but what comfort was there for anybody?

At midnight two police captains arrived with fifteen extra men in case of trouble. There was no trouble; the district was dying, quietly. One light flickered out, then another. A last madame reached into her stocking to tip the professor. Down the block a trumpet was lifted in a treble cry of defiance; then it subsided in a low, sobbing run. A Negro began a hymn, a mournful chant. The old, good days is gone, Papa, new times is on us. . . .

A few madames tried to slip back, among them Gertrude Dix, but they were arrested. Not even Tom Anderson could help now. A certain amount of prostitution continued, but on a much-reduced scale and in scattered localities. Orleanians protested: "Nowadays you never know what your next-door neighbor is!" With the ending of the war there were sporadic attempts to revive the district, but they all failed. Many a professional was cynical about it: What's the use? These days, the free talent gets there first.

For a time Tom Anderson kept on with his saloon; then he too reformed. His constituents elected him for sixteen years to the state legislature, and he went into another get-rich-quick business—oil. When he died in 1931 at seventy-three, white-haired, truly a jurist in appearance, the newspapers treated him kindly: "Few men in New Orleans were better known; few will be missed more." They praised his "forceful character," his ability to "make friends," his piety. Toward the end Tom went to church two and three times a week.

The octoroon Lulu White hit the toboggan. Her diamonds disappeared, her red wig grew frazzled, her face sodden. It was the same story for many others; their sweet men quit them and they went to the dogs. A few who had salted away their money turned respectable, moving uptown and attending concerts and entertainments that must have seemed tame after the giddy nights when pianos tinkled to the tune of "Elgin Movements in My Hips, with Twenty Years' Guarantee." Perhaps they had earned the right to enjoy being acutely bored.

For a time Basin Street lost even its name. Orleanians wanted to forget that old harridan of a thoroughfare. The squares above Canal Street were renamed "Elks Place"; below Canal they became "North Saratoga"—both titles lamentably drab for a place full of garish memories. For years the district turned gray and fell apart at the seams. It housed tenements and hovels, until even they were torn down to make way for the Iberville Housing Project.

The main product and relic of the district that flourished and kept on flourishing was jazz. The country had beckoned, and—jobless as a result of the district's closing—scores of players started up to Chicago and the other places that were clamoring for them. North and south, men and women were listening with eager enthusiasm to the sounds that had stirred New Orleans. After some band dates on river boats, Louis

Armstrong, too, was headed for fame. The white Dixieland jazzers went north—Nick LaRocca and Leon Rappolo and dozens of others. Everybody was singing it, everybody doing it: Milneburg Joys, Mahogany Hall Stomp, Basin Street Blues. Papa, play it right. I got Elgin Movements. . . .

Jazz had started on its triumphant way around the world. It was being listened to, analyzed, described in dignified print. Stokowski had a kind word for it; in France, Maurice Ravel tried to use it in some compositions. Soon an esoteric cult was growing up—a cult that spoke of polyphony and other mysterious things that made the boys feel guilty. As one put it, "To hear them fellows talk, sounds like it's a sin!" New Orleans had produced what many regard as the first truly native American music, had altered the trend of popular taste for a generation or more.

Basin Street had lost its name, true, and for many years was in eclipse. Yet in a sense it was eventually brought back by jazz. For a time, a few last, empty houses hung on despite the housing project. Lulu White's name was still to be read in her stained-glass transom, and Tom Anderson's in tile in the pavement in front of his Arlington Annex. Afterward Lulu's bagnio was turned into a teen-age community centre, while Tom's establishment became a garage and his name was paved over. *Sic transit gloria mundi!*

Then, in the 1940s, New Orleans, catching up with the rest of the world, began to realize its jazz heritage. The National Jazz Foundation set up shop, to talk over old days, to recall the great figures, to play phonograph records from the years before the thing had gone glossy and big-band and refined. So it was that, on a day when Orleanians with memories felt sad, the title of Basin Street was restored to the street signs. Hardly its old self, of course. But something.

South Rampart is still South Rampart—the smell of frying pork chops, drugstores and pawnbrokers', shoe shops and phonograph stores. It is nearly all "dark," feet shuffle endlessly, and everywhere sounds the deafening blare of the music that South Rampart helped give to the world. On the side streets little boys beat their drums and tootle their horns, with the old wild light in their eyes. Will another Satchmo come along, one of these days?

CHAPTER 16

Cities within the City

A FEW squares away from Basin Street stand the earliest cemeteries, those places that many think the strangest of New Orleans' strange sights. Cities within the city, "cities of the dead"—these phrases have often been applied to them; there are none more appropriate. New Orleans has long buried most of its bodies aboveground in tombs that suggest narrow residences with peaked or rounded roofs, ranged along lines of streets. Like the traditional Creole houses, these tombs are frequently of brick, stuccoed and whitewashed; they have miniature "galleries" of ironwork, and in some cases narrow banquettes. Thousands are fitted with iron gates, and metal garden chairs and benches are grouped in front, so that the effect is given that the people inside are "receiving" guests.

For generations, because the law forbade burial in the city's moisture-saturated grounds, coffins had to be deposited in well-sealed receptacles aboveground, and soon such upright resting places spread in every direction. The older cemeteries gradually became so crowded that in some spots only a few inches of space intervene between tombs, no ground being left for trees or bushes or even grass. The similarity to city streets grows on the stranger. Those who are used to green lawns and white headstones—all that the word "cemetery" connotes in other parts of the country—stand incredulous. Nor is there anything of the chaste look of, let us say, a New

England graveyard. The Creoles are as neighborly in death as in their close-packed residences. Here is serenity without chill, pervading friendliness, even pleasant humor.

One of my early recollections is of visiting a downtown cemetery. To a five-year-old it seemed a wonderful spot, full of stage scenes and temples; I did not associate it with death. The plump angels trumpeting away, the pretty marble girls in Grecian robes—they looked distinctly cheerful. And, when I look today, they still give me that impression as they tootle away, pointing brightly toward the sky. The whole place seems cheerful, with everybody lying near his old friends, comfortably settled in a populous neighborhood. . . .

More than most cities do, New Orleans remembers its dead, keeps them in mind, visits them, leaves flowers for them. The oldest cemeteries are within walking distance of Canal Street; the dead are next door to the living. As I have watched Orleanians paying a call at a tomb, I have often been reminded of nothing so much as a family party having a pleasant time. Why not? As the Orleanian asks, aren't there more ways of showing respect than to beat your head against a wall?

Mark Twain was delighted with those resting places. Deploring the public buildings erected here during the "gingerbread" period, he said that the only real architecture in New Orleans was to be found in the cemeteries; and he suggested—none too tactfully—that Orleanians would be better off if they "would live as neatly while they were alive as they do after they are dead." And certainly they erect for themselves tombs that are models of good design and appearance. For the simpler folk there are plain receptacles in long, tidy rows; for the rich ones, marble structures like the houses in the French quarter or the Garden District, with pillared entranceways, Greek Revival pediments, and elaborate cornice work. Some are gabled; others have marble courts and vestibules and stained-glass windows.

There is a profusion of sculpture: weeping willows and

weeping widows in bas-relief, carved seraphs, soldiers, sphinxes, sheep being driven homeward—and even the figure of Death itself. A surprising number of persons have expressed a wish to have the dark angel set in front of their tombs, some specifying that he must be carved "looking pleasant"! Other demands have been for obelisks bearing mystic Egyptian figures of men or animals; pyramids in rosy marble; a Chinese tomb complete with tinkling bell (this for a Chinese person); and one with a heavy steamboat bell above it in memory of the river captain who lay beneath. To my mind, however, no tomb in New Orleans is more affecting than the one bearing the phrase, below the name of a fifteen-year-old girl, "Ma Pauvre Fille."

In the earlier, uncongested days bodies were apparently placed in the earth. But the water table lay within three feet of the surface, and the grave-diggers would find water pouring into the hole they had just prepared; whereupon they stood on the casket to force it down. Indeed, if the family was not present, they might even break holes in it to make it sink! In such cases the remains were virtually drowned; as an observer said, this was truly to "write one's name in water."

For a time the community was served by a burying ground within the narrow town limits, on the block bounded by Royal, Chartres, Bienville, and Conti. Then a new one was chosen toward the ramparts, and in time there was another that used a field outside (through which Basin Street was later cut). The problem throughout was space; nobody wanted graves in his back yard, but almost the whole area beyond the town limits had the consistency of a marsh. Nowadays, men digging in the earth still discover forgotten spots where interments once took place.

After 1800, as the city grew more crowded, officials began to fret over sanitary conditions. There were more and more epidemics, for which the authorities, as was noted earlier,

blamed "miasmatic exhalations." This led to bickering with
the officers of the St. Louis Cathedral over the funeral services customarily held there. Every Creole wanted to be buried
from the old church, as his fathers had been; but the city
authorities replied that—no matter how Creole a dead body
was—it still emanated "effluvia," which undoubtedly added in
time to those "miasmatic exhalations." Therefore, an order:
No more burial rites at the cathedral. A mortuary chapel was
built, in about 1827, safely beyond the ramparts; and it is
still in use as a church, even though the cathedral services
were later restored.

It was these fears of "miasma" that produced a second
order: Hereafter, all interments must be aboveground. As a
consequence old St. Louis Cemetery No. 1 filled rapidly,
as did St. Louis No. 2 several squares away on North Claiborne Avenue. A little later, No. 3 was established along
Esplanade near Bayou St. John. When a resident of the
locality tried to enjoin this, the Louisiana Supreme Court
decided against him: Cemeteries could be so planned as to
rank among "the most attractive ornaments of a city"—which
is just what they have become in New Orleans. Nearly
100,000 persons are interred in the three St. Louis resting
places, which Orleanians keep quite distinct by their numbers. One Creole said to me, "These worries will drive me
straight into St. Louis No. 2!" And another assured me that
"we are of good blood—we have maintained our place in
St. Louis No. 3."

Here is demonstrated, in the names of the persons buried
in these cities of the dead, the growing diversity of the New
Orleans population. The name recorded on a tomb may be
entirely French, or entirely English, or a mixture of the two.
It may combine Spanish, Spanish-English, and Spanish-
French; or Italian (a surprising number), Italian-French,
and Italian-English; and there are names of German, Jugoslav,
and North European origin. Here are true international settlements.

The shape and appearance of the tombs frequently bring astonished comment. One day years ago, after spending hours at one of the cemeteries, a breathless visitor wrote home: "The Creoles bake their dead in ovens as we do our Brown Johns for breakfast." And *oven* was no bad term for these rectangular receptacles. Some are built in two or three layers, or in tiers of four or five. Such types, which commonly form the long outer walls of the cemetery, have been compared also to beehives and even to filing-cabinets.

It has long been customary, after a body has been placed in a vault, to plaster over the front with great care. By the end of a year, when the body has usually turned to bones and dust, the law permits the tomb to be opened if necessary. When someone else in the same family dies, the coffin is removed and burned and the bones are pushed or dropped to the back. Occasionally the tomb contains a small crypt underneath to receive the older remains. This procedure may be repeated many times through the years until—though the tier actually holds only one body at any given time—the list of names on its front has grown long. Some are shocked; but, after all, space is limited.

The receptacles are usually owned outright, though not invariably. In the line of wall ovens it is possible to rent space for a body at a cost of a few dollars a year. If the responsible family ignores the annual bill for rental, a warning is issued; and if payment is still not forthcoming the coffin is destroyed and the bones buried, so that the vault can be rented again.

Then New Orleans has its "three-day burials." If you want to impress your friends you pick out an ornate tomb and make a payment on it. When you die you will be interred there with gratifying éclat. Then, a few days later, you are discreetly removed to some humbler receptacle, where you stay. But you have died well!

In St. Louis Nos. 1 and 2 the ancient names predominate: DeBoré, who made sugar granulate commercially; the Chalmettes, on whose field was fought the Battle of New Orleans; Gayarré the historian; Myra Clark Gaines, half-Creole, half-Irish, who sued the world to prove her right to her name; and Alexander Milne, the tight-fisted Scot who wouldn't powder his hair for a duke.

In St. Louis No. 2 lies Pierre Soulé, perhaps the most undiplomatic of all American diplomats. A hot-tempered Frenchman, Soulé went to Spain in the 1850s, during one of the recurrent crises over the Cuban question. He was a glowing orator, an impressive personage; he had everything except tact and common sense. He infuriated the Spaniards by fulminating against them, threatening them, and mixing in Cuban intrigues; he got into duels over Madame Soulé's costumes, and he almost brought on a war.

To return to St. Louis No. 1, here is Paul Morphy. (His ancestor was a certain Mike O'Murphy, who left Ireland for Spain and there became Don Miguel Morphy.) Paul was a well-born Creole, son of a justice of the Louisiana Supreme Court. His life was that of any other child until, at five, he happened to be watching his father play chess. M. Morphy thought himself quite a chessman; but now the boy leaned over and told Papa that he had made a wrong move! After considerable study, Papa agreed. The child had taken no lessons; he had merely watched his elders. Though the Morphys now realized that Paul was a prodigy, they tried not to force his education. At eleven he met a world chess authority and trounced him. Still, he manifested no extraordinary interest in the game; he and his father were planning that he should become a lawyer.

Paul grew up a slim, good-looking youth with a suggestion of aristocratic hauteur in his bearing. At nineteen, having finished legal training, he was as yet too young to practice. Idle for the moment, he agreed to take part in the Manhattan Chess Club's first Congress. There he astounded the world, achieving unprecedented feats. Blindfolded, he met chess champions and worsted them. Diffident, sometimes bored, the young man received praise calmly; even his admirers thought him a bit of a prig. He went on to Europe, and Europeans who had scoffed leaped up to applaud. He was almost certainly the world's greatest chess player.

Then little things began to happen, puzzling things. Home once more, Paul became distrait, oversensitive, taking offense at minor slights, angered when called a "professional." Monsieur, *he* was a gentleman! He announced that he wanted to forget chess, would never play it again; he would be a lawyer. When he tried the law, however, he failed. Moodily he wandered alone, behaving ever more strangely. As the years passed he acquired delusions of persecution. In a big house at 417 Royal Street (now the Patio Royal) he lived an ever more secluded existence, a worried-looking dandy who left the house once or twice a day in a theatrical cape to follow exactly the same route for a walk. And secretly, as if it were a vice, he played chess with himself.

Sorrowfully the family took Paul to a mental hospital, where, removing his gloves with a precise gesture, he argued that he was sane—and did it so convincingly that the officials refused to accept him! He went back to his stuccoed mansion with its fragrant courtyard, arched carriageway, and curved double staircase that was an essay in grace. He had reached glory at twenty, and he lived on dully until he was forty-seven. Now, in his quiet gray tomb, Paul Morphy sleeps easily at last.

In St. Louis No. 1 lies Dominique You, once a soldier in the Grande Armée of France, later one of the Laffites' piratical associates, who at the Battle of New Orleans transformed himself from freebooter to patriot. But Dominique did not slip away afterward like the Laffites; he remained on the scene. In these quieter days he turned honest, or at least reasonably so, becoming a ward politician. Romanticists who had respected him as a proper pirate were dismayed by this fall from grace. For Dominique at least, politics opened no treasure houses, and he died poor and ill and obscure. Then, like the quixotic place it is, New Orleans remembered Dominique again, and gave him one of its great funerals. Stores closed, military companies fired guns, ladies dropped roses. On his tombstone are the words *sans peur et sans reproche.*

For years an anonymous Orleanian marched annually to Dominique You's tomb to place flowers. He was J. W. F. Moore, copy-desk editor and soldier (artillery, like Dominique), with whom I worked for years. There was no blood relationship; Bill said he simply *liked* the piratical old sonofabitch. When Bill himself died recently, the mourners moved from his grave to Dominique's to leave part of Bill's flowers there—because Bill would have had it so.

Here, too, lies Marie Laveau, the Voodoo Queen—or does she? St. Louis No. 1 contains a well-preserved tomb with the inscription: MARIE PHILOMÈNE GLAPION, *décédée, le 11 juin 1897.* But there were two Maries, and this was the daughter, a lesser Voodoo. The real one, it is claimed, rests in the tier below, without inscription; otherwise, too many people would come. Yet over in St. Louis No. 2 there is still another "Laveau tomb," and the informed swear *this* is the one. A nameless oven in a line of ovens, it appears at first glance no different from dozens around it. Look hard, however, and you see that the concrete is marked by dozens of red crosses and on the ledge lies a piece of red brick. Thousands believe that if you scratch a cross mark and pray, Marie will make certain your wishes are carried out. And they can cite evidence —didn't she once turn men into barking dogs? A bold one, Marie did everything from simple curing to the concocting of bad- and good-luck charms; from dancing around a pot with snakes in it to the brewing of mixtures containing Spanish flies (cantharides) to spur the virility of older cavaliers. The sextons say she was really placed in that first tomb, "but they hadda move 'er—too many prayin' and hollerin', huntin' luck." So, one night. . . .

Still, people found out. "They creeps in here, quiet, and talks to her. Mumbles and cries. Thinks she can hear 'em and

do like they wan'." It is not only Negroes; white women also
seek Marie's help. "They comes along, preten's they jus'
amblin' aroun'. Minute I turns, over they goes. Even digs
holes in the plaster. They throws in dimes and nickels and
quarters—more they gives, better chance they wish come
true." A few leave presents—soft drinks, roast chicken with
oyster dressing, a fresh chocolate cake.

"That ought to be nice for you," I suggest.

He gives a horrified start. "Me, tech sech stuff? I don' fool
with no hoodoo!"

So much for the French places. Eventually the Americans
decided they wanted their own cemetery. In about 1825 the
first Protestant one was located uptown adjoining a former
pauper burial spot. Christ Episcopal Church took over the
property as fashionable Girod Cemetery, or—in the words of
the French—"La Cimetière des Hérétiques." It was a period
when elaborate ornamentation was the fashion, and the
Americans built tall and ornate vaults enriched with dentil
lines, Corinthian motifs, and fine cornices. They were prodigal, too, of versified inscriptions lamenting the virtuous dead.
Some of the epitaphs for small children are especially touching, even though couched awkwardly.

By contrast rises the tomb sacred to Dr. Dow, physician,
who ordered carved on his shaft a skull and crossbones. No
less an individualist was John David Fink, bachelor. Born in
Germany, he died here at seventy. Back in his youth he had
fallen in love with a girl who hurt his feelings by laughing at
his suit; she wanted, she said, to "work out her own destiny."
Though Mr. Fink at the end of his life showed himself a
charitable man, leaving a large sum for an asylum for Protestant widows and orphans, he decreed that it was to admit no
old maids. "Let them," he said, "work out their own destiny."

Through the 1870s the Girod Cemetery prospered. Then
the neighborhood of South Liberty and Cypress deteriorated,
and industry moved in—warehouses, factories, a railroad.

Families acquired tombs elsewhere, and Nature began her reconquest of the place. Today it is a scene of crumbling ruin. Insistent vines and weeds have caught at walls and tombs; from empty receptacles grow luxuriant ferns; grass has taken possession of other stretches, and where bricks have fallen away bones can be seen inside the ovens. At a turn in an aisle, weeds with plumelike tips burst from a cornice against the sky.

From low spots fig trees crawl upward, their pressure breaking through a wall, and the branches dig within like twisting hands, thrusting aside weakened bricks. A forgotten rosebush forces its way desperately along the corner of a deserted row, blooming briefly out of the weeds. And over there a stray honeysuckle springs from a ruined tomb, the edge of its coffin exposed to the light. Gradually the weight of the upper rows of ovens has pressed down so that the bottom tier is almost under the surface. An attendant points: "Them poor mens down there, they gettin' crushed on!" And you recall old tales of people buried alive. . . .

For years Girod Cemetery has constituted a problem for the city. Vandals slip in at night and tear away ironwork, urns, and slabs. Long ago the church sold the lots to holders of the tombs, who then resold the space to persons unknown, so that by now the title is uncertain. The authorities have declared the spot a possible health hazard, and hundreds of vaults have been "posted" for repair or demolition. But no final disposition of the problem is in sight.

Before the 1860s a showplace of New Orleans was the élite Métairie Race Track, at what is today Métairie Road and Pontchartrain Boulevard. During the postwar period it fared less happily. A story exists to the effect that a man who sought membership in the racing club was turned down, whereupon he swore he would turn the place into a graveyard; and, it is added, he did so. Whether the tale be true or not, the track management encountered a series of financial crises, with splits among the shareholders, and the place was eventually sold. The location, on a well-drained natural ridge, made it an admirable spot for a cemetery, and a cemetery it became, for people of all faiths.

Métairie's main drives cover the site of the old track; where thousands once cheered the horses there is now the quiet of New Orleans' great place of the dead—an expanse of lagoons, bridges over canals, and magnificent tombs. The water table having dropped in recent years, there is now some interment in the earth, but the custom of tomb burial still predominates.

John Erskine thought that Métairie recalled Père la Chaise Cemetery in Paris but was far more beautiful. Here lie, in a mausoleum covered by a green mound, the bodies of 2500 men, Louisianians in Lee's Army of Northern Virginia, topped by a thirty-foot monument of Stonewall Jackson, who was mortally wounded in battle with these soldiers. The inscription is simple: "From Manassas to Appomattox, 1861 to 1865." Here lie, not far away, Louisianians who fell under General Albert Sidney Johnston in the Army of Tennessee; here, too, rests Louisiana's General Beauregard. Before the monument a marble sergeant calls the roll of his companions.

Nearby, as in the other cemeteries, are massive structures in which lie Orleanians who banded together in societies and other organizations; in death also they are together. But most visitors hasten to see, instead, the pink marble tomb of Josie Arlington, the Basin Street madame whose story was told in an earlier chapter. Though it now bears an unrelated name, the stone torches remain and the bronze virgin still knocks.

They also enjoy hearing about Mr. Moriarity, whose odd fancy stands near the entrance—a shaft with four ponderous female figures about it, erected in honor of the late Mrs. Moriarity. A special railroad track had to be laid in order to convey the ladies to the desired position. It is said that the sculptor stared in amazement when the widower ordered "the Four Virtues."

"But there are only *three* Virtues," the artist protested.

"I don't care. I want four!"

So he got his four, and to this day New Orleans calls them Faith, Hope, Charity, and Mrs. Moriarity. (Martin Dooley, Finley Peter Dunne's philosopher of Archey Road, has been credited with the phrase, but old-timers insist that it was a spontaneous local growth.)

In 1867 the Archbishop of New Orleans, visiting Europe in search of new priests, induced two Germans to come and serve Holy Trinity Church, located in a thickly settled German section downtown. They arrived in winter, and with spring the yellow fever struck. Men and women died on every side; the older priest went quickly. Young Father Peter Thevis remembered that in the old country the devout put their faith in Saint Roch, patron of plague victims. Falling to his knees, he made a pledge: If Saint Roch would save his people, Father Thevis would build a shrine in the saint's name.

The epidemic ended; and, though people had died all over town, it is said that none of Holy Trinity's congregation was lost. Father Thevis then went to work to create an American version of the "Holy Field" of the Germans in Rome, a chapel with burial ground. He himself laid the marble floor, and helped with the carpentry and brick-setting. Slowly rose a tall, narrow Gothic chapel, of brick with tiny stained-glass windows, arches, and carving. (Because of its unusual shallowness, one observer thought it resembled a kitchen clock.) The years and the climate settled quickly on it, tenacious ivy did the rest, and today Saint Roch's chapel looks as ancient as many in the Old World.

Before its wooden altar New Orleans came to pray. Men and women with every kind of ailment made pilgrimages to ask recovery. One parishioner had a marble-worker fashion a heart-shaped ex-voto offering and hung it near the altar; others added theirs, until hundreds were in place. A man who declared that his arm had been cured ordered a plaster replica of it, realistically painted, and hung it up. A girl who had had to walk with a crutch placed it near the altar when she had no further need of it. Not far from these were the wax casts of a baby's hands and of a woman's foot. One elderly woman who had received a great favor installed a life-size statue of herself.

Never have I been to the chapel and found it empty; its pews are filled with believers who kneel in the flickering light. In the yard outside are New Orleans' only open-air Stations of the Cross. Here women move slowly from one to the other of the fourteen niches; vines twist about the ornamented wood, and here and there a flower blossoms along the frames of statuary.

Several generations of New Orleans girls have sworn by Saint Roch. On every Good Friday they pray to him for a mate, each sure that before the year is out she will have hers. Many "make" nine churches in a novena for their husbands-to-be, and they try usually to end at the Saint Roch Chapel. In the burial ground grow four-leaf clovers, and they pick one as they leave. This helps, too, they tell you. The Catholic Church of today does not encourage the practice, though it cannot stop it. Father Thevis, before he died and was buried beside the altar, smiled: "Why shouldn't they pray to God to direct them in the most important step of their lives?" Most Orleanians would agree.

Every November 1 the city observes its occasion of supreme remembrance, All Saints' Day, by thronging its cemeteries in order to place flowers at the graves. Next to Mardi Gras, this is the great day of the people; in his devotion to the two occasions there is a clue to the Orleanian's philosophy. One occasion is of the flesh, the other of the spirit; he will not neglect either.

For days in advance, the cemeteries are astir. Women appear, mops in hand, with scrubbing brush, scissors, and paint. All must be prepared—grass trimmed, stucco whitewashed, lettering redone. Negro boys go about, offering to "wipe down your tomb, Mister"; attendants have sand, shells, and ornaments ready. Whole families appear, each member with a service to perform. They bring lunches, sit on the edges of graves, and rest between sessions in the sun. The provident carry bucketfuls of soft drinks, and the scene drones with activity as friends call greetings. They have not met since last All Saints'. A woman once told me: "Whenever I want family information, I wait till then, because I'll see everybody I know." And there will not be many resting places without signs of refurbishing. To the true Orleanian it would be close to sacrilege to "neglect his dead." The departed would feel it, and neighbors would talk.

The iron doors swing open early on All Saints'. The tramp of feet is endless; special policemen are assigned to keep traffic moving. Banks and public offices close; stores lock up, or employers excuse their workers for several hours. ("I'd never work for a man heartless enough to keep me from going to my grave!") Before the entrances stand vendors of ice cream, pralines, tamales, and toys. Others, appealing to those who have waited until the last minute, sell paint and scrubbing brushes.

Hourly the crowds increase, and all bring flowers. November provides the grandeur of chrysanthemums, huge white and yellow blooms. Nearly every Orleanian who can afford it will carry them, as well as some who cannot. Some bring flowers out of their own gardens, from plants they have nursed for this one day. "I hope my carnations bloom for All Saints'." "Jus' like those hard-headed things to come up too late!"

Women make a living by fashioning "permanent" flowers. Also popular are wide wreaths of beads in black or white and pink, sprinkled with silver or gilded. Along some graves holy statues are placed for the day. And a friend of mine once saw an elaborate cloth wreath, with a stuffed white bird swinging in the centre.

As the hours pass, greetings grow louder: "Yes, I heard how they lost two in a year. A shame!" "No, they never call *us*, not since that Carnival argument we had over how to make gumbo." "Say, look at that girl down there in white. Never saw her at that grave; can't be related to the Hodginses."

A dark-clad woman, eyes downcast, kneels in prolonged prayer; it is a "new death," and she will receive sympathy and understanding glances. Yet by and large, All Saints' mood is less than tragic. It is a family day, when people gather as their fathers and grandfathers did, and the tone of regret is often tempered by philosophy. "Poor Nonc' Terence—I can see him now, kneeling before his *prie-dieu* every morning. A fine man. And did it do him any good? That second wife left him flat the minute he got arthritis!" "My sister Marie, I say she earned any good time she's having up there. If she hears me now, she can tell God it's the truth."

After a moment of silence the family rises. "We got four more places to make, two of 'em way uptown." The listeners understand. When there are many connections, people work hard on All Saints'; if they pass up a cousin, there will be questions. . . . Continuing mysteries stir the cemetery-goers. A grandmother or a bachelor brother dies; every year thereafter the immediate family arrives to find flowers already brought by somebody unknown; who can it be? The possibility of an unsuspected *tendresse* is raised, and the relatives may delegate one of their number to come very early next year and watch to see who it is. Things grow only more controversial when the man or the woman, on discovery, refuses to disclose his or her identity. "That ain't right!" one matron cried. "She ought to give her name, or else stay away from our tomb. We got rights!"

Despite informalities, it remains a day of profound meaning. The living show the dead that they are not forgotten; those who now give a day to the departed will themselves be remembered in the next generation. And often natives are so touched by the spirit of the day that, when they spy an unornamented grave near theirs, they go over to put something there.

Years ago a young girl, on her way to New Orleans, was taken sick on the train and died. City officials made inquiries, but her family could not be located and she was placed temporarily in a humble cemetery plot. Finally her brother, learning what had happened, came to New Orleans, arriving on All Saints' Day. When an official guided him to the burial place they found there a wreath and a bouquet, though the girl had known nobody in the city. Some passer-by had noticed. . . . This is the kind of thing that makes Orleanians like New Orleans.

The saints are very close to the Orleanian, who begs them to intercede in difficulties, to find jobs, to persuade evil women to stop annoying virtuous families. Because certain ones swear by one saint, and others have *their* favorites, jealousy often arises.

"Saint Rita—that's a stuck-up saint!" one woman cried to another. "What does *she* know about poor people?"

"Hunh!" her neighbor retorted. "Saint Rita's forgot more about the poor than your saint ever knew. She's as plain as I am. I talk to her woman to woman!"

New Orleans is fond of Saint Expédite. Saint Rita is hailed as the "advocate of the hopeless." There may be "runs" on certain saints; if word gets out that one of them has done a particular service, the demand will be prompt, and overnight he will become a best-seller at the religious stores. Year in, year out, however, Orleanians retain their favorites. A continuing one is Saint Joseph. "Him, he can be a mean saint when he wants," an old woman says with a shake of the head. "But you get him in a good humor and he'll give you the shirt off his back." She has a method of countering his "meanness"; when he proves stubborn she stands him upside-down in his metal holder, and this, she says, brings him around!

In all this there is naïveté, of course, but also a direct simplicity. Who would wish to take from the devout the solace they derive from such faith? Their lively gratitude has been expressed for years through the newspapers' classified advertising columns in such items as these: "Thanks to the Infant Jesus of Prague in answer to the Flying Novena for favor granted." "Thanks to Holy Ghost for prayer answered." "Thanks to St. Anna. My dogs were all returned to me." "Thanks to St. Jude, Blessed Martin, Lily of the Mohawks, Blessed Mother and Her Son in helping my boy to walk." "Thanks to St. Jude Iscariot, St. Jude Thaddeus, Infant Jesus of Prague." When the phrase "Publication promised" is added, it means that, in praying, the petitioner pledged that the saint's name would be printed along with the thanks.

Mrs. Maud Ronstrom, in charge of want ads in the *Times Picayune-States,* recently made an appeal to the users of that column. It seems that too many were assuring the saints that she would run all such mentions of favors granted. "Please, ladies," she begged, "don't make such promises." There was simply not enough space to print them all, and nobody would want the saints to be disappointed.

CHAPTER 17

The Art of Eating

AS SOON as a Creole enters into Heaven, it is said, he waves a hand to Saint Peter: "Comment ça va, M'sieur?" Then he turns to the nearest angel: "Where's the pot of *jambalaya?*" If he finds there is none of that strongly accented combination of shrimp, oysters, tomatoes, rice and other items, he rubs his chin, sidles over, and inquires about the food customs in the other place. . . .

Mark Twain sat with fork poised over a dish of fragrant New Orleans pompano, and his friends held their breaths for the verdict. That pompano, he sighed, was "as delicious as the less criminal forms of sin." William Makepeace Thackeray, whose stomach did not protrude without reason, also sampled the city's delectations. Almost dreamily, he wrote that he was here in the spring, "Just when the orchards were flushing over with peach-blossoms and the sweet herbs came to flavour the juleps." His judgment was definitive: "It seemed to me the city in the world where you could eat and drink the most and suffer the least."

Orleanians of today would agree with Mark Twain and Thackeray, save that in the latter's statement they would change the word "most" to "best." This appears to them only the simple truth, and there are gourmets far and near who agree. The town has long been a home of gastronomic joy. In certain other parts of America the preparation of food seems to be a chore, its consumption a race with the clock. An Atlanta woman once observed: "You people not only like to eat; you like to cook, too." This is undeniable; the consumption as well as the preparation of edibles à la New Orleans has all the ramifications of a fine art.

When very young, I shocked a French quarter chef by speaking of one of his "gravies." "Gravy! It is never a 'gravy' here. It is always—the sauce." I have never repeated the error. . . . For New Orleans, wines and stronger liquors are the essentials of many dishes. *Filet de sole bonne femme* is not *filet de sole bonne femme* without the undertone of white wine. That turtle dish—omit the touch of brandy, and what have you? A beautiful woman with no sparkle in her eyes.

The Creole cuisine is the end-product of an original affection for good things, imagination in combining them, and—the factor without which the finest chef is powerless—critical judges to appreciate. The city has no place for the visitor with mind on higher things, or the New Englander whose notion of a good meal is the "boiled dinner." Orleanians are repelled by the pale art of the white sauce, or the salad compounded of raw carrots or of stuffed prunes with marshmallow whip. They favor, rather, the pungent touch, the delicate "lift" of aromatic herbs. With something approaching passion they relish adroitly mixed offerings of land, river, and sea. And they have always been as quick to "Bravo!" a good cook as a good tenor.

Those who look on eating as a duty, who watch their waistlines and count calories—New Orleans is no town for them. In a restaurant they will be met politely, but they will gather that they have entered the wrong establishment. I overheard one out-of-town visitor tell a manager firmly: "I don't want any of your dressings or your seasonings. Just vegetables with cottage cheese." "I am sorry, Madame," was his courteous rejoinder, "but I fear you would not like *any* of our food." And Madame could only leave.

Authorities who sample New Orleans' food may reflect and seek to identify its elements, but they always encounter difficulty. The cooking is not simple Southern (this has never been truly a "Southern" city), nor is it that of rural French Louisiana, nor entirely French or Spanish, Negro or Indian. Yet it reveals elements of all of them, plus something best identified as "of the lowest Mississippi." From the French it derives an elementary flavoring, a delicacy of taste. To this the Spanish have added fragrant spices, concocted piquant combinations; the Indians, roots and herbs; the black man, skills in mixing mouth-warming ingredients. Although in most warm countries there is a tendency to prefer rather hotly flavored foods, the seasoning here is seldom fiery. Never dominating the distinct taste of seafood or of meats, it brings them out instead. In Creole cooking, what counts is the soupçon— not the handful.

No less important are the basic materials. Nearby are marshes and swamps, brackish shallow lakes, the teeming brown river, and the Gulf itself; and across Lake Pontchartrain stands higher earth that supports upland life. From the soil Louisianians harvest fruits and vegetables in almost tropical abundance; in the city's environs three crops a year may be raised. A New Orleans restaurateur has refused to open branches in New York and Chicago because—as he maintains —without a ready supply of these foods his dishes would be impossible.

The French colonists experimented with strange fish and game, substituting wild ducks for tame geese, tender shrimp for veal. In their gardens the Creole housewives raised their indispensable herbs—bayleaf, thyme, parsley, peppers, cloves. And soon they were learning from the Choctaw Indians, receiving the gift of *filé* (powdered leaves of dried sassafras) for their *gumbo*, Creole soup extraordinary. Into this gumbo go shrimps or oysters or crabs, or all of them, or perhaps chicken, each making a fragrant dish. In any case, bits of ham and other meat are tossed in—almost anything in the kitchen, indeed. The gumbo just gets thicker and better. Okra sometimes replaces the filé as a thickener, and is equally acceptable.

An essential ingredient is that staple, rice. Creoles say that only the Chinese eat more rice than they do. At every old-style meal a large bowl of rice has a prominent place. If the diner does not find it he knows that something catastrophic has happened in the kitchen. Rice goes into stews and soups and stuffings, is served with meats and gravies and seafood. It makes puddings, too—not the mild "rice pudding" found elsewhere, but rich savories with wine and fruits and spices. Nor does the rice turn up at the table in that gummy mass that most Americans meekly accept. Boiled quickly, with cold water then run through it, and finally steamed over warm water, its grains stand separate and flaky. When it is served with gumbo—its aroma floating up in light steam, a crab claw on the surface, tips of pink shrimp visible beneath—the Louisianian will tell you that life holds few more satisfying delights.

A second major Creole dish is the jambalaya which, as already stated, the Orleanian confidently expects to meet in Heaven. For this, shrimp and oysters may be used together, or separately, or pork sausage instead. Like gumbo, a jambalaya tastes a little different wherever you find it. Every cook has his own opinion on which combination is best; each modifies the ingredients with his temper, the weather, or what he finds in the icebox.

Crawfish (in Louisiana, never *cray*fish) can be turned into a dish that its advocates consider the best that le bon Dieu allows man to know. Every spring ditches are acrawl with millions of these small, lobster-like things, three to six inches long. Caught in baited nets, they are boiled with peppers, bayleaf, thyme, salt, and other seasonings, and eaten either hot or cold. But the crawfish's noblest apotheosis, his pre-ordained destiny perhaps, is to be served as bisque. One recipe calls for about forty-five of him, well boiled and drained. These are then broken in half, their heads are cleaned, and about twenty-five of the heads are laid aside to be used for stuffing. All the tails are peeled, chopped carefully, and combined with a cup of well-soaked bread, salt, pepper, parsley, several garlic pods, and a spoonful of chopped onions. This mixture is then stuffed into the heads.

Now for the soup. The contents of the crawfish heads are dropped into a quart of water and boiled for a bouillon. At the same time into another pot go a cupful of green onions, a cupful of chopped parsley, two bay leaves, a bit of thyme, an onion, and butter to fry it all until browned. Then in goes the bouillon with salt and pepper. For a half-hour or so this must boil, with more water added if required. Shortly before serving, the stuffed heads are rolled in flour, fried in butter till crisp, then dropped into the soup. And rice goes into the soup plate with the bisque. The crawfish's beady eyes may seem to watch from the mixture; but surely he has died in a good cause.

Close to the bisque is redfish *courtbouillon*, a stew of delicately flavored fish with a gravy of tomatoes, peppers, thyme, parsley, olive oil, garlic, and white wine. The whole is poured over toasted bread, or mashed potatoes, or rice. Orleanians will argue for hours over the nuances of its preparation.

The old Marseille favorite, *bouillabaisse*, has taken on a Louisiana coloration. Redfish and red snapper become major ingredients, with sheepshead, crabs, shrimp, crawfish, trout, and other fish. Thackeray, here in 1855, told how he went to a lake inn for a bouillabaisse "than which a better was never eaten in Marseilles." As proof: "And never the least headache in the morning. I give you my word; on the contrary, you only wake with a sweet refreshing thirst for claret and water." Also, I suggest, for more bouillabaisse. . . .

Orleanians have developed into an art their tricks of handling crabs. They eat the hard-shelled ones cold or warm, after boiling in spiced mixtures; they add crabs to stews and soups; they use the meat in salads. But foremost, perhaps, are the crabs in their soft-shell phase, caught after they have shed and before they can re-acquire armor-plating. Broiled or fried in a buttery sauce, they are eaten down to the thin shell and paper-crisp claws. Years ago fishermen began to scoop up such crabs in their final fat hour, when they were about to shed the hard shell that had grown too constricting. Working carefully, the men pulled off the old coverings, and there were the "busters," ready for an epicure. If an Orleanian doesn't consider you an epicure he won't waste this delight on you!

Distinct from the spectacular restaurants have been the Creole family cuisines—distinct, but just as flavorsome. A New Orleans home cook, white or black, has a way with a kitchen stove that many a chef has difficulty in matching. Like a language or an art, a living cuisine borrows, assimilates, expands. With a population so multilingual, Creole cooking has been modified with the years. A Frenchman has married an Italian girl; some Jugoslavs move into the French section; a German cousin comes to live with the Creole family—and each adds something.

Take my family as an example. Though it is of Irish descent, the present generation grew up on gumbo and café au lait. We like jambalaya as thoroughly as any Creoles do, but we also enjoy Italian stuffed artichokes, as well as an emphatic crab mixture suggested by a Dalmatian friend from the lower Delta. Since one family branch is German, we have long appreciated pot roast and noodles; yet in the main, no matter what goes onto the family stove, it emerges with a strong French-Spanish seasoning.

The Creole home cook has never been wasteful. The French économie revealed itself from the start. Good materials, but no waste, no tossing away of scraps; for everything a use must be found, from left-over cuts to fish broth to the vegetables remaining in the pot after the soup has been served. These last would go into a salad; the boiled beef would go into a second salad; and the family thus had three dishes instead of one.

For years I ate Creole *grillades* before realizing that they were what most Americans might call a meat stew. But with what a difference! Grillades are made from a veal or beef round, tomatoes, and a half-dozen seasonings, cooked slowly in a pot. It is practicable to use these less expensive meat cuts because by stewing for a long time in their own juices they become softer and more savory. And Creole hands are especially skillful in the art of braising, which can turn tough meat tender and juicy.

Simplest of old-time New Orleans family dishes is that of red beans and rice. It is a kind of symbol of New Orleans, and many have never known a week to pass without at least one meal at which it is the *pièce de résistance:* sometimes the Monday meal, again the Saturday one. The dried beans are soaked overnight; the water is poured away and fresh is added; then the whole is cooked slowly with onions, green onions, bits of meat, ham, or bacon, lard, parsley, and pepper. It turns soft and creamy and is served over warm rice. With a salad, it constitutes a complete and inexpensive meal. During poor times, families have often subsisted on red beans and rice.

More elaborate is the *daube glacé.* Those to whom jellied meat means "American style" jellied meat can have no conception of the toothsome dish that the Creoles achieve in that direction. With the addition of pepper, bayleaf, cloves, and the rest, their daube glacé becomes a superb dark brown thing with taste to match. This is the kind of magic that is displayed by a Creole cook of my acquaintance who can turn even tripe into magnificent edibility.

Through the years men of New Orleans have sipped, sampled, and swilled their liquors. It was one of Jenny Lind's troupe who observed: "In New Orleans, indeed, drinking seems to hold its chief abiding place in the New World, and

I suppose that more spurious liquor and more genuine brandy is sold and consumed in this city than in any other part of the Union."

Every chronicler of New Orleans life concedes that the city has always been the tippler's paradise. If it had ever been authoritatively bidden *not* to drink, it would have drunk the more heavily, or—at least—merely raised an eyebrow and gone on as before. To national Prohibition the Orleanians paid little heed. There are bars here that boast they hardly closed their shutters throughout the "dry period," and their customers will be quick to hiccup an agreement. Yet the city's prevailing tradition has always been one of moderation. It was the rivermen, the sailors, the inexperienced Americans —it was these who tumbled into the gutters. The Orleanian said he knew when to stop, and usually he did know.

At any moment, it might have seemed that everybody in town was having a drink, or on his way to have one, or just back from having one. When the weather was hot, people took sherry cobblers; when it was cold, hot toddies; and brandy and whisky the rest of the time. At home they had their *bière douce* (sweet beer) made from the skin and "eyes" of pineapple mixed with sugar, water, and rice. The ladies made cherry bounce, geranium wine, and two or three other drinks; among themselves they sipped mild white anisette.

For generations, well-known drinking places flourished, changed hands, and still flourished. Discreetly euphemistic were the terms used for them: coffee houses, cafés, exchanges, even confectionaries. At one time a visitor counted forty-five bars in one block, on both sides of the street, just above Canal, and many of these never closed. From this zesty stretch rose an aroma that was either scandalous or delectable, depending on your viewpoint. So dense and pervasive was it that the susceptible claimed they could get drunk merely by prowling slowly past!

The bartenders became glamorous personages. Developing

their own followings, these philosopher-friends of mankind moved from one establishment to another, in some cases eventually opening places for themselves. Men trained their sons in the art and passed on the fragrant traditions. There were wars among these saloon operators, not in the Chicago manner but arising from the spirit of competition over the quality of their respective liquors; it was a kind of warfare that New Orleans loved.

Old, honorable, and extraordinary is the Sazerac, the golden-brown drink that many insist is the city's most glorious contribution to the art of drinking. Two small, heavy tumblers are required for it. While the first is being chilled with ice inside, the mixer works on the other. In it he crushes a lump of sugar moistened with water, then pours in a jigger of rye or bourbon, a half-jigger of vermouth, a dash of bitters, and a dash of orange bitters. In go several pieces of ice, and the mixture is stirred with a spoon.

Now back to the first glass. Removing the ice, the mixer drops in a touch of absinthe, swishing the glass in his hand until the liquoricelike stuff has caressed all the inside, then throwing out the drops. Into this scented glass the mixture is now poured, lemon peel is twisted over it, and voilà—a small drink but a magnificently potent one. Once upon a time the following dialogue was current:

"When you go to New Orleans, my son, drink a Sazerac cocktail for me, and one for yourself."

"And a third one?"

"*That* must be for the Devil, my son, for no mere mortal could down it!"

(However, there have been courageous Orleanians who have tried to. . . .)

Another school inclines toward the New Orleans dripped absinthe. At Bourbon and Bienville streets stands a tall brick building, with good ironwork and Spanish arched windows, whose coatings of worn stucco reveal its age. It served many uses until, about 1860, it became a place for good drinking—

the Absinthe House. Here the cool green stuff has dripped, dripped, dripped through the decades.

It was a French Opera bartender who gave it its name and reputation. Having notably succeeded in that place, he transferred his miracles to the Absinthe House. There he installed a fountain faucet with a marble base. Beneath this he placed one tumbler at a time, partly filled with cracked ice. He touched the faucet and the absinthe came out, one round drop of liquid jade at a time. As it touched the ice he stirred. The mixture clouded, whitened a little, and still more dropped. Presently he removed the spoon and the concoction was ready for the quivering throat of the man who watched.

A few, especially women, look to the gin fizz, combining the appeals of a foamy ice-cream soda and a firm liquor. Like a proper martini, it housebreaks gin into something else. One recipe calls for a jigger of gin, an egg white, a teaspoonful of powdered sugar, the juice of half a lemon and half a lime, an ounce of sweet cream, and a few dashes of orange-flower water. Shake earnestly, steadily, until the drink is filled with froth, and serve. So mild does the fizz look and taste, with its flower-water fragrance, that blue-noses have been persuaded to try it without realizing its gin content, and have burbled happily over their discovery. During the 1890s Henry Ramos, originator of one particular fizz, owned a number of places at which long lines of assistant bartenders did nothing but agitate the mixtures that the top men served. To shake the right way became an art. Today the Roosevelt Hotel owns the rights to the original recipe.

At the old Absinthe House at 240 Bourbon the specialty is a Pirate's Dream, served in a 28-ounce vase, holding four kinds of rum, crushed mint at the bottom, much ice, a number of syrups including a "passion fruit" variety, a handful of cherries, slices of orange, and a final ounce of the heaviest rum floating on the top. A dozen or so straws stick out of the ice, to make things easier, and the fruit topping makes the drink look like a salad—though there the resemblance ends.

The St. Charles Hotel's specialty is Planter's Punch, a long drink with two kinds of rum, especially fine if you ask the bartender to skimp the sugar he is intent on adding. Down at Café Laffite at 941 Bourbon they serve a quite dry Martini with absinthe added—title, the Obituary. Which seems a good place to drop the subject and return to more solid things, the great restaurants of the city.

Madame Begué, of sainted memory, was a lady known mainly for two things, her breakfasts, and her liver. "What dishes that woman made with liver!" Old men's moustaches quiver at the thought. Madame's story is that of the "better mousetrap." For years she operated a plain upstairs restaurant on old Levee (now Decatur) Street at Madison opposite the French Market. She had a French husband, lost him, then married a second Frenchman, Hippolyte Begué. Short, stalwart, and rather silent, she herself was a German; but so thoroughly had she combined her own arts with the Gallic ones around her that the world considered her a Creole cook.

Hers was a butchers' eating place; the portly Begué had been a butcher before the widow invited him to come up and tend her bar. He ended by seeing his name given to the restaurant. Daily the butchers, with their helpers and wives, stopped work about eleven o'clock and trooped over for a big breakfast. They had last eaten at about dawn—coffee, rolls, claret; and by now, after hours of strenuous bargaining, had worked up an appetite. Well they knew good food; these critics would sniff at inferior fare. A trencherman's feast was the result, going on for three to four hours.

If you went there, you found a single room, low-ceilinged and unpainted, and a single table stretching back almost to the kitchen, which stood on a higher level in plain view. There moved Madame with her helpers, under ropes of garlic, hanging game, and red peppers. In the dining-room Negro waiters brought wide-mouthed claret bottles and piles of crisp French loaves. Madame gave a signal, Monsieur whistled to the waiters, and your food came into sight, with aromas that, some swear, no other woman ever coaxed out of food.

Your meal usually opened with soup—a heavy one such as meets the masculine taste—followed by succulent *bouilli* (boiled meat from the soup) with spiced sauce. If crawfish were in season, they emerged in steaming platters. Probably you then ate a sweetbread omelette, savory and packed with ingredients. As the boys jumped to clear your table, out walked Madame, holding a platter of redfish in Creole sauce, cooked in wine, and with it potatoes in butter. After this you had chicken in red-brown sauce with mushrooms, and a salad of choice lettuce, oil dressing, and shrimp. Then came the course for which, like everyone else, you had been waiting—Madame's liver, always the best for miles around, larded with bacon, pre-broiled in butter, then merged with bay leaf, cloves, and other herbs and, not least, with red wine. From here on, you had nothing to do but sit around, smoke, nibble cheese or an apple or a peach, and wait for the coffee, which was liberally laced with brandy. When it was all over, you realized why a meal at Madame Begué's took several hours—it was almost beyond you even to get up from the table.

It was at the time of the Cotton Exposition in 1882 that Begué's was "discovered." Outsiders took to dropping in. Couldn't they join the butchers? They would pay anything. Room was made for a few, then for more; before long much of the place was reserved for weeks in advance. Madame died in 1906; Monsieur, marrying again, carried on until his death in 1917. The food continued much as before, though the sightseers had long ago frightened away the butchers; these original patrons did not enjoy sitting next to ladies who found them "quaint, and so interesting." In time, Begué's closed, but today—downstairs in the same building—the family-style Tujague's restaurant flourishes. You do not order at Tujague's; you accept the day's dishes, usually things like soup, bouilli,

veal with sauce, chicken, salad—and coffee in glasses. Tujague's is *sui generis*, including waiters whose friendly ways
approach chumminess. A girl I took there hesitated over a
dish. "Look, lady, try it," our waiter urged, "it's good for
you!" Her acquiescence made him beam for the rest of the
evening.

Few of the present-day French places have the décor that
New Yorkers seem to expect. Rooms are plain, with gas fixtures recently converted to electricity. There is no music;
patrons go because they enjoy good eating. The restaurants
have maintained themselves year after year because Orleanians like what they offer and tell their friends about it.
Several have been tempted to expand, but have resisted. They
have, in kitchen and dining-room, only enough trained service
to take care of a certain number properly, and beyond this
number they refuse to go.

Antoine's has functioned at or near 713 St. Louis Street
since 1840, in the hands of a single family. The first Antoine
Alciatore started at twelve in the kitchen of the Hôtel de
Noailles at Marseille. Nearing sixteen, he won marked attention when he was allowed to prepare a beef order called for
by Monsieur Talleyrand. It was served very rare, as the
statesman preferred it. He summoned the youth for commen-
dation. "What do you call the roast?" As Alciatore looked
at the contents of the plate they reminded him of nothing
so much as his father's description of the gory beheading of
Robespierre. So he christened it *Bœuf Robespierre*.

From Marseille, Antoine went to New York, then to New
Orleans, where he served at the St. Charles Hotel until he
opened a *pension* opposite the St. Louis. His specialty was
now *Dinde Talleyrand*, a cannily seasoned turkey dish. Wishing to let New Orleans know its quality, he adjusted the
kitchen shutters so that the aroma would seep out. New
Orleans came. A son, Jules, succeeded; today Jules' son, Roy,
is the proprietor of what is one of the country's memorable
restaurants.

Here pompano *en papillote* (in a paper holder) was concocted. Early in the present century the balloonist Alfredo Santos-Dumont arrived in the city, and officials appealed to Jules Alciatore to devise something new and appropriate. Jules recalled that his father had once enclosed a mixture in a paper bag fastened at the top; Jules would improve on this. He cut out a new paper shape—like a flattened balloon—and waxed it inside. Then he put into it delicate pompano covered with cream, fish flakes, spiced egg yolks, and shrimp. Into the oven went the whole thing, the bag puffing slightly with the heat. When the waiter cut it open it gave forth a seductive steam—and Jules' day was made.

The second Alciatore also conceived Oysters Rockefeller, *Huitres en coquille à la Rockefeller*. For years a related sauce had been used for snails, but fewer people now ordered *les escargots*. Jules' product is the new and authoritative covering composed of green lettuce, spinach, parsley, butter, green onions, chevril, tarragon leaves, breadcrumbs, anchovy sauce, and a little absinthe. The mixture is crushed in a sieve and poured over oysters on the half-shell; the oysters are placed on rock salt in a pie pan to hold the heat, and then baked. When the first lot came out, years ago, another day was made.

Also notable at Antoine's are *filet de truite Amandine*, trout covered with melted butter, almonds, and seasonings; and *poulet chanteclair*, a plump chicken carefully done to death. After being dropped into claret to soak, it is baked with mushrooms, bacon, and other ingredients. As the chef told me: "The fowl, it must swim in the claret until the delicate white meat is tinctured, *aromatique*." And that is just what the dish is, tinctured, aromatique beyond description.

Galatoire's, at 209 Bourbon, has remained for decades in one family and grown immensely in repute. For certain dishes qualified judges are inclined to rate it first. Surely Galatoire's *Truite Marguéry* is a gourmet's dream. The fish is smothered (happy fate!) in a sauce compounded of the richest cream, shrimps, and Creole ingenuity; or the mixture can be poured over large coral-pink shrimps to make a dish that I consider close to New Orleans' best.

Chickens in a dozen sauces, eggs with artichoke, eggs enveloped in golden mixtures, sautéed liver—Galatoire's is a restaurant of surprise for the stranger, of continuing satisfaction for the native. Its omelettes are remarkable even in a town that has a tradition of good omelettes. It offers a brilliant combination of eggplant and shrimp, and its ripe, garlicky salads are uniformly well prepared. Galatoire's disdains publicity and advertising; its proprietor shrugs away suggestions that his establishment be written up here or there. Instead, it concentrates on cuisine.

Arnaud's, 813 Bienville Street, breathes the flavor of its late owner, "Count" Arnaud Cazenave, raconteur, gay dog, smiling showman. In his seventies he had a young-old, Mephisthophelean twinkle. Born in France, he appeared here as a champagne salesman; he was called "Count" because people said he looked just like one, and the title stuck. Under his direction New Orleans has eaten, through the years, uncounted quantities of vivid *Shrimp Arnaud*, with a sauce of high voltage; *Oysters Bienville*, a warm, provocative covering made from cheese, meats, and other unnamed ingredients, all baked over the oysters; magnificent steaks with two sauces; and dozens of other dishes in the Arnaud manner, not to mention his after-dinner "Ambrosia" drink. A native always knew when the "Count" liked your looks; he sent you one of his Ambrosias, as Ken Gormin pointed out.

A man who had a zest for life, the "Count" built a swimming pool atop his house on Esplanade Avenue, with a tower to enable him to see the Carnival parades from a distance. He invariably started the day with a pint of champagne; toward the end of his life, however, his doctor made him substitute orange juice. "You know," he sighed, "I held my nose for a long time. But a man can get used to anything, even orange juice." Another unvaried practice—said to be his recipe for a happy life—was drinking endless cups of coffee, half of each cup strong Bourbon. He used to drink a good thirty cups in an evening. Though he developed or improved more than a dozen rare dishes, he himself always ate steak and potatoes, and he liked hamburgers! His big restaurant continues under his daughter's management; and sometimes a waiter thinks he can hear the "Count" laughing to himself in a corner, remembering how good life was. . . .

La Louisiane, 725 Iberville, established by another Alciatore, is known for its *Turkey Rochambeau*—strips of rich meat and ham in a brown sauce, with a golden one on top. In the courtyard of Broussard's at 819 Conti there is a statue of Napoleon which is saluted ceremoniously whenever a bottle of Napoleon brandy is opened. My preference here is either *Oysters Broussard* or the *Broussard Surprise*, a dessert akin to Crêpes Suzette but with a fluffier interior.

Deserved reputations are maintained by the Vieux Carré, 241 Bourbon; Patio Royal, 417 Royal; Maylie's, 1001 Poydras; Kolb's, a stoutly German establishment at 125 St. Charles; and Crescent City, 1001 North Broad, for its steaks. Farther uptown one finds the late Corinne Dunbar's establishment at 1716 St. Charles Avenue, with personalized Creole dishes; Commander's Palace, 1403 Washington Avenue, known for its soft-shell turtle stew, canapés, and fish dishes; and Manale's, 1838 Napoleon Avenue, with many Italian dishes, including spaghetti *bordelaise*. These are the ones I myself know and like best; other Orleanians will suggest still others as their favorites.

Then there is coffee. To the native it is a revivifier, an aid to digestion and to life itself. One man swore that when he was motoring home he could estimate his distance from New Orleans merely by stopping at intervals for a cup of coffee—each cup a milestone.

This *café* catches hold of a man and never lets go. To be

sure, outsiders may take a first sip and decide they have made a mistake. It is vigorous stuff; there is a saying that, unless the spoon stands up in the cup, the coffee isn't a New Orleans mixture! And Orleanians are given to quoting the epigram to the effect that coffee should be "as pure as an angel, strong as love, black as the Devil, and hot as Hell." They scorn the notion that it may shorten their lives. Look at Uncle Térence; he lived to be ninety, and would have died before he'd give it up. Anyway, a short life *with* coffee— wouldn't that be better than a long one *without* it?

The true Orleanian sips coffee, black, as he gets out of bed, "to pull myself into one piece." With breakfast he has it again, perhaps *café au lait*—half coffee, half milk, not boiled together but mixed just before drinking. In midmorning he stops for another small coffee. At lunch, again; during the afternoon, time out for it; at dinner and perhaps as a final drink before sleep. Many, waking in the night, go to the stove for more. And all day long those at home may keep a pot handy for convenient sips—"convenient" meaning "whenever they feel like it," and they feel like it almost continuously.

In smaller restaurants or hotels, the question is put to you: "Northern coffee, or New Orleans kind?" The latter contains chicory—from ten or twenty percent to a much higher proportion; the town consumes about sixty percent of America's chicory. Creole coffee is never boiled, but is dripped slowly, with only one dripping to the grounds. "The only bad point about our coffee," an Orleanian explained to me, "is that it spoils you for anything else." This man, when he travels to New York, Chicago, Atlanta, Dallas, Houston, Nashville, Tulsa, St. Louis, or Memphis—to any place outside of southern Louisiana, that is—takes along his own coffeepot. Once he forgot it and had to have it sent on to him by air express. "It ruined two days! How other people can stand what they do stand . . ."

We Orleanians admit but one improvement on our coffee,

and this one is an intensification, a glorification, of the beverage itself—*café brûlot*. Dousing their lights, restaurants serve this flaming coffee with ceremonial flourish, and Orleanians often do the same thing at home, drawing friends about the bowl with its soaring flames. A silver container is used, and a ladle; into the dish go sugar, brandy, cloves, allspice, orange and lemon peel, and cinnamon sticks. The brandy and ingredients are set afire in the bowl; slowly the coffee is poured in, ladled, and lifted blazing into the air. As they sip this transcendent mixture at the end of a meal, Orleanians give thanks that they live in a city which makes such things available. In an age of wars and world problems, is this too little to be grateful for?

CHAPTER 18

"If Ever I Cease to Love"

THE girl belonged to a once wealthy family that now had to count its quarters. For years she had watched older friends as they took roles in Mardi Gras royalty. Now she herself had reached eighteen, and Maman laid a problem before her, a choice. The years of scraping and saving had at last produced a certain sum of money, which was now to be used. It could send the daughter through college—or it could finance her début, with a chance at Carnival queenships. Which did the girl prefer to use it for? Without a flicker came the reply: Carnival! "Who in her right mind would choose otherwise?" she demanded, and hardly any *jeune fille* in the city would have dissented. That's Mardi Gras in New Orleans.

In 1882, Rex's Queen and her maids, all in gold and silver, were leaving their carriages. As one of the maids, Leona Jackson, stepped down, the door slammed on her little finger. Though the pain was intense she only said, as she wrapped a bit of tulle around it, "It'll be all right!"—and, smiling, went on to the glory of the grand march and the toasts in champagne. But her finger soon proved to be infected, and when that was over, the nail came off. Just then an admirer was calling on her. After commiserating with her he begged, "Give it to me." When finally she consented, he had the nail mounted in gold for use as a scarfpin, told his friends it looked like coral, and wore the pin to the next ball! Another friend, not less taken by Miss Jackson's beauty at Carnival time, pronounced her hand so comely that he insisted she have it photographed; and he carried its picture in his watch. And this, too, is Mardi Gras in New Orleans.

It is a state of mind—something that pervades the air and gets into the Orleanians' bloodstreams. The stranger protests, "I don't believe it—but there it is!" And there is not much exaggeration in the saying that the city has just two seasons: Carnival, and after-Carnival. It is not usual nowadays for a mass-scale celebration to be repeated year after year with undiminished success; this one has, in fact, grown with its age. Today, a hundred and twenty thousand or more visitors come to join the excitement every year.

Christmas is hardly over when Carnival opens, and it goes on for two months, more or less, depending on the date of Lent. During its last week it gathers momentum, with ever grander balls and street parades, shimmering floats in the daytime processions, and night floats whose gold and scarlet hues are caught by flambeaux in the hands of cakewalking blacks.

Eventually comes Mardi Gras itself—Fat Tuesday, the day before Ash Wednesday—the supreme fête celebrated by thousands in costumes ranging from ornate to casual, by "marching clubs," and by truck and wagon parties, with competitions among weirdly masked contestants dancing on the corners. In the midst of all this moves Rex, official King of all the Kings for the day, a crown on his head, a rhinestone-encrusted sceptre in his hand, leading his parade while his Queen waits on a draped reviewing stand. And throughout the day will be heard on every side that foolish but memory-stirring song which is Mardi Gras' theme:

"If ever I cease to love,
  If ever I cease to love,
  May the fish get legs and the cows lay eggs—
  If ever I cease to love!"

This is a day of gusto and illusion, of buffoonery and satire, of the brilliant and the ridiculous. Fat Tuesday brings the sparkle of delighted eyes, the tap of feet in jazz rhythm, the bubbling of champagne, the magic of the hot-dog (with Creole dressing), the fun of wondering who it is that is talking to you. By and large it is a day marked by pleasant behavior. Obstreperous drunks are few, fisticuffs negligible. Through the decades New Orleans has learned how to have a good time within reasonable bounds.

Somewhat paradoxically, Mardi Gras has become two celebrations. The first is the genial, free-for-everybody affair. Have a drink with us. Where are you from? That's the damnedest get-up I ever saw. . . . But there is another side, more reserved, more exclusive, which lies at the heart of New Orleans' inner social system. The two celebrations touch hands, but hardly more than that.

The older Carnival traditions are carefully preserved, kept as they have been kept for generations. The rules of the "krewes"—the men's organizations with their great balls and courts—dominate the lives of the city's inner circles, and on the way the tradition is carried out depends the happiness of many a man and woman. To be invited to a ball, to be a member of the King's court—this lends a new savor to life. *Not* to be invited—this may mark the beginning of a life-long addiction to Bourbon.

"See that young fellow?" a friend asks. "Carnival ruined his life. He got so much interested in the krewe that he stopped paying any attention to his law practice."

Some doctors, finding themselves absorbed in the season, close their offices temporarily and refer patients to friends. The octogenarian who "never leaves the house" will manage to reach a ball with the help of canes or a wheel-chair and equipped with a muffler and a hot-water bottle. Miss it? He's been going for sixty years, and he'd rather die than not go. (In some cases, after exposure, he does die.)

Yet the system is changing, at least around the edges. The ocean fortress still holds, but the currents are swirling higher around it. To an extent that dismays the old-timer, Carnival organizations have multiplied until there is now a krewe for nearly every element of the population, and there is a distinct trend toward democratization. "Every man a King, every woman a Queen," Huey Long used to say, and the promise seems to be coming true. In a little more than a year some fifteen new organizations sprang up. If a man finds that he cannot become a King in one krewe, he may form a new krewe in which he *can* become one.

The celebration goes back to the pagan rites of spring, which in time were taken over by the Christian Church. Carnival, the season when the devout must look forward to denying the flesh for the forty days of Lent, ends with Mardi Gras; the morrow, Ash Wednesday, marks the start of the penitential period. All this must have been in the minds of the French pioneers as, moving through the Delta in 1699, they realized that on this day their compatriots at home were dancing and masking on "Fat Tuesday"; so when they went ashore they gave the name "Bayou Mardi Gras" to the winding stream they came upon.

The French colonists had their casual Carnival balls, and the Spanish found the custom well established. Noticing with alarm that the mulattoes and the Americans were devoting the day to boisterous violence, the Spanish put a stop to the custom of masking. Later, when the Americans took over and the mysterious Aaron Burr came downriver, the panicked authorities revived the ban. Orleanians, however, whether masked or not, continued to enjoy balls and gallivant about in costume. In the 1820s or a little later certain Creole youths returning from Paris decided to liven things up, in Continental style, with masked processions of substantial size. They appeared on the streets in "every variety of costume, from the fantastic Harlequin to the sombre Turk and wild Indian,"

while women leaned over galleries to throw roses and bonbons.

For a time, then, things got out of hand. Urchins filled bags
with flour and broke them over people's heads; then mud was
substituted, and finally quicklime. Owing to such abuses, the
celebration of Mardi Gras fell off, and it was some years before it was resumed on any considerable scale. In 1857 a new
organization was formed to do what roisterers over in Mobile
had done for years—present a parade with floats and torch-
lights. The organization called itself "The Mystick Krewe of
Comus," and it put on two floats—one carrying the King, the
other showing Satan in a blazing hell. As scarlet flames cast
their glow on iron galleries, a new Mardi Gras was born.
But it was to have strong American overtones, for—though
the Creoles had established the festival—the newcomers assumed an ever more dominant role. The hostilities of the 1860s
interrupted the celebrations, but since that period only major
conflicts have interfered, the Spanish-American War not having been considered "major."

Yet Mardi Gras might never have become what it is today
but for a twenty-two-year-old Russian Grand Duke, who
was present only by chance and who can hardly have treas-
ured the memory of his experience. It was 1872, and Alexis
Alexandrovich Romanov, brother to the Tsar's heir apparent,
was rattling around America, being bored by welcoming
committees and ogling the girls, who ogled right back. Alexis
Alexandrovich was handsome, blond, moustachioed, and—if
an eighth of the stories told of him are true—an amatory
prodigy. He liked everything feminine, including Indian maidens. Invited to hunt buffalo, he preferred pursuing the sister
of Spotted Tail, one of the braves.

The climax of the Grand Duke's tour was reached in New
York when he beheld the rosy blonde Lydia Thompson, then
acting in the comedy *Bluebeard*. As she sang the song "If
Ever I Cease to Love," Alexis' moustaches twitched, and it
was not long before she was singing it to him alone over

midnight suppers. Then, bestowing on her a diamond necklace and other *bijoux*, he sighed, buttoned his greatcoat, and departed to inspect other American wonders.

But the more he saw of America, the more he wanted to see of Lydia. When presently she went south on a tour, he trailed her. He had no luck at first, however; he kept missing her. Then he learned that she was headed for a place called New Orleans, and to New Orleans he proceeded. Mardi Gras was almost upon the city, and when it was discovered that an honest-to-God Grand Duke was on his way there, the Orleanians sat up. Something very special must certainly be staged. Already a new Carnival Krewe was being planned, as a method of quieting Reconstruction tension; and the project was elaborated.

A new King was proclaimed—Rex, Lord of Misrule. (Pedigree: by King Cole out of Terpsichore. Origin: a plantation on Olympus.) An official holiday was announced and street maskers were bidden to form a united procession. Carnival colors were chosen—purple, green, and gold. City Hall's columns were to look down on their first Carnival reviewing stand, and there was to be a thronelike seat for Alexis, under a red silk canopy. Could Russia do any better than this?

When the Grand Duke's steamer tied at the wharf the female Orleanians ran like mad to the scene; and had their labor for their pains, since it was not until the next day—the eve of Mardi Gras—that Alexis showed himself. With formal bows only, he proceeded at once to the official ceremonials: welcomes by the committees, receptions, and the like. And that night he witnessed Lydia's performance at the Opera House; perhaps saw her privately afterward—nobody could be sure.

The next day, in the uniform of a lieutenant of the Russian Navy, he walked briskly up the stairs at City Hall. But faces fell when, on seeing the throne prepared for him, he said he preferred to stand—which was very hard for the ladies who had been practicing curtsies for days. What was the use of having a Grand Duke present if he acted just like other people? Alexis only smiled. Surely, he said politely, in a democratic country no special reverence would be accorded to royalty? And he had the cruelty to quote from the Declaration of Independence to the effect that all men were created equal. . . . And, however much New Orleans resented it, Alexis continued to stand.

Now started a mile-long parade of some ten thousand people. Rex himself, cantering up on his horse, bowed deferentially to the Grand Duke. Meanwhile somebody had been struck with an inspiration: Since they all knew how much Alexis liked "If Ever I Cease to Love," why not play it? Whereupon one band after another was playing the song every five minutes or so. Surely this would please Alexis? If it did, he concealed his pleasure admirably, for not a flicker of response came from him. Finally, some of the crowd broke into an improvised chorus:

> "If ever I cease to love,
> May the Grand Duke ride a buffalo
> In a Texas rodeo—
> If ever I cease to love!"

But Alexis still stared straight ahead, silent; and the general conclusion was that, no matter what or how many his private love affairs, he preferred to keep them private, even in a democracy. . . . Nor was his behavior any more satisfactory that night when, at Comus' ball, though he watched the tableaux politely, he was deaf to every hint that he should dance. He had an engagement with Lydia but broke it, and he did not see her again. The explanation seems to have been that, after a long chase that had taken him as far as New Orleans, Alexis suddenly realized that Lydia bored him—that he no longer loved her, *tout court*. And there was another actress in town—Lotta Crabtree, playing in *The Little Detective*—and toward her the grand-ducal fancy soon turned. Though scheduled to leave, he kept putting off his departure

in order to see Lotta again and again. At their final parting
he is supposed to have given her an arm-band set with diamonds, pearls, and turquoises, the last-named to match her
eyes.

Willy-nilly, Alexis Alexandrovich had helped to fix the
pattern that Mardi Gras would follow thenceforth: official
holiday, Rex, and (not least) "If Ever I Cease to Love" as
its song.

In the social activity built around Mardi Gras it is the men
rather than the women who rule. The oldest "krewes" dominate—half a dozen or so of them, with memberships ranging
from one to two hundred. In each, the man who dictates is
not the "King" but the captain, who earns no salary but
wields vast influence. One of his major responsibilities is the
preparation of the krewe's annual parade. For scores of workers Mardi Gras is a year-'round task. No sooner is one season
ended than work must be started for the next. The artist
chooses a dominant theme for the krewe's floats—a legend, or
a series of related myths. From delicate pictures, designs are
fitted to the floats, which are twenty-four feet long and
eighteen high. There are usually about eighteen of them,
and the work moves on a strict schedule, men laboring at
plaster molds and wooden columns, fashioning papier-mâché
lions, great birds, and trumpet flowers that will rise in the air.
At the end, other workmen apply rich blues and yellows and
finally silver and gold leaf.

Who will be King? Each krewe will have one. This important question is being weighed by the krewe's captain. In
any of the old-line organizations the choice soon narrows.
The King must not be a poor man, for he may have to spend
more on the honor than he has earned annually for a long
time. He will hardly be young, but usually a middle-aged to
elderly merchant or lawyer. He must provide his own costume, jeweled train, and accessories, give suppers and parties,

buy presents for the Queen and her maids, meet a hundred obligations.

For all this he is granted the privilege of displaying his legs in full-length tights; if he is sixty or past, the pleasure in this privilege may be confined to himself alone. In most cases (Rex being an exception), he hides his face behind a mask; as somebody observed, men fight in New Orleans for the right of anonymity. Yet no one objects to being King, and few say No. The city remembers many a lovable old gentleman who, with one highball, had been almost irresistibly tempted to tell you about his day of splendor as Rex; after two, he was not to be restrained; with the third, out came the precious mementoes—photographs long carried around and by now so creased as to be almost falling apart. . . .

Yet kingship is a mild issue compared with queenship—the question of who will be chosen Queen for each of the oldest and most celebrated krewes: Comus, Rex, Twelfth Night, the Atlanteans, and a few others. This is the burning issue for thousands, especially for such Orleanians as looked on World War II chiefly as an annoying interruption between one Mardi Gras and the next.

To be Queen of one of these older krewes a girl must usually belong to the well-defined group of the season's dé-butantes. She has to make it this year, or not at all. A man, even one nudging seventy, may wait to be a King. ("Lord, I pray Thee let me live—my wife would never forgive me if I died before . . .") But the girl can't wait at all, and this lends acute tension to the situation.

The Carnival expenses of a Queen's family may be over-powering—costume, gifts, supper, and the like. Occasionally a father has staved off creditors for years while working and saving toward his daughter's supreme hour. The hour arrives; having begged, borrowed, bought on credit, the family is ready to splurge—and nobody can say he ever saw more rhinestones, more wine, more oyster patties. Later may come bankruptcy, or at least a long struggle to pay off the debts.

But does the family regret it? Hardly ever. It has had its moment.

The choice of the Queen is governed by a number of factors: family tradition, general social standing, wealth, business affiliations, political obligations. When a candidate's mother has been a Queen it is understood that the daughter will reign in her turn. Whatever the Grand Duke Alexis might have thought, Mardi Gras has its own system of royal inheritance.

As in the case of the King, the decision here too rests with the krewe's captain, either alone or in consultation with a committee. There may be bitter battles, with furious infighting. If a girl's father is a bank official he may swing a lot of influence. Yet some captains refuse to submit to such influence; they have been known to create situations when, among nearly equal claimants, they have chosen on as whimsical a basis as beauty and disposition. So, after all, it does help a girl to be pleasant and show good manners. . . .

Parents who set their hearts on having a Queen in the house will start preparing for it a long time ahead. Sophonisba is but four at the moment, but that is none too early. She must be given the right pre-school course, go to the proper dancing class and summer camp. Her preparatory and finishing schools must be selected with equal care. Shortly the child herself begins to hear about Carnival, and Mardi Gras balls are a part of her playtime activities. At dancing school she and her friends learn how to hold themselves, how to enter a room. "When you're a real Queen, think what people will say." And in time Sophonisba will join some teen-age organization having its own Carnival gaieties.

Meanwhile, year in and year out, teas and receptions must be given for Sophonisba's friends and friends' mothers. Father pitches in, cultivating the krewe, frequenting the right clubs, drinking with the boys, working cheerfully on floor and reception committees at the balls. Almost before he knows it, Sophie, aging fast, has reached seventeen, then eighteen, and is ready to come out. If her parents are wise they choose her début year with care, picking a season that promises to present the fewest opponents; no matter what obligations have been built up, Sophie's chances may slip away in a glutted market. Yet accidents have happened; in a dead heat between two equally formidable candidates Sophie may turn out to be the dark horse, the new winner. By a similar fluke, however, she may just as easily lose; when she is almost under the wire, some unanticipated entry may overtake her—Philomène, say, whose people have lost everything but whose popularity or family background carries her through. Her début may have been a modest affair, but everybody likes her and her parents, and so she edges out the newcomer.

The same girl may be a Queen twice, or even (though rarely) three times; or she may be Queen at one ball and maid at others. If Father has worked too hard he may secure too many honors for her, and the family is sure to hear about it. The story is told—it inspired a song—of a girl who took nearly everything in sight until, apprehensive, she pleaded, "Daddy, don't make me Queen of Comus!" Yet any girl who shook her head at Comus would be a phenomenon indeed.

Christmas becomes a momentous day, since it is then that the glorious news is brought (or isn't). A male friend calls with a box of roses and a scroll that bids the girl to the court; and on that overwhelming moment she will look back all her life. Or no one comes, and she will remember the day as the one on which she tasted gall and wanted to die. . . .

The newly appointed Queen and her mother now set quickly about their secret tasks. A Queen's gown may cost four thousand dollars or more; it is of the richest white fabric ornamented with sequins, rhinestones, or pearls. The krewe artist provides a general design for it that will fit his theme—Oriental, Viennese, classic; and, within limits, she has it made to suit her own preferences. Generally she is given her crown and sceptre, and often her brilliant mantle, yards long. Most Queens of the traditional balls retain their costumes for life;

occasionally one will keep hers draped on a mannequin in the drawing-room. Only the Queen who later runs into bad luck will sell or pawn her finery; most would starve first. Among the curious stories told in connection with these regal wardrobes are some about girls who considered the ensembles planned for them hardly grand enough. One, for instance, was not satisfied with the mere dozen aigrettes in her headgear, and she added fifteen more. The artist shrieked, but she paid no attention. She would go on with the twenty-seven aigrettes or not at all. She went on.

Who will be invited to the ball? Committees meet for weeks in advance to pass on lists sent in by krewe members, each of them being allowed a limited number of invitations, and many a clash ensues. Souls are searched, and the social register is worked through. (Who *is* Mr. S——, anyhow?) After the lists are finally made up, the chairman is still harassed by continual telephone calls, appeals, pressures. By the night of the ball he is likely to admit that he wishes he had been tossed over the levee at birth, for he has had to watch women cry, has alienated friends, has made permanent enemies.

At last comes parade night. The "dens," warehouses near South Claiborne Avenue and Calliope Street, begin to fill with members arriving to don costumes and mount floats, on which each has a specific position assigned to him. According to the rules, nobody under the "slightest influence" of liquor may ride; but "influence" is a matter of definition. To fortify the wavering, a generous buffet supper is provided. A man clambers to his perch on a float only to find himself at a precarious point—atop a serpent's head, or emerging from a rose ten feet above the ground. Seeing an iron rod at his elbow he grabs for it, and rolls away.

Bands are blaring along the route. Slowly the floats move along, the path being cleared by police on horses or motor-cycles. Mothers hold their children up to see better, or fathers carry them on shoulders or in boxes fixed on the ends of poles.

As each float passes, its maskers reach into bags holding the throw-outs: beads, whistles, and other trinkets for the crowd. "Throw me something!" "Gimme something, Mister!"—and the gifts fly in a shower as the float moves by. There is no Carnival excitement to match that of reaching out and catching a gift, no disappointment like that of realizing that the man in front of you has the longer reach.

This custom of throw-outs has given rise to odd incidents, as when one slightly muddle-headed young masker mixed among his flat souvenirs a special present he was holding, and then discovered he had tossed out the emerald bracelet intended for his fiancée. He advertised, of course, but the lucky recipient never revealed himself.

The parade moves up St. Charles Avenue to Washington or Louisiana Avenue, then down St. Charles to Canal Street and along it or into the French quarter for its destination, the Municipal Auditorium at Beauregard Square. Here the audience moves through closely guarded doors for the approaching ball. Each person must show an invitation in his own name. Years ago two invitations to Comus were stolen; a two-thousand-dollar reward was offered, but they were not returned.

Will a visitor see a Carnival ball? In the case of the older organizations, only if he is a relative or a good friend of a member. And it can be arranged, too, for certain celebrities. Two organizations, Rex and Hermes, have invitations available for out-of-towners, though these are in considerable demand. Some newer groups are less rigid, but their members, too, are anxious for invitations. Wise visitors expect to be disappointed; then, if things turn out well, they are happily surprised.

Meanwhile, inside the auditorium the participants are dividing off. Usually an invitation entitles a guest merely to look on from a seat upstairs. But various women have received call-out cards, permitting them to sit below and be called forth for dances with members of the masked krewe. Each member is allowed a limited number of call-out cards; they are major prizes. As each dance begins, committee members go about calling the names and finding the ladies that match them. Handsome, popular women are brought forth frequently; for the less glamorous, husbands may trade promises, each anxious that his wife or daughter have her hour in the spotlight. Those in the front row smile and smile. (A dowager friend once said to me: "Look, that's the toothpaste row!") And these brilliant smiles are rewarded, for they often catch the confused and nervous man.

A masker may be so ancient that his partner must lead him about the floor; such elderly couples "promenade," walk slowly around the room to the music. If browbeaten at home, a man may take this annual chance to rebel, dancing with anything good-looking that meets his eye. And a few bolder ones manage to introduce a friend of lighter moments as a "little cousin from the country." Younger men have slipped in as many as three such *amies;* those of maturer years are limited by their capabilities.

On the floor the lady maintains an illusion that she does not recognize her partner. The men's masks are all-concealing, but it is a rare woman who cannot identify her husband's legs and paunch. In any case she always gets a favor, some handsome trinket of durable value. Also, young men may take this opportunity to give a present or two such as a girl could normally not accept. Tales are told of one who slipped diamond clasps about the wrist of his best friend's wife. Her husband, oddly, believed her when she said they were "just junk." Less romantic is the incident of the deaf old party who reached into his bag for a favor and handed his partner his hearing-aid device. Not recognizing what it was, the poor girl spent half an hour before she succeeded in prying it open. . . .

The floor committee has its difficulties. Members must catch a name correctly, and then find the lady—and sometimes neither is easy. ("I am positive I was asked for," protests one red-faced woman; "but those ninnies never get the names right!") Ultimately the committee members go numb, or—with a few drinks—become sportive. One exuberant gentleman called out, "Josie Arlington! Josie Arlington!" Then he tried "Lulu White!"—and, as a last touch, "Countess Willie V. Piazza!" With that he collapsed. Later he was dropped by the krewe, to be restored to grace only after a season of penance.

Always, meanwhile, there is the more public part of Carnival. The week before Mardi Gras finds parades multiplying. On Thursday and Friday two major organizations, Momus and Hermes, have night marches that all the city comes out to see. Saturday brings a child King of the Krewe of Nor, with a line of "princes" riding Shetland ponies, floats with older boys to pull them, and a Queen awaiting His Majesty. Older monarchs stop at City Hall and at one of the social clubs to toast, first the Mayor, and then their Queen. Nor does much the same thing, with lemonade or hot chocolate in place of champagne.

Sunday presents a comparatively new organization, Venus, the only Queen who sits on a float with her women krewe members riding on floats behind her. The usual rule is reversed: Ladies, wearing masks, pick King and dukes, whose names are then given out while the ladies' identities are supposed to remain secret. Traditionalists shudder, but Venus keeps rolling along. On Sunday also, Alla, King of Algiers, chugs down the river with a procession of tugs and ferries; on Monday night Proteus of the sea has his march through the streets.

And now Tuesday morning—Mardi Gras itself. The children get up soon after dawn, hunting their costumes and trying to hurry their elders. On the streets trucks are being loaded with masked youths; crowds gather at the corners. Along St. Charles Avenue for thirty-five blocks the banquettes are filling with early arrivals, for here they will see the main parades.

At City Hall a little girl is posing in a new dress; she is an orphan who will stand beside the Mayor and help preside over the day. At the head of the Krewe of Crescent City, a line of trucks with maskers, is another child to whom the city's heart goes out; one year it was a boy who had lost both feet in an accident, and another it was one who was going blind.

But meanwhile here comes the first King on the scene— earthy, ever-human Zulu from Africa. Zulu's every act is a satire on self-conscious whites and their pretensions. He wears, not ermine, but a rabbit skin and a grass skirt; he generally arrives on a barge snorting audibly; his floats are decorated with moth-eaten palm trees. His knights strut in the guise of medicine men and black-face Keystone cops. Nor does Zulu sip delicately at champagne; he takes heavy swigs of Bourbon, gin, rye—anything in sight. When he stops, it is not to toast the Mayor but to salute bars which in return give him bottles of free stuff. Autographing coconuts as he goes, he visits the Japanese Tea Room in the heart of the Negro section, and his Queen and her maids await him at the Geddes & Moss Funeral Home. He has a route, though it doesn't count for much; Zulu is good for all day, rambling over town.

At about eleven in the morning, sirens sound and out rides Rex with his procession of pastel floats. By this time Mardi Gras is loud and furious. Peanuts are being thrown from wagons, and colored paper hangs everywhere. Amateur bands are picking girls to serenade. Here is a man dressed as an alligator, with a cigar in his mouth, and there's a woman who was hanged three weeks ago but who has climbed out of her grave to waltz with her executioner, the red rope in his hand.

Men walk by disguised as sandwiches or as bales of cotton, and girls in flappers' costumes of 1925, with Irene Castle bobs. And that's Governor Claiborne hiccuping absinthe, and there goes the Baroness Pontalba arm in arm with a quadroon Sirène. With them are Bernard de Marigny and Josef Stalin. Duelists pass, on their way to death under the Oaks; and

Manon Lescaut with a hillbilly. One undersized fellow, his hand thrust into his coat-front, is obviously Napoleon Bonaparte; but curiously he has two other hands, one at each side. Following him come steamboat captains sporting dollar-sized diamonds; gorillas; girls garbed as playing cards; and a baby made up as a spider. One bright old dowager, who never misses a chance to mask, is a shoeshine boy.

The day is one of smells—of popcorn, beer, cotton candy, dust stirred by jigging feet, and people. It is a panorama of the life of New Orleans—Creole, American, black, white, brown—compressed into twenty-four hours, with something of everything that the old city has meant. There is French *joie de vivre*, the endless capacity for a good time, the willingness to let others have theirs. To appreciate it requires humor, a relaxed mood, and an aspirin. . . .

How to enjoy it best? Most Orleanians would suggest that you be up early, by eight o'clock or so, to see Zulu at the New Basin Canal and follow him for a time. Then go to St. Charles and Howard avenues, wander uptown to watch the marching clubs and the beginning of Rex's procession, then downtown on St. Charles to City Hall. If you feel in the mood, you might try the Sazerac Bar on Carondelet Street—if you can fight your way in on the one day when women are permitted in this dim male retreat.

Afterward, for early afternoon masking, the Orleanian will recommend the Canal Street business section, where you'll see nearly every sight you have ever imagined and some you haven't. You might try North Claiborne Avenue for the remarkable "Indians"—Negroes in ornate and lavish disguise; or the "Baby Dolls"—dark girls of more than good will. Afterward head back to the French quarter where, on Bourbon Street, you'll find a bar wherever you look, all sizes, all kinds, ranging from those ten feet square to others with spacious courtyards. With good luck, if you pick a quiet hour, you may get into one of the good restaurants.

You'll mask, of course. Take your own costume; or better, stop in at a cobwebby shop on Royal or Bourbon; or bring along any funny hats or old garb in your attic. The average visitor comes prepared to drink a little, but not too much; you'll enjoy it better through a mild glow than from behind a Scotch fog. Forget your inhibitions; dance on the street if you feel like it, sing and hold hands with strangers. By dark you will do well to work your way toward Royal Street, near St. Peter, for the last parade of the year, Comus'—the one that some think the finest.

It is all at its best when the flambeaux cast grotesque shadows along the canyon that is Royal Street, and the lights give a richness to the fading walls behind the galleries. As the parade passes along Orleans Street toward the auditorium, Comus prepares to alight for his own tableaux and ball. As midnight nears, Rex, the other king, leaves with his court to go and salute Comus, the older monarch. A grand march follows, with a promenade of the two courts; a supper follows and officially Mardi Gras is over.

For thousands, however, it goes right on. Families take tired and cross children home to bed; but parties continue in homes, restaurants, bars, and hotels. Though all masks must be off by six o'clock, countless men and women will stay in costume, a saint sipping crème de menthe, a devil drinking milk. If you feel the way most Mardi Gras devotees do, you won't want to turn in yet. In any case, you might try to arrive after midnight for coffee and doughnuts at French Market, that assembly spot of débutantes and fishermen, muskrat trappers and dowagers, where even the most confirmed non-coffee-drinkers applaud the café au lait.

In the first dawn the dark façades of the nearby buildings will brighten a little and you will spy pieces of discarded tinsel here, a forgotten mask there. A couple passes quickly, stepping over a sleeping man in clown's attire. A church bell rings, and lines of people appear in the pale light, on their way to services. Lent is beginning, the forty days of sack-cloth and ashes. *Carne vale*, farewell to the flesh. . . .

"He who tastes of Mississippi water, he'll be back." He who tastes of Mardi Gras, he will also return. It's the maddest, fastest, giddiest, most absurd, most magnificent thing in New Orleans. Yes, you'll be back.

SUGGESTED TRIPS
IN AND AROUND NEW ORLEANS

TRIP I—THE FRENCH QUARTER

THE best way to see any part of the French quarter is on foot, taking as many hours or days as can be spared for leisurely strolls with side explorations into courtyards and carriageways and shops. An appropriate point from which to start is Jackson Square, bounded by St. Peter, St. Ann, Chartres, and Decatur streets.

In the centre of the square General Andrew Jackson rides his horse. Facing the square is the cathedral, on the spot that has had a church building ever since the town's earliest days. This is the third such structure, finished in 1794 and extensively remodeled or restored several times since. To its left is the Presbytère, formerly official church property, and to its right the Cabildo, the old building of state. These latter buildings are now the property of the Louisiana State Museum. In them may be seen colonial documents, portraits, and various rare objects such as the death mask of Napoleon (given to New Orleans in 1834 by Dr. François Antommarchi, one of the Emperor's physicians); and also the Louisiana Transfer Room in which Louisiana officially changed hands in 1803; a slave block and a plantation bell; ancient prison rooms; and a collection of natural science exhibits characteristic of Louisiana.

Near St. Ann Street is a Civil War pioneer submarine. Flanking the square are the two Pontalba apartment buildings built in 1829. The one on the St. Ann Street side, now owned by the state, has an apartment display dedicated to the Baroness Pontalba, as well as the Museum library.

Beginning at St. Ann and Decatur streets are the five buildings

349

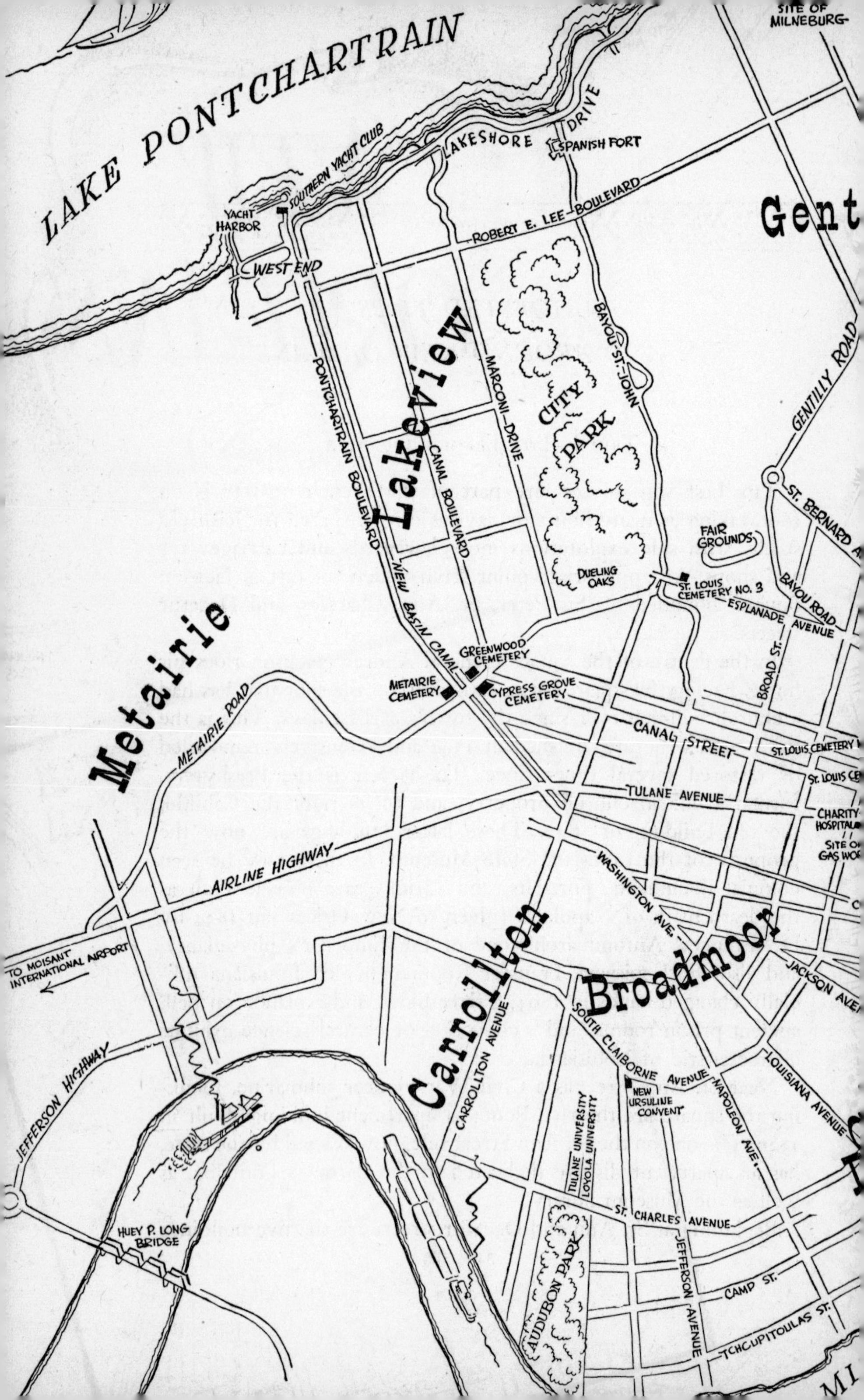

LAKE PONTCHARTRAIN
SITE OF MILNEBURG
SOUTHERN YACHT CLUB
LAKESHORE DRIVE
SPANISH FORT
YACHT HARBOR
ROBERT E. LEE BOULEVARD
WEST END
Lakeview
PONTCHARTRAIN BOULEVARD
CANAL BOULEVARD
MARCONI DRIVE
CITY PARK
BAYOU ST. JOHN
GENTILLY ROAD
ST. BERNARD
FAIR GROUNDS
DUELING OAKS
ST. LOUIS CEMETERY NO. 3
BAYOU ROAD
ESPLANADE AVENUE
NEW BASIN CANAL
GREENWOOD CEMETERY
METAIRIE CEMETERY
CYPRESS GROVE CEMETERY
Metairie
METAIRIE ROAD
BROAD ST.
CANAL STREET
ST. LOUIS CEMETERY
TULANE AVENUE
CHARITY HOSPITAL
AIRLINE HIGHWAY
WASHINGTON AVE.
Carrollton
Broadmoor
TO MOISANT INTERNATIONAL AIRPORT
JACKSON AVE
SOUTH CLAIBORNE AVENUE
CARROLLTON AVENUE
NEW URSULINE CONVENT
TULANE UNIVERSITY
LOYOLA UNIVERSITY
NAPOLEON AVE.
LOUISIANA AVENUE
JEFFERSON HIGHWAY
ST. CHARLES AVENUE
HUEY P. LONG BRIDGE
AUDUBON PARK
JEFFERSON AVENUE
CAMP ST.
TCHOUPITOULAS ST.

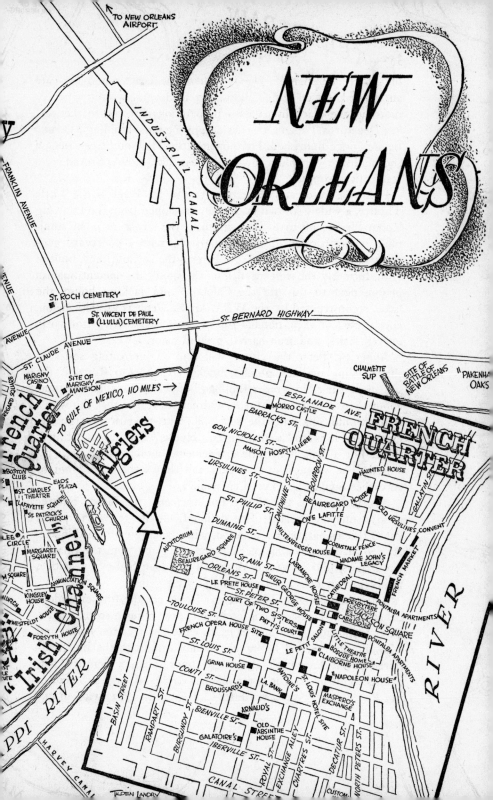

of the French Market. Many go here the year 'round for café au lait at the two coffee shops. On Friday night and Saturday morning the place hums with preparations for the market. At 823 Decatur is Tujague's restaurant; in the same building Madame Begué's once flourished. Here opens little Madison Street, once a thoroughfare of sailors' dives and the like, now restored as a residential property.

From St. Peter and Chartres: At 616 St. Peter is the Little Theatre, a widely known institution developed from the Drawing Room Players of 1916. Built in 1922, the structure is an admirable reconstruction of the Creole style, with a courtyard generally open to the public. 615 St. Peter is the Battle Abbey, built in 1839, formerly the state arsenal, on the site of the ancient Spanish prison; next to this are the Calobozo and Jackson house, the latter reconstructed by the WPA. 620 St. Peter is Le Petit Salon, constructed in 1838, notable for its "bow-and-arrow" ironwork, curved stairs, and iron-barred ground floor.

Along St. Peter the visitor will find an interesting series of shops selling pralines, gumbo, books, etc. At 640 Royal is the so-called "First Skyscraper Building" of the quarter; at one time, about 1810, it had three stories, and natives feared that the whole thing would sink into the soft soil. The novelist George W. Cable used it as his "Sieur George's House." It now has a fourth story. For a time it became a tenement, but has since been restored. The wrought-iron gallery rail shows the monogram of an earlier owner, Dr. Yves LeMonnier.

At 710 Royal is the Coffee Pot, formerly the Green Shutter shop, a fine one-storied place dating from the 1790s. At 718 is Pat O'Brien's bar, once a mansion, with its large courtyard intact. At 726 St. Peter is a simple, picturesque place from the Spanish days, the studio of Wood Whitesell and Dan S. Leyrer, with a richly grown courtyard and double iron gates.

Returning along St. Peter, at 701 Royal are the former Cadet's bakery, and Manissier's confectionary, now a chain store. 732 St. Peter is the site of Le Spectacle, an early theatre. 700 Royal and adjoining are several LaBranche family buildings, the much-admired "Iron Lacework Buildings," more than a century old; painted light green, the ironwork has design of oaks and acorns. 712 Royal is the Arts and Crafts Club, built in 1823, with an im-

pressive gallery view. Here is the rear garden of the cathedral—
St. Anthony's garden, where men once dueled over quadroons.
It also contains a monument to thirty French marines who died
in 1857 while helping to nurse yellow-fever victims. The shaft
was ordered by Napoleon III, was first erected at the Quarantine
Station, and in 1914 was transferred to the site.

Between Chartres and Royal, along each side of the cathedral,
are Orleans and St. Anthony's alleys, the second called "Pirates'
Alley" though it wasn't cut until long after the pirate days.
Facing Orleans Alley are some hundred-year-old residences; along
St. Anthony's the St. Louis church house, residences, and a shop
selling religious articles; adjoining streets also have such shops.
Across Royal is Orleans Street, widest in this section, leading out
toward Old Congo Square, now Beauregard Square, on which
stands the Municipal Auditorium.

At 717 Orleans is the three-story building identified as the
scene of the quadroon balls. It has been successively a legislative
chamber, a court, and Carnival headquarters; the Sisters of the
Holy Family now occupy it and operate the St. John Berchman's
Orphanage on the adjoining site of the old Orleans Theatre.

At 718 Orleans is the former Orleans restaurant, erected in
1809.

Back to Royal, at 721 is the former home of Mayor Joseph
Roffignac, a count who fled the French Revolution and became
a merchant here. For several squares are one-, two-, and three-
storied structures of good design and considerable age. At 823
is a notable home and courtyard, that of Daniel Clark, father of
the Myra Clark Gaines who sued the world. Built in the first
quarter of the nineteenth century, it is now the home of the
artist Alberta Kinsey. At 840 Royal is the birthplace of the
historian Charles Gayarré.

Turning into Dumaine: At 632 is "Madame John's Legacy,"
which in G. W. Cable's story was owned for a time by the quadroon Zalli. This square presents one of the quarter's finest vistas
of varying rooflines. At 707 Dumaine is a one-storied house with
unusual rounded Spanish roof tiles; here Cable placed Kristian
Koppig of the same story. Back to 841 Royal: Here is the tall
structure in which the quadroon Zalli lived. At 902 begin the several notable Miltenberger homes, built about 1840. At 910 was

born Alice Heiné, of the same family, who first married the Duc
de Richelieu, and then, on his death, Prince Louis of Monaco;
after twenty years as the Princess of Monte Carlo, she won a
divorce.

At 915 Royal is the house of the Cornstalk Fence; the ironwork, perhaps a hundred years old, shows cornstalks, ears of
corn, flowers, and butterflies painted in various hues. At 919 is
the courthouse in which Andrew Jackson, after the Battle of New
Orleans, was fined $1000 for contempt of court. At 934 Royal
lived Confederate General P. G. T. Beauregard for about eight
years after the war; the courtyard gate shows a love-bird design.
At 1027 is the tall house used by George Cable as the home of
"Madame Délicieuse," and at 1026 his "Dr. Mossy's Office."

At 1132 Royal is the home of the architect James Gallier, Jr.,
with granite steps and a fine doorway. At 1140 Royal is the
former "Haunted House," a towering structure of cemented
brick built in 1832 in the French Empire manner. Here lived
fashionable Madame Lalaurie, of whom it was said that she
mistreated her slaves. One day the house burned and, according
to newspapers and contemporary writers, in it were found six
or seven emaciated wretches. A mob broke in and Madame fled.
Descendants deny the story, regarding her as the victim of
jealous connections. The ornate doorway is often commented
upon.

Off Royal, at 724 Governor Nicholls, are the Préval Stables,
with arched quarters cutting far into the square. Built in 1834,
they figure in a derisive Negro gombo song about Judge Préval,
who charged Negroes for use of the place for a ball. A little farther on, at 706 Barracks, is the small house in which the famous
naturalist Audubon lived while awaiting fame. At 822 Barracks
is the Maison Hospitalière, home for aged Creole women, with
a striking courtyard surrounded on three sides. At 1003 Barracks
is "Morro Castle," finished about 1840, a tall, heavy structure,
marble-faced, once supposedly haunted.

Trip II—The French Quarter

The élite Creole section of the 1830s and 1840s began near
the river and Esplanade Avenue. At Esplanade and Decatur stands

the former U. S. Mint, built in 1836, now a Federal prison, a massive structure utilizing bricks of river mud, covered with stucco and granite. At this spot Jackson reviewed his troops before the Battle of New Orleans. During the Federal occupation under Ben Butler, William Mumford was hanged here for insulting the American flag.

A short way off is once-bawdy Gallatin Street, now two squares long between Barracks and Ursulines. Mafia gangs once clustered here. In the 1930s part was removed to make way for the improved French Market. At 1121-23 Chartres is the home built by the Swiss consul Peschier, who married Bernard de Marigny's daughter Angèle. At 1113 Chartres is the birthplace of chessplayer Paul Morphy, with pillared gallery and curving iron stairs; it dates back to the 1830s and General Beauregard once rented part of it for several months. Across the street is the historic Ursuline Convent. Joined to it is St. Mary's Italian church, built about 1845. On March 19 it is always the centre of Saint Joseph's Day observances; scores of Italian families put up altars in the vicinity.

Back to Esplanade: At 524 is an old house dating from the early 1800s, later the home of the historical collector, Gaspar Cusachs. At 604 Esplanade once lived Paul Morphy's father. 606 Esplanade was owned by Michel Doradou Bringier, of the flavorsome Bringier clan, whose paterfamilias picked eligible young bachelors and asked if they would marry his wealthy daughters. (They usually did.) At 704 is the impressive former home of John Gauche, built in the 1850s, with a courtyard and distinctive gallery work showing Cupid figures.

Between 730 and 740 are homes once owned by the New Englanders Abijah and Alvarez Fisk of Natchez and New Orleans; a brick wall with fine iron ornamentation stands before the garden and the older house. At 820 is the former Guérin home, dating from the 1820s; at 833 Esplanade live the Perrilliat family, connections of Bernard de Marigny; a short distance off, at 1436 Bourbon, is Marigny's old gambling casino, now owned by Lewis Clapp. At 908 Esplanade once lived the widow of Prosper Marigny, who later married Alexandre Grailhe, precipitating a remarkable duel. At 1016 Esplanade is a massive brick place built before 1840.

Going back to Royal and up Royal to the 700 block, we retrace stretches already covered in Trip I. At 631 Royal is one of the oldest houses of the quarter, a simple two-storied one with courtyard, dating back perhaps to the 1780s; it was here that the famous soprano Adelina Patti stayed when she sang in New Orleans in 1860. At 628 Royal is the "Royal Castilian Arms," built in the 1790s under Spain. At 616 and 624 Royal are "twin houses" built about 1830 by Dr. Isadore Labatut. The first Labatut came here in about 1780, and his descendants remain in the old house. At 612 Royal is a house, at least a century and a quarter old, in which the Crawford family has lived for generations. All along Royal—once the Creoles' most fashionable street—one finds restored homes and antique shops; it was a Creole custom to have the business establishment below and the living quarters above.

At 621 Royal is the home of Alexandre Grailhe, the duelist, and at 613 the Court of the Two Sisters, dating from the 1830s, eventually occupied by the sisters Emma and Bertha Camors, who operated a store. It is now a restaurant and drinking place, with great ironwork gates. At 611 is the former home of Governor André Bienvenue Roman, a sugar planter. At 601 (corner of Royal and Toulouse) stand a series of brick buildings with second-story galleries and a procession of tiny galleries at the third level.

Off Royal on Toulouse, at 708, is the Court of the Two Lions, with figures of lions atop a pair of pillars. Dating from the 1790s, it was occupied by that Vincent Nolté whose memoirs, *Fifty Years in Both Hemispheres*, provided basic material for Hervey Allen's *Anthony Adverse*. At 727-29 Toulouse, the druggist Peychaud is supposed (according to Stanley Arthur) to have created the institution of the cocktail.

Back to Royal: At 528 to 534 are a series of stuccoed structures in the finest Creole style, once occupied by merchants, attorneys, and others. At 529 is a notable structure built during Spanish days, reputedly the home of Governor Estéban Miro. The long gallery has cast-iron of unusual simplicity, and there are fine staircases and a courtyard. At 520 is the home, built about 1815, occupied by François Seignouret, wine-seller and furniture-maker whose designs were much favored. He often worked the letter "S" into patterns, and here a *garde de frise* (ornamental gallery screen) shows it. Eventually Pierre Brulatour occupied the house. A descendant, Jules, married Hope Hampton, the actress and first-nighter. No galleried and fanlighted courtyard in the city has been more greatly admired.

At 519 Royal is a less pretentious building, going back to the 1770s; one legend calls it the quarters of the Spanish mounted police. At Royal and St. Louis is the site of the St. Louis (later Royal) Hotel. In the 1870s it became the state capital; then, damaged in the 1915 hurricane, it stood forlorn until it was torn down a few years afterward. Out St. Louis, at 713, is Antoine's restaurant, there since the 1860s. Opposite, at 716, is a house dating from the 1830s, home of the Reconstruction governor Henry Warmoth, and also of the diplomat Pierre Soulé.

Back to Royal: The 400 block, river side, is occupied by the New Orleans Court building, a miscarriage in architecture for which a full square of quarter houses was torn down in 1910. At 437 Royal is Feldman's Antiques, formerly the drugstore of Peychaud of cocktail fame. At 417 Royal is the Patio Royal restaurant, built about 1800, once occupied by the Banque de la Louisiane, whose initial LB may be seen in the balcony; here also once lived Paul Morphy. The courtyard is unusually good. At 413 Royal was born Adrien Rouquette, Creole poet-missionary to Indians. 401 Royal (now Manheim Antiques) once also housed the Louisiana Bank, and the initials LSB are still to be seen; it has a striking domed ceiling.

At 344 Royal is the old mortgage office built in 1826, a classic structure with handsome iron gate; it is now the American Legion Hall. Along intersecting Conti Street is Exchange Alley, extending to Canal Street; it was once the fencing masters' section. Back to Royal: At 339 is the former Planters' Bank, later the quarters of the Gas Light and Banking Company (now Waldhorn's Antiques). Continuing up Royal, at 333 is the site of the original U. S. Post Office, now Harmanson's bookstore. At 312 lived the politico, "King John" Slidell.

At 301-307 Royal is the structure that housed Prudent Mallard, furniture-maker extraordinary. At the corner of Iberville is Solari's restaurant; a short distance out Iberville, at 725, is La Louisiane restaurant, dating back to 1834. Back to Royal: At 126 is the former Merchants' Exchange, at one time a post office and courthouse, in which the adventurer William Walker was acquitted of filibustering charges. At 127 was the former Gem, a saloon above which the Carnival Krewe of Comus was organized in 1857. At 121 Royal was the former Cosmopolitan Hotel, now St. Regis restaurant, with memorial windows. At 116 Royal is the former Sazerac bar, which gave the world the drink of that name.

Trip III—The French Quarter

Starting from Canal, at Decatur Street stands the block-square U. S. Custom House. The cornerstone was laid in 1849 and the building partly occupied in 1856. Then work was delayed, and eventually discontinued. Its present height was not reached until 1881; the fourth floor and the dome were never finished. The Greek Revival columns, oddly, show Egyptian lotus capitals; niches that were intended for statues remain empty; the cornerstone is lost because the building sank about thirty inches at one side. Once it was a Federal prison, again the home of city police, and in Reconstruction saw killings and riots. Its second-floor marble hall is a magnificent chamber.

Down Chartres from Canal: At 301 Chartres was operated the New Orleans branch of the United States Bank in the early 1800s. On this spot, too, Governor Bienville lived, and nearby the Ursulines took up quarters. 440 Chartres is the building of the former Exchange Coffee House or Maspero's Exchange, where the Barataria pirates held their conferences. Here, when Andrew Jackson was fined after the Battle of New Orleans, the crowd paid him enthusiastic tribute. Just off Chartres, at 533 St. Louis, is the Lafitte Bank, dating from 1800; as Stanley Arthur has noted, the real estate firm of Lafitte & Dufilho, once here, had no connection with the privateers of that name.

At 500 Chartres is the "Napoleon House," former home of Mayor Girod, who proposed to house the ex-Emperor here on his escape from exile. A popular story says that, with Dominique You, Girod promoted a plot to rescue Napoleon from St. Helena; but Napoleon died before anything could be done. At 514 Chartres is another "Napoleon House," dating from about 1822, formerly an old pharmacy; it is to be restored. Off Chartres, at 628 Toulouse, is a three-story structure with carriageway, and one of the widest of the city's fan windows; it was put up in about 1812 by Jean François Jacob, and legend inaccurately calls it a home of Governor Claiborne.

Back to Chartres: At 614 is the Court of the Twisted Vine; the great wistaria that once covered the whole patio was cut down in recent years. At 617 Chartres is the former home of Bartholomé Bosque, with the "BB" curiously reversed in the ironwork. And here we are back again at Jackson Square and the Pontalba Buildings.

Trip IV—The French Quarter

Starting from Canal, down Bourbon. At 209 Bourbon is Galatoire's restaurant. At 240 is the Old Absinthe House, built about 1805, with its entresol and high balcony. Across is the Vieux Carré restaurant. Just off Bourbon, at 813 Bienville, is Arnaud's restaurant, the building dating back from the 1830s. At 327 Bourbon stands the three-story house of Judah Benjamin, built by his Creole father-in-law; its ironwork has a bow-and-arrow pattern. At 400 Bourbon is the bar from the Old Absinthe House at 240. At 439 Bourbon the grape ironwork motif is notable. Off Bourbon at 819 Conti is Broussard's restaurant.

A block down, again off Bourbon, at 820 St. Louis, is the Grima house, dating from about 1820, a handsome house with fine doorway and courtyard. In the back is Courtyard Kitchen, with authentic New Orleans specialties. Along Bourbon are a number of former pensions patronized by opera singers of a former day. At 601 Bourbon is the one-time residence of the historian Gayarré. At 800 is the refurbished building occupied by a night spot, La Lune. At 819 Bourbon an unusually large building with striking ironwork was formerly the property of the Junior League; it was built about 1859.

Off Bourbon, at 824 Dumaine, is the former Sacred Heart Convent of the Creoles, now occupied by the Society of Saint Teresa of Jesus; its bow-and-arrow ironwork is noteworthy. At 941 Bourbon stands the "Lafitte Blacksmith Shop," or Café Lafitte, a single-storied structure *briqueté entre poteaux* (bricked between posts).

Along St. Philip Street, at 817, is the day school of the Mother Cabrini Nursery, with a fine courtyard. Proceeding to Dauphine for the last lap of this trip, we find at 716 the Le Prêtre house with a high gallery and much-photographed ironwork. Here a male relative of some Turkish ruler is supposed once to have brought part of a harem; the ruler schemed revenge-at-a-distance, and one morning the relative and all the girls were found bloodily dead—or so the story goes. Here also lived Dr. Joseph Gardette, who married the enigmatic mother of Myra Clark Gaines.

At 633 Dauphine is the J. B. Debois home, with letters in the ironwork, and (just above) the Masonic square and compass. At 625 is Major Latour's School, with tiled roof, dating from the period before the 1788 fire. At 521 is the Xiques mansion, with classic columns and a double-curving stairway. At 505 Dauphine the naturalist Audubon had another studio. And at 920 St. Louis the Forstall family reigned during the 1850s.

Trip V—The Garden District

This uptown American residential section is best traversed by automobile, but a St. Charles streetcar or a Magazine bus will take the visitor from Canal Street to First for a trip by foot.

At 1134 First is the white-columned home, well maintained, in which Jefferson Davis died, with his wife Varina Howell Davis beside him. It was built in the 1850s by J. U. Payne; he and his son-in-law, Judge Charles E. Fenner, were close friends of the Davises. Mr. and Mrs. Frank Strachan now own it. At 1239 First is the Brostrom home, with unusually fine ironwork, iron fences, and a gallery marked by both square and fluted columns.

At 1427 Second Street is the Musser house, unusual in several respects. Miss Miller's school formerly stood here; another house, built by the D'Arcys in the flush days before the War between the States, was divided and a portion brought here and embellished. The short columns, with elaborate capitals, extend along a simple gallery with an imposing doorway.

At 1213 Third is the Hero house, about a hundred years old, serene amid its shrubbery. James Gallier, Jr., is named as the architect; the Heros have lived there during most of its existence. At 1206 Third is the General Hood home, built a little later, with an unusual mansard roof. At 1415 Third is the Pescud house, a handsome white establishment of the "flush" days, with Doric columns below the more ornate Corinthian above, and a striking mahogany stairway twisting up toward a stained-glass dome. Thomas Jordan is the present owner.

At Third and Prytania is the former McStea house, later Redemptorist church property, a many-roomed establishment with brick walls, covered; imposing gates, and considerable ironwork ornamentation. It was built during the decade before the War. At 1604 Fourth is the Grima house, about a hundred years old, with a series of lawns and gardens that have elicited praise during many years.

At 1538 Fourth Street is the Moore house, notable for its wide drawing-rooms and for ironwork that makes each gallery a work of art. Begun just before the War, it was not finished for years afterward. At 1450 Fourth Street stands the Britten house, built shortly before the War, its covered brick brown in hue. Its ironwork, curving with the house, is much admired; before the front extends a cornstalk-pattern iron fence similar to that at 915 Royal—New Orleans has no others like these.

Farther uptown, at 1313 Eighth Street, is the George W. Cable home, a simpler and older house with brick columns, old pivoted windows, and ironwork gate; it was built in 1870. On Washington Avenue at Coliseum Street is Lafayette Cemetery, with ancient walls and tombs. Across from it is Commander's restaurant.

At 2627 Coliseum is the Eustis place, bricked, showing Swiss influence; now occupied by the architect Richard Koch, it was built by Julius Koch for James Eustis, ambassador to France. The Walmsley house, 2507 Prytania, goes back to the 1850s and is known for its iron ornamentation and finely maintained plantings; it contains twenty-nine rooms. At 2520 Prytania stands a house built by James Gallier, Jr., the Ewin home, boyhood residence of former Governor John M. Parker. Its single-story gallery has iron lacework, and there is considerable elaboration of the ceilings and interior mantels.

At 2423 Prytania is a low "cottage," the Woodruff George home, with a wide, six-columned front gallery and a curved one at the side (both with square columns), good cornice work with dentil lines, and tall French windows. At 2426 Prytania is the Harry McCall house, a structure of somewhat simpler lines, with long ornamented columns two stories high, and a wooden balustrade. At 2405 Prytania is the James house, of covered brick, two stories and a half tall.

At 2343 Prytania is the former Bradish Johnson home, built in 1870 in elaborate postwar style, with pairs of gallery columns. Inside is one of the city's notable curved stairways. It is now the Louise S. McGehee School for Girls. At 2340 Prytania is the Westfeldt house, a raised plantation type dating from the 1820s when this was Livaudais family property. Thomas Toby, manager of the Livaudais lands, built this heavy structure, with rectangular columns, for his overseer; then his own house was destroyed and he moved in.

At 2211 Prytania is the Henderson home, designed by the active James Gallier, Jr., in the style of an Italian villa. At 1238 Philip is the Pipes residence, a stately home with double galleries, four-pillared, and a handsome doorway, the whole surrounded by well-planted gardens. At 1410 Jackson Avenue is the large former home of Cartwright Eustis, its three and a half stories marked by Ionic columns; it is now Soule College. At 2127 Prytania is the former Maginnis home, now headquarters for the Red Cross, New Orleans chapter; about eighty-five years old, it is of the raised-garden type, with slender columns, ironwork, elaborate cornices, and dormer windows. The lower floor has been enclosed at front.

At 1220 Washington Avenue is the Baptist Bible Institution; before 1918 it was Newcomb College. James Robb built the central structure in Italian Renaissance style, with fine exterior marble stairs; it has an octagonal "Pompeiian room." The chapel is often admired.

A short distance downtown, at Race Street, begins Coliseum Square, an irregular green expanse between Camp and Coliseum streets dating back to the 1830s. At that time there was projected a scheme for a "classic revival" in the vicinity, with street names such as Prytania, Melpomene, Euterpe, Thalia, and Erato; with a university, a stadium for Olympic meetings, and a forum for great gatherings. The project never materialized, but the street names hung on.

At 1228 Race is the Caffery house, three-storied and stuccoed; constructed during the War, it was started by slaves and finished by free men. At 1322 Felicity is the former McGinty house, striking in that it has wooden columns for the lower gallery and ironwork posts above; and the cornice work is elaborate. At 1805 Coliseum is the Kelly house, a raised cottage with delicate columns, unusually wide windows above, and a long stairway at the front. At 1749 Coliseum is the Grace King house, long occupied by the late writer—a two-and-a-half-story structure with double galleries, each four-columned, and many rooms.

At 1420 Euterpe, also fronting Coliseum Square, is the Thornhill house, occupied by the Freedmen's Bureau during the War. At 1221 Orange is a simpler type, set close to the ground, with square wooden pillars, many rooms, and an unusual second-story projecting chamber, supported by posts below. It is now the home of Mrs. Coleman Moore.

At Camp and Prytania streets is Margaret Square, with a marble statue to Margaret Haugery, a charitable Irishwoman; this is said to be the first statue erected to a woman in the United States, or at least in the South. She gave some of her continuing efforts to the Louise Home, facing the square. Nearby, at 534 Howard Avenue, is the Sarpy home, a plantation residence dating far back to 1765, now hemmed in by later buildings.

From about Magazine Street to the river, between St. Joseph Street and Louisiana Avenue, is the former "Irish Channel." At 1600 Constance is Kingsley House, well-known settlement house occupying a former cotton warehouse property. About nearby Annunciation Square are former mansions of earlier residents. Mercy Hospital, at 1321 Annunciation, was once the Saulet plantation, built about 1815.

GENERAL

The Bayou St. John area near City Park, which can be reached by Esplanade bus, has a number of older-style plantation houses, including the Schertz house at 1300 Moss, sometimes called the "Spanish Custom House," dating back to the 1770s or '80s; the Aristée Tissot house, built in the early 1800s; the Walter Parker house at 924 Moss, built in the late 1700s; the Cucullu house at 1370 Moss; Our Lady of the Holy Rosary School, 1342 Moss; the Elizabeth Wisner home, and others. In the nearby park may be seen the Dueling Oaks and Suicide Oak.

Along St. Charles Avenue, from Lee Circle to a point above Broadway, may be seen some of the most impressive residences of the city, some built in the 1820s and '30s, others later.

Out beyond Pontchartrain Boulevard and beyond Métairie Cemetery is the lake-shore, with old resorts of the West End, ruins of the Spanish fort, the settlement of Bucktown, and the new seawall and built-in area, formerly part of the lake. A curious sight is the lighthouse of Milneburg, left "stranded" a half-mile inland by the creation of new land.

Just above New Orleans the Huey Long Bridge provides a striking panorama of river and city. From Eads Plaza, at the Canal Street ferry landing, there is a close view of the river. At Pauline, Erato, and other wharves automatic banana-loading may sometimes be seen; at others, such as the Poydras Street wharf, Negroes are guided by varicolored flags in the loading of coffee. The public grain elevator is at the foot of Bellecastle Street. From Jefferson Avenue to a point beyond Carrollton are a number of squatter settlements on the *batture*—the shelf of land between the levee and the river in low season. When high water comes, many lose their stilt-houses.

Audubon Park, from St. Charles Avenue to the river in the uptown section a short distance below Broadway, has the city's only hill, built by the WPA to show New Orleans children what a hill is and what it can be used for.

From New Orleans automobile trips may be made to the Delta section below the city; across the lake to Mandeville, Slidell, and the state park on Bernard de Marigny's old estate; to Bayou Lafourche; to the Teche country and Grand Isle; and to the sugar plantation country along the Mississippi and False rivers.

OVER a period of years many people, in New Orleans and elsewhere, have helped me in gathering data used in this book. (Sometimes they helped when they didn't know it.) Among them are:

Miss Isabel Puig, Mrs. F. X. de Verges, Mrs. Louis Perrilliat, Mr. H. R. Baker, the late Mr. André Lafargue, Mr. Sidney Villere, Mr. Roger Baudier, and Mrs. Eleonora Waldmann Wharton.

Mr. Pierre F. Choppin, Mrs. J. N. Roussel, Mrs. A. C. Bates, Mr. Clarence L. Johnson of the National Park Service, who has done considerable work on Bernard de Marigny; Mr. William Wells, formerly of the State Park Service; Mr. Mandeville Arnoult, Miss Jeanne Delery, Mrs. George A. Hero, and Miss Anna Minor.

Mr. and Mrs. Albert Voss, Mrs. Albert Sidney White, Mr. and Mrs. Walter J. Stauffer, Mrs. Thomas Sloo, Mr. Howell Morgan, Mrs. R. G. Robinson, Mrs. Lise P. Fowler, Mr. P. J. Rinderle, Mrs. Sarah Towles Reed, and Mr. Lionel Bourgeois.

Dr. Garland Taylor, librarian of the Howard-Tilton Memorial Library of Tulane University; Miss Marguerite D. Renshaw; Mr. John M. Dawson, formerly assistant librarian, and others of the staff.

Mr. John Hall Jacobs, librarian of the New Orleans Public Library; Mr. George King Logan, assistant librarian; Miss Margaret Ruckert, Miss Gladys Peyronnin, and others of the staff; Mr. James J. A. Fortier, director of the Louisiana State Museum; Miss Josie Cerf of the Louisiana State Museum Library; Miss Essae M. Culver of the Louisiana Library Commission.

Dr. William McCain, director of the Mississippi Department of Archives and History, and Miss Charlotte Capers, his assistant; Dr. Wendell H. Stephenson, chairman of the History Department and professor of Southern History, Tulane University, and

Dr. Fred Cole, dean of the College of Arts and Sciences, Tulane University; and Miss Marguerite Fortier, curator of the Confederate Memorial Hall, New Orleans.

Mr. G. R. Lyle, Director of Libraries of Louisiana State University, and Mrs. Ruth Campbell, curator of the Louisiana Room, Hill Memorial Library, Louisiana State University; and Mr. Paul North Rice, chief of the reference department of the New York Public Library.

Miss Virginia Westbrook, Mr. Allen Dowling, Miss Mary Railey, Dr. Rudolph Matas, Mrs. Burdette Huggins, Mr. S. Sanford Levy, Mr. A. J. S. Harmanson, Mr. Guy Bernard, Mr. and Mrs. Harry McCall.

Miss Eleanor Riggs, Mr. and Mrs. Lewis Clapp, Mr. and Mrs. Marc Antony, Mr. Richard Koch, Mr. Sam Wilson, and Mrs. Elizabeth Kell Perkins.

Miss Anna Marie Kane, Mrs. William J. Kane, Mrs. Warren Reynolds, Mr. Stanley C. Arthur, Hilda Phelps Hammond, Mrs. Corinne Legier Gleason, Mrs. Jean Sully Smyth Floweree, Mr. E. P. Lastrapes, and Mrs. Maud O'Bryan Ronstrom, want ad columnist of the *Times-Picayune* and *New Orleans States*.

Mr. Henri Wehrmann, Mr. G. William Nott, Mr. Albert Lieutaud, Mr. Dan S. Leyrer; Mr. Leonard Oppenheim of the Tulane University Law Library; Mr. Wood Whitesell, and Mrs. Yvon du Quesnay.

Miss Marie A. Ragon of Paris; Mrs. Merrill Parish Hudson of Memphis, Tenn.; Mr. Herman Diers of Washington, D. C.; Mr. Weeks Hall of New Iberia, La.; the late Miss Helen Gilkison of Baton Rouge; and Mr. Ralph S. O'Leary of St. Louis.